D0712391

Transforming folk

WITHDRAWN
UTSA Libraries

MANCHESTER
1824

Manchester University Press

WITHDRAWN
UTSA Libraries

Transforming folk

Innovation and tradition in English folk-rock music

Robert G. H. Burns

Manchester University Press

Manchester and New York

distributed in the United States exclusively by Palgrave Macmillan

Copyright © Robert G. H. Burns 2012

The right of Robert G.H. Burns to be identified as the author of this work has been asserted by him in accordance with the Copyright, Designs and Patents Act 1988.

Published by Manchester University Press
Oxford Road, Manchester M13 9NR, UK
and Room 400, 175 Fifth Avenue, New York, NY 10010, USA
www.manchesteruniversitypress.co.uk

Distributed in the United States exclusively by
Palgrave Macmillan, 175 Fifth Avenue, New York,
NY 10010, USA

Distributed in Canada exclusively by
UBC Press, University of British Columbia, 2029 West Mall,
Vancouver, BC, Canada V6T 1Z2

British Library Cataloguing-in-Publication Data
A catalogue record for this book is available from the British Library

Library of Congress Cataloging-in-Publication Data applied for

ISBN 978 0 7190 85338 hardback

First published 2012

The publisher has no responsibility for the persistence or accuracy of URLs for any external or third-party internet websites referred to in this book, and does not guarantee that any content on such websites is, or will remain, accurate or appropriate.

Typeset
by Toppan Best-set Premedia Limited
Printed in Great Britain
by the MPG Books Group, UK

Library
University of Texas
at San Antonio

Contents

List of figures

List of tables

Preface

Despite initial detachment from folk revivalism, English folk-rock has moved closer to aspects of tradition and historical status and has embraced a revivalist stance similar to that of the folk revivals that occurred earlier in the twentieth century. Whereas revivalism often rejects manifestations of mass culture and modernity, the early combinations of folk music and rock music demonstrated that aspects of preservation and commercialisation have always co-existed within this hybrid musical style. English folk-rock, a former progressive rock music style, has emerged in the post-punk era as a world music style that appeals to a broad spectrum of music fans, and this audience does not regard issues such as maintenance of authenticity and tradition as key factors in the preservation process.

Rock music has remained a stimulus for further change in folk music and has enabled English folk-rock to become regarded as popular music by a new audience with diverse musical tastes. When folk music was adapted into rock settings, the result represented a particular identity for folk music at that time. In a similar way, as folk music continues to be amalgamated with rock and other popular music styles, or is performed in musical settings representing new cultures and ethnicities now present in the United Kingdom, it becomes updated and relevant to new audiences. From this perspective, growth in the popularity of British folk music since the early 1970s can be linked to its performance as English folk-rock, to its connections with culture and music industry marketing and promotion techniques, and to its inclusion as a late twentieth-century festival component presented to audiences as part of what is promoted as world music. The popularity of folk music presented at world music festivals has stimulated significant growth in folk music audiences since the mid-1990s, and consequently the UK is experiencing a new phase of revivalism – the third folk revival.

Acknowledgements

My gratitude extends to many people and institutions whose assistance has been integral to the completion of this undertaking. I would like to thank Sue Court and Henry Johnson whose enthusiasm for my research has always been a key source of motivation. I must also thank my family, Sue, Jake and Alex, who demonstrated patience and understanding on the frequent occasions when I needed to become a recluse. I would like to thank my colleagues in the Music Department at the University of Otago, whose support has been invaluable. In particular, I thank Peter Adams and John Egenes for their help with various music technologies, Louise Kewene, Dorothy Duthie, Mary-Jane Campbell, Lisa Johnson and Sandi Jull for their support in non-music related areas, Patrick Little and Dan Bendrups for their wisdom and wit, Graeme Downes for his musicological expertise, Oliver Wilson for his assistance with editing, and Ian Chapman for his patience whenever I needed to discuss the origins of progressive rock music. I extend my gratitude to Misha Nikolic, Laudin Nooshin and former colleagues at Brunel University and Thames Valley University, who were all at the genesis of this project, as was my friend Roger Knott, who introduced me to the music of Fairport Convention in the early 1970s.

Finally, I must thank my informants, whose willingness and openness towards this research was vital to its completion. The cooperation of Martin Carthy, Simon Nicol, Rick Kemp, Gerry Conway, Ashley Hutchings, Georgina Boyes, Jim Boyes, Bob Pegg, Bob Lewis, David Arthur, Malcolm Taylor, Diana Campbell-Jewitt, Ian Smith, Derek Schofield, Karl Dallas, Ed Bicknell, Keith Benniston, Steve Heap, Eddie Barcan, and staff at the Vaughan Williams Memorial Library was integral to this book.

Material in this book has appeared in the following publications:

Robert Burns, 'Continuity, Variation and Authenticity in the English Folk-Rock Movement', *Folk Music Journal* 9:2 (2007): 192–218.

Robert Burns, 'Authentic vs. Inauthentic: Towards a Resolution of the "Folk-Rock" Conundrum', *38th World Conference of the International Council for Traditional Music* (Sheffield: University of Sheffield and the British Forum for Ethnomusicology, 2005), 12.

Robert Burns, 'British Folk Songs in Popular Music Settings', in *Folksong: Tradition, Revival and Re-creation*, ed. Ian Russell and David Atkinson (Aberdeen: Elphinstone Institute, University of Aberdeen, 2004), 115–129.

Robert Burns, 'Continuity, Variation and Selection: Sharp's Views Validated as Modern Folk Music is Amalgamated and Presented with Popular Music', in *Music and Locality: Towards a Local Discourse in Music* CD Rom (Wellington: Victoria University of Wellington, 2004).

Introduction

During the late 1950s and early 1960s, the folk music revivals that took place in the United Kingdom and the United States of America became a means of expression for modern social and political views, as well as a means by which elements of an idealised past might be preserved. While revivalists in the second British folk revival (which arguably took place between the late 1940s and the late 1970s) regarded the amalgamation of folk music with popular music as inauthentic, notions of authenticity validated by perceptions of tradition have been present in English folk-rock since the late 1960s. This book examines the re-contextualisation of British folk music into contemporary rock music. English folk-rock occupies a space contested by folk music purists and modernists through the dialectics of authenticity and heritage on the one hand, and the influence of commercialisation on the other. This space is a continuum that gives English folk-rock a powerfully symbolic presence in modern folk music performance in the UK. At one extreme of the continuum folk music is validated by invented tradition and nostalgic views of an idealised past, and at the other extreme is a folk-rock performer view that this music is transitory and constantly undergoing change. The space between the extremes of the continuum consists of commonalities that provide British folk music and folk-rock with a unified identity.

As a result of this idealised and invented past, folk music became an alternative to the visceral nature of rock and roll and the perceived vacuousness of the pop music that followed in the early 1960s. Folk music was often televised during the 1960s in the UK with artists such as Val Doonican singing traditional Irish songs while seated in a slowly rocking chair, and with variety show appearances by folk groups such as The Spinners (who appeared in matching sweaters not unlike those worn by Doonican), The Settlers and The Seekers. Ensembles such as these often used names connected to forms of labour and pioneering, possibly for the purpose of promoting credibility with the folk audience. One characteristic of all this folk 'representation' during the 1960s was that the folk music made available to the general public by the United Kingdom media in the 1960s sounded insipid and dull, and bore no relation to the music that was, as I later discovered, originally a social commentary and narrative and a means of binding communities together. With a negative media image, British (and American) folk music's popularity waned as pop and rock music styles were exchanged between the UK and the United States. This trend was, however, broken in the late 1960s and 1970s with the emergence of English folk-rock, a sub-genre of the progressive rock movement that was pioneered by bands such as Fairport Convention and Steeleye Span.

By the early 1970s, my own musicality had developed with the dedicated help of two fine music teachers at my school and, despite a significant parental nudge towards the health sciences, I decided to make a career from music. One of the first steps towards this goal was taken in 1971 when I performed as a semi-professional musician at a folk club near London at which my band was supporting folk guitarist Wizz Jones. The band was predominantly acoustic, with understated support from my electric bass and a drum kit. When we set up our amplifier and drums, there was a loud expression of disapproval from the audience, which continued to respond negatively as we performed. At this time, I was at the beginning of my musical career and the audience response may have related to the band's inexperience in live performance, although six months later the band also performed, and was well-received, at the Marquee Club in London, a significant rock venue during the 1960s and

1970s at which The Who and Jimi Hendrix had often performed. It was at the folk club performance that my first experience of audience disapproval (before I had actually performed) led me to consider differences in audience reception that often relate to musical preconceptions.

In 1972, I became a professional musician and entered the world of constant touring that eventually led me to a career as a studio musician, and to work with performers such as Eric Burdon, David Gilmour, Pete Townsend, James Burton and Jerry Donahue. I will discuss issues of audience reception to combinations of rock and folk music in a later chapter, but my experiences with Donahue led me to think about a contemporary identity for English folk-rock music. While performing with Donahue, a former member of Fairport Convention, I played in the UK and in Scandinavia at festivals and in clubs and theatres, and I witnessed first hand how a member of a seminal English folk-rock band was still revered in the 1990s. Moreover, this experience led me to question what English folk-rock had become in the era of Brit rock and during the growth in popularity of world music festivals that often promoted English folk-rock as a world music genre. Most significantly, my research from this period onwards led me to the conclusion that English folk music, in all its contemporary guises, was entering a new phase of revivalism that is separate from the two folk revivals that occurred during the twentieth century.

Firstly, however, we need to examine the concept of English folk-rock itself, and indeed briefly address the notion of Englishness divorced from xenophobia in the early twenty-first century, which is addressed in detail in chapter 2. 'English folk-rock' was the first of many descriptions that have been used to identify British folk music performed with other musical styles outside the rock idiom since the late 1970s. Others include 'electric folk' and 'British folk-rock'. The term 'English folk-rock' was initially used by the UK record industry to promote and market Fairport Convention and Steeleye Span. This classification remains despite these bands' re-contextualisation of folk songs from all of the British Isles into rock music settings, and despite a longstanding usage of 'British' to describe indigenous folk music in the UK. English folk-rock, which is distinct from folk-rock styles emerging in the United States of America in the late

1960s, generated change in the folk music world in the after-math of the second British folk revival, while initially remaining detached from aspects of revivalism. I retain the term 'English folk-rock' as a means of describing a musical hybrid that at once embraces indigenous folk music of the British Isles, while at the same time adapting it for rock performance drawing upon Afro-American influences.

During the progressive rock period, bands in the UK recorded albums fusing rock music with other musical styles, aided by financial support from their respective record companies. These combinations included fusions of rock music with Western art music, jazz, Eastern music and early music.[1] Fairport Convention was a progressive rock band, and their critically acclaimed fourth album, *Liege and Lief* (1969), changed audience perceptions of folk music. Significantly, the artwork for the cover of *Liege and Lief* included information on the work of the Edwardian folk song collector Cecil Sharp (1859–1924), whose contribution to the preservation and dissemination of folk songs has been seminal to this musical movement and has been acknowledged in many of the interviews carried out in fieldwork.

At the Folk-Song Society Centenary Conference held in the UK in 1998 there were several discussions concerning the re-evaluation of late twentieth-century criticism of Sharp's work.[2] There was a groundswell of support for Sharp, notably from Vic Gammon, who maintains that his own historical criticism of Sharp should not be regarded as denigration and states that Sharp was 'undoubtedly the greatest folk song collector England has ever seen'.[3] In a later discussion of Sharp's definition of English folk music, Gammon refers to aesthetic Darwinism in Sharp's attempt to align aspects of the music with the theory of evolution.[4] Sharp proposed three principles – continuity, variation and selection – as a means of explaining what he thought was the communal origin of folk songs.[5] Gammon correctly maintains that Sharp's defining principles are flawed, although he suggests that they provide areas for further discussion.[6] While Sharp's framework can be criticised for its lack of specificity, in that it is not confined to folk music alone, his three principles can be taken out of their original context to provide useful descriptors that may be applied to various aspects of English folk-rock performance. This is especially so in light of the change that has occurred since folk music has become amalgamated with popular musical styles.

Sharp's three principles can be re-applied to contemporary folk music, and in particular to English folk-rock, on the grounds that the music continues to be performed in new stylistic formats by performers who have adapted the music into contemporary settings. Variation has thus occurred as performers at once move away from notions of preservation, which existed during the first and second folk revivals of the twentieth century, while maintaining their own perceptions of folk music authenticity. Contemporary, folk-influenced amalgamations develop through processes of performer and audience selection. Folk songs are often recontextualised because of their pertinence to more recent social settings in a process of contemporisation that presents folk music to new audiences to which issues of authenticity are no longer central issues.

While Sharp's principles thus provide a useful framework in which to position English folk-rock, they are only used as an illustration and do not underpin this analysis. Authenticity is a key concept and notions of authentic performance practice often limit the potential lifespan of folk songs, and performer and audience notions of authenticity often differ. Performer interviews in this study demonstrate performer willingness to acknowledge the co-existence of authenticity and innovation (tradition and change) in performance practice, although these interviews also demonstrate that audience reception of change has often been hostile on the grounds of perceived inauthenticity. Authenticity in folk music is a false construct most often based on the idealisation of Victorian and Edwardian folk song collectors, many of whom edited their transcriptions to make them acceptable to Victorian and Edwardian audiences. The authenticity debate in folk music is thus similar to that which exists in early music and it is discussed more fully in a later chapter.

This book thus identifies what continuity, variation and selection in folk music performance practice mean for the concept of authenticity in traditional folk music. I discuss means by which rock music styles have been combined with British folk music and given the description 'English folk-rock'. I also ask whether the hybridisation, which occurs as British folk music becomes amalgamated with musical styles of the many cultures present in the United Kingdom, acts as a contemporary means of preserving traditional British folk music, given that English folk-rock bands have often drawn upon a variety of folk music from different parts of the British Isles.

In the context of folk music combined with popular music, I argue that continuity, variation and selection in British folk music adapted for performance within an amalgam of the mainstream styles of world, roots and rock music attract larger audiences, while retaining performer and audience notions of tradition, heritage and national identity. However, traditions such as those in folk music are often invented, constructed and formally instituted within a short space of time.[7] The invention of tradition and heritage in English folk-rock, as a means of validating continuity with the past, became apparent towards the end of the twentieth century following folk music variations such as 'folk blues' in the 1950s, as well as other folk-influenced amalgamations in the progressive rock movement during the late 1960s and the 1970s.[8] Promotion of Englishness in the first half of the twentieth century has often drawn upon folk signifiers such as Morris dancers, maypoles on the village green and orchestrated folk songs.[9] The meaning of pageantry and ritual in the twentieth century can only be interpreted by the rediscovery of the actual social and cultural milieu within which they first existed, which is often relatively recent.[10] This view is apparent in aspects of English folk-rock marketing and promotion methods since the 1980s, such as the appropriation of nineteenth- and early twentieth-century working-class imagery that, while remaining connected to relatively recent practices, draws upon notions of authenticity based on perceived history that is presented to audiences as invented tradition. It is significant that music-industry promotion of English folk-rock in the 1970s made use of folk signifiers in order to promote notions of invented tradition and heritage among rock music audiences.

Since the late 1960s, performers and promoters of English folk-rock have utilised promotional strategies familiar to the popular music industry. These include the marketing and distribution of folk music as a commercial commodity that draws upon notions of tradition and heritage for its promotion. Initiatives towards the commoditisation of folk music combined with rock music were anathema to many folk performers and members of the folk audience who regarded folk music as above the potentially corrupting commerciality of popular music. English folk-rock performers interviewed in fieldwork do not regard the involvement of aspects of the popular music industry in modern folk music as having a detrimental effect on the nature and meaning of folk music. The convergence of folk music and popular culture may, however, reinforce sociological perceptions of the devaluation of folk music through commoditisation, a process that followers of Adorno regard as de-humanisation by the effects of mass culture, and consequently worthy of ethical opposition. The adoption of aspects of music-industry-related commerciality and promotion processes in English folk-rock does, however, facilitate enhancement of performance reputation and status that arguably reinforces notions of separateness between performer and audience.

As preservation becomes linked to commercialisation, continuity, variation and selection in folk and folk-rock settings provide a connection between performance styles that preserve folk music in both modern and traditional contexts. Although revivalists often reject manifestations of mass culture and modernity, early amalgamations of folk music and rock music might be regarded as a unifying factor, further linking aspects of preservation and commercialisation. This unification has gradually enabled English folk-rock to establish a commercial, world music identity that retains belief in the music's 'timelessness, unbroken historical continuity, and purity of expression', while attracting a new audience with diverse musical tastes.[11]

Some folk music critics regard commercial trends in modern British folk music performance and promotion as hyperbole that was once only associated with the pop scene. Aspects of commercialism and notions of 'star' status in folk music are contrary to the open performance platform policy available to floor singers in many folk clubs, where new performers are encouraged to participate in a communal environment.[12] Despite this view, music-industry-related commercialism also enables English folk-rock performers to become 'producers' of folk music in terms of new recordings distributed in several kinds of media and in terms of concert tours outside the established folk club scene.[13]

Chapter 1 provides an overview of the book, including methodology, a short review of related literature and analyses of statistical information related to music-industry perceptions of the popularity of folk music and folk-influenced music. Chapter 2 discusses aspects of folk music and English folk-rock from a consumerist standpoint to identify aspects of heritage that are promoted within a commercial construct by a national 'culture industry'. This chapter investigates perceived identities within the folk music of the British Isles and identifies a contradictory stance adopted by the political establishment in the promotion of national heritage and identity.

Chapter 3 provides a historical overview of the various approaches taken by folk-rock bands that maintained a philosophy of retaining elements from what they regarded as source versions of songs in order to validate invented notions of authentic British or English tradition and heritage. The chapter identifies differences between bands that were referred to as English folk-rock in the 1970s. Most of these bands drew upon a variety of influences other than folk and rock music or were influenced by one dominant style that overshadowed any influence from folk music. Several of these bands later moved away from their original style. Moreover, the chapter establishes difference in the approach to performance between the two principal English folk-rock bands, Fairport Convention and Steeleye Span.

Chapter 4 presents a musicological view of several folk songs adapted for English folk-rock performance from the perspectives of instrumentation, use of combinations of regular and irregular metre, use of variable and constant pulse, and changes to texts. I have also examined means by which English folk-rock performers have adapted folk songs of the British Isles into popular music settings for the purpose of presenting a contemporary view of British folk music. As a consequence, English folk-rock as a popular music context for folk song performance located within the world music genre now attracts larger audiences than folk song performance in the traditional folk club scene.

In chapter 5, I investigate audience reception of English folk-rock from the perspective of performers interviewed in field research, as well as my own experiences as a professional musician and as an audience member. I propose an audience reception concept for English folk-rock that demonstrates a contemporary view of a musical style that combines aspects of rock music performer status with the concept of 'audience and performer as a community' familiar in the folk club scene.

Notes

1 Edward Macan, *Rocking The Classics: English Progressive Rock and the Counterculture* (New York: Oxford University Press, 1997), 30.

2 Material from this conference has been published as essays in *Folk Song: Tradition, Revival, and Re-Creation*, edited by Ian Russell and David Atkinson (Aberdeen: Elphinstone Institute, University of Aberdeen, 2004).

3 Vic Gammon, 'One Hundred Years of the Folk-Song Society', in *Folk Song: Tradition, Revival, and Re-Creation*, 15.

4 Vic Gammon, 'Introduction: Cecil Sharp and English Folk Music', in *Still Growing: English Traditional Songs and Singers from the Cecil Sharp Collection* (London: English Folk Dance & Song Society in association with Folk South West, 2003), 13.

5 Cecil J. Sharp, *English Folk-Song: Some Conclusions* (London: Simpkin, Novello; Taunton: Barnicott & Pearce, 1907), 18–31. The International Folk Music Council adopted these principles as a means of defining folk music in 1954.

6 Gammon, 'Cecil Sharp and English Folk Music', 14–15.

7 Eric Hobsbawm, 'Introduction: Inventing Traditions', in *The Invention of Tradition*, edited by Eric Hobsbawm and Terence Ranger (Cambridge: Cambridge University Press, 1983), 1.

8 Respectively, Charles Ford, '"Gently Tender": The Incredible String Band's Early Albums', *Popular Music* 14:2 (May 1995) 178, and Macan, *Rocking the Classics*, 30.

9 Georgina Boyes, *The Imagined Village: Culture, Ideology and the English Folk Revival* (Manchester: Manchester University Press, 1993), 3.

10 David Cannadine, 'The Context, Performance and Meaning of Ritual: The British Monarchy and the 'Invention of Tradition', in *The Invention of Tradition*, 105.

11 Tamara E. Livingston, 'Music Revivals: Towards a General Theory', *Ethnomusicology* 43 (1999), 69.

12 Niall MacKinnon, *The British Folk Scene: Musical Performance and Social Identity* (Buckingham: Open University Press, 1993), 29 and 48–9.

13 Email correspondence with folk festival promoters.

Setting the scene

An overview

This book follows a Marxian axiom of culture industry hegemony of notional national heritage supplied to the performer whose interpretation and production of English folk-rock are packaged for audience reception and consumption. English folk-rock is situated within a culture industry that is linked to political initiatives aimed at promoting notions of unified Britishness. The presentation of contemporary British folk music as English folk-rock becomes a nationalising, communal artefact produced within the hegemony of a socio-political culture industry as a means of re-branding of notions of national identity within the British Isles, particularly during the period following devolution.

I have drawn qualitative evidence from interviews conducted between 1997 and 2007 that provide essential information on aspects of continuity, variation and selection in traditional folk music and English folk-rock from performance, authenticity and commercial promotion perspectives. Information has come from established folk and folk-rock performers such as Simon Nicol, Ashley Hutchings, Martin Carthy, Gerry Conway and Rick Kemp. While this is not an exhaustive list, these musicians are representative of English folk-rock because they are, or have been, members of bands that pioneered early folk-rock performance, combining traditional folk songs with modern instrumentation and performance practices since the late 1960s and early 1970s. These artists are still active as performers, and their views provide an insight into change in folk music performance, as well as the maintenance of notions of authenticity, as folk songs are adapted for performance in a folk-rock context. It is also significant that, during the latter parts of their careers, many of these performers have performed simultaneously in both the English folk-rock and the traditional folk music spheres, providing them with comparative experiences of both, a further valuable aspect to their contribution to this study. These experiences add to the qualitative nature of their inclusion in this study, and, for this reason, English folk-rock and the traditional folk music scene are sometimes discussed interchangeably.

An initial point of contact was Simon Nicol, who later introduced me to both Ashley Hutchings and Martin Carthy. I first met Gerry Conway when we were employed as session musicians backing James Burton, Elvis Presley's guitarist, in 1993, and we later performed with Fairport Convention guitarist Jerry Donahue on a Middle Eastern tour in 1997. I replaced Rick Kemp in Donahue's band in 1991, and Kemp and I have maintained contact ever since. Whereas Simon Nicol remains a member of Fairport Convention, a band he joined in 1968, former member Ashley Hutchings left in 1970 to form Steeleye Span, as well as many later folk-influenced bands that have amalgamated British folk music with popular music styles. Both Nicol and Hutchings were members of Fairport Convention during the period of the first amalgamations of folk and rock music. Hutchings was replaced in Steeleye Span by Rick Kemp, who is also currently a member of the electric ceilidh band Whapweasel as well as The Gathering – an ensemble consisting of former members of Fairport Convention, Steeleye Span and Jethro Tull. Martin Carthy was also a member of Steeleye Span in the early 1970s, although he had established his reputation before that period as a solo performer and as a member of a duo with violinist Dave Swarbrick. He still performs as a solo artist, and as a member of Waterson: Carthy. Carthy was awarded the MBE in 1998 for services to English folk music. Gerry Conway performed on the first Steeleye Span album, *Hark! The Village Wait*, in 1970 and has also performed with the rock band Jethro Tull, with songwriter Cat Stevens, as well as with the folk-jazz ensemble Pentangle. He is currently a member of Fairport Convention. I regard Conway's contribution as valuable because he was one of the first two drummers to amalgamate the folk and rock styles into an authentic rock music setting.[1]

I also interviewed folk music critics such as Georgina Boyes, Karl Dallas and Bob Pegg, whose combined inputs provided a contemporary overview of folk revivalism in the United Kingdom, in particular the second folk revival, as well as aspects of change in modern folk song performance. Malcolm Taylor (Library Director at the Vaughan Williams Memorial Library), Diana Campbell-Jewitt (National Education Manager of the English Folk Dance and Song Society between 1995 and 2007), and Keith Benniston (Chief Examiner of Trinity College, London) discussed the teaching of folk music as English folk-rock and modern folk music education methods in the UK. I corresponded with folk singer Bob Lewis, a veteran singer from the British folk club scene, who offered his personal views on aspects of traditional folk song performance between the 1960s and 1990s. From a music industry perspective, the book includes information gleaned from interviews with Derek Schofield, the editor of *English Dance and Song* (the house magazine of the English Folk Dance and Song Society (EFDSS)), Ian Smith, the founding chairperson of the Musicians' Union Folk and Roots Section, and Ed Bicknell, manager of the rock band Dire Straits. Bicknell was entertainment secretary at the University of Hull during the late 1960s and became a booking agent for many of the late 1960s' and early 1970s' progressive rock bands, such as Pink Floyd. Bicknell situates Fairport Convention among the most popular progressive rock bands of that period. I have also been in correspondence with Steve Heap, former promoter of the Sidmouth Folk Festivals, and with Eddie Barcan, promoter of the Cambridge Folk Festival.

Interview questions related to personal experiences that led informants to involvement, and participation where appropriate, in folk music. I asked performers about their training as musicians, their early influences and their introduction to folk music, particularly in the case of performers whose backgrounds were in rock music. I also asked performers about the adaptation of folk music for performance in other musical genres and what type of changes were made, as well as their views on the significance of these changes and issues concerning notional authenticity. Informants also expressed views on the commercialisation of British folk music, folk music as a means of promoting notions of heritage and its globalisation within the world music arena. This area of questioning led to further discourse on the location of a modern British folk music that was relevant to a multi-ethnic United Kingdom.

Finally, I have drawn on my own ethnographic experiences as a professional musician playing in a variety of musical settings in the UK between 1970 and 2000. These performances included playing in folk clubs in the early 1970s and at UK, European, Middle Eastern, Canadian and Scandinavian folk and rock festivals throughout the 1980s and 1990s. While evidence of these experiences is limited, and exists mainly in performance reviews, artist websites and in various rock narratives of rock singer Eric Burdon, I was fortunate to be in a valuable position to witness and experience differences between audience reception patterns while performing in diverse styles and in diverse locations. In this case, my performance experience represents extensive 'insider' fieldwork that is key to my investigations into audience reception. My performance experiences led to my initial interest in how rock music, in all of the diverse forms it is performed, is received, especially when it is amalgamated with styles that factions of the audience may regard as contentious. This insider fieldwork extended into my attendance at folk festivals throughout the 1990s as an audience member, at which I witnessed a change in the artist rosters being presented to audiences familiar with folk festivals being an extension of the folk club scene.

New folk identity in the festival scene

The inclusion of modern British folk music, including English folk-rock performers, on artist rosters at world music festivals, such as those staged at Sidmouth and Cambridge, provides this music with a significant international profile that can be equated with its increased popularity. A broader folk music audience is demonstrated by growth in audience attendance at world-music-orientated folk festivals since the mid-1990s, which has far exceeded that of earlier decades.[2] English folk-rock music has often been performed at folk festivals referred to as world, roots and international events, and information supplied by festival promoters supports the notion of a rise in the popularity of various performance styles of British folk music presented at these festivals. While there are many other annual UK folk festivals that promote a variety of British folk music styles, I focus on Sidmouth and Cambridge because these are two of the largest folk-orientated festivals in the UK and they have demonstrated audience growth annually throughout the late 1990s and into the twenty-first century.[3] The presentation of British folk music at Sidmouth and Cambridge festivals has arguably become part of what Philip Bohlman describes as the 'commodification' of folk music. Bohlman maintains that revivalism and 'contemporary institutions' in folk music are inseparable, and argues that the use of modern technology along with music distribution networks enables past traditions to become new ones in the present.[4] In a similar way, the term 'contemporary institutions' can be applied to aspects of the music industry present in folk music, such as record companies, promoters, agents and marketing networks. Modern folk festivals are consequently linked to the popular music industry through commercialisation and business practices.

I also focus on Sidmouth and Cambridge because of the cosmopolitan nature of their artist rosters, particularly the Sidmouth festival's long tradition of including artists from other countries, and the Cambridge festival's inclusion of British folk music performers alongside popular and rock music artists.[5] At the time of writing, in 2011, these festivals have been promoted for approximately fifty years, although stylistic variation within their artist rosters has been recent in comparison with rock festivals in the UK. Variation in musical styles presented at modern folk and rock festivals in the UK suggests a blurring of stylistic boundaries. The inclusion of performance areas aimed at recreating a folk club atmosphere at both the Cambridge and Sidmouth festivals can also be regarded as a means of authenticating continuity in the festivals' folk identity. Moreover, folk festivals such as these provide a means of making traditional British folk music available to new audiences unfamiliar with notions of a national heritage – albeit an invented one.

A few key terms

I have found Michael Peluse's use of terminology in musical styles to be valuable in my own use of terms to describe folk music and amalgamations of folk and rock music in the UK. In his discussion of Japanese folk and pop music, Peluse notes that, in Japan, the term 'folk song' is used for songs that originated in rural areas and the term 'traditional' implies what Japanese audiences regard as the indigenous nature of this music.[6] Moreover, Peluse observes that, while 'traditional' can have a variety of meanings, in this sense it also implies continuous change over time. Peluse also maintains that the term 'pop' is multilayered and implies a relationship with mass media, urbanisation and the involvement of professional performers.[7] I use the term 'British folk music' to distinguish between indigenous traditional folk music of the British Isles and the non-British folk music of new cultures that now reside in them. 'Traditional' is also used as a means of distinguishing between earlier styles of folk music performance and more recent electrified folk music performance. I use the term 'English folk-rock' not only as an established commercial term, but also to distinguish between this music and the folk-rock styles originally popularised in the United States of America by performers such as Bob Dylan and The Byrds in the late 1960s, as well as between the folk-influenced rock music of Wales and the predominantly Celtic-influenced folk-rock music of Scotland and Ireland. What is most significant about Peluse's observations above is that folk music amalgamated with other styles Japanese audiences perceive as 'remaining true to its roots' by evolving and changing, while still maintaining links to the past.[8] Peluse also argues that an audience selection process governs whether the music lasts or fades from the popular sphere, an aspect particularly apparent in British folk music and English folk-rock.[9]

Britta Sweers maintains that the term 'folk-rock' was first used in the UK in the promotion of Fairport Convention's album *Liege and Lief* (1969), and she adds that the term did not become fully established until the period between 1973 and 1975.[10] Sweers prefers the description 'electric folk' on the grounds that it was borrowed from the original American term 'folk-rock', and that it reflected the newly invented fusion of folk and rock in the

United Kingdom. She notes that music producers and music journalists regarded 'electric folk' as one of several collective labels for a particular style of progressive rock.[11] 'Electric folk' may be aptly applied to Steeleye Span, whose structured approach to English folk-rock followed a blueprint established by its members with the aim of performing traditional folk music on electric instruments.

Taking a slightly different tack, Paul Stump argues that 'the marriage of folk and rock was always on rock music's terms'.[12] I support Stump's view for the reason that other folk-rock performers interviewed in fieldwork prefer the inclusion of the rock descriptor, a preference arguably related to a majority whose musical origins are in rock music.[13] Moreover, Sweers' and Stump's descriptions raise further questions concerning performer perceptions of the amalgamation of folk music with other musical styles, as well as the methods used in the exchange of musical elements between folk music and popular music. The adoption of folk music influences by musicians in the popular music genre is not the only change to have occurred in a broad variety of folk music performance practices during the latter part of the twentieth century, given that there has been a symbiotic exchange of influences between the genres. The 'traditionalist/modernist' debate discussed in this book concerns issues arising from the adaptation of folk music for performance in popular music contexts.

A few key concepts

This book addresses issues that have often been the subject of debate among scholars and fans of folk music during the second half of the twentieth century. There has been little scholarly work in the field of English folk-rock. The first work to address the combination of pop music and folk music was *The Electric Muse: The Story of Folk into Rock*, which was originally published in 1975.[14] The work was intended to accompany a set of three LPs but it has never been regarded by musicologists as anything other than a work by music journalists who often wrote for the *Melody Maker* and *New Musical Express* magazines, and was intended only for rock and pop fans. The work was published at a time when English folk-rock had become an established progressive rock genre, and when Steeleye Span had also achieved success in the mainstream popular music charts. While *Electric Muse* remained the only work to address English folk-rock for thirty years, it can only be regarded as an enthusiastic attempt to document a musical trend that was still in its early stages by comparing the new style to what had occurred in the United States during the late 1960s, and by proposing stylistic comparisons between folk and rock music. A new collection of recordings, which features a selection of the original tracks with the addition of some more recent ones, was released as a triple CD, *The New Electric Muse* in 1996. Sleeve notes were written by one of the original authors, Karl Dallas.

The first work to adopt a scholarly approach to this field was *Electric Folk: The Changing Face of English Traditional Music* (2005) by Britta Sweers. *Electric Folk* reconstructs and narrates the events and challenges taken up by musicians from both sides of the folk/rock divide during the late 1960s in which period followers of the second folk revival regarded pop music and its later incarnation, rock music, as a potentially corrupting commercial influence. Sweers provides the reader with a comprehensive insight into a period in which all forms of 'popular' music experienced change. There are, inevitably, elements that can be explored more fully, given that Sweers adopts an 'outsider' approach in contrast to my 'insider' evaluation.

Michael Brocken's *The British Folk Revival 1944–2002* (2003) focuses primarily on acoustic folk and its politics in the post-war period, although he provides a chapter acknowledging the rise of folk-rock in the United Kingdom in the 1970s and the consequent discussions of notions of its authenticity.[15] More recently, Rob Young's *Electric Eden* (2010) also focuses on the 1960s and 1970s, and provides a broad and comprehensive overview of folk music in the UK in the second half of the twentieth century, including its amalgamation into other musical styles, although this study does not address any particular aspect in great detail.[16]

Following the continuity, variation and selection concept, my own study expands into an analysis of a folk music industry supported on commercial and political levels, it provides a musicological analysis of the adaptation processes adopted by English folk-rock performance supported by performer accounts of this process, and it investigates audience reception of a sometimes contentious musical hybrid.

How did Cecil describe it?

Before beginning any discussion of the use of Cecil Sharp's three broad principles as descriptors for English folk-rock, it should be noted that Sharp attracted scholarly criticism throughout the twentieth century. Criticism of Sharp was levelled at his self-promotion and personal lionisation, and Sharp's principal biographer, A. H. Fox Strangways, was critical of his autocratic relationships with his peers and associates.[17] Sharp was further criticised by Marxist-orientated scholars such as Georgina Boyes, David Harker, A. L. Lloyd and Michael Pickering for editorial changes he made to folk songs, his collection methods, his dissemination of folk music to middle-class Edwardian audiences, his support for the inclusion of folk music in the national music curriculum, and his misrepresentation of informants.[18] On the other hand, C. J. Bearman refutes Marxist criticism of Sharp on the grounds that it erroneously maintains that Sharp described folk music in terms of his sources' class rather than their culture, and he argues that 'careless assumptions' made by these critics 'seep their way into social history', misleading later scholarship.[19] Bearman's criticism of Boyes is concerned with her suggestion that Sharp misrepresented residents of small towns as 'peasantry', and Bearman also counters Lloyd's attempt to redefine folk song in Marxist social history terms as 'lower-class' song as conforming with Marxist ideology, 'in which dislike of the "peasantry" *tout court* plays an important part'.[20] Bearman argues that Marxist ideology condemns English folk song to becoming a prisoner of a class war and that it is necessary to reject 'unfounded and limiting assumptions' in order to regard it, not as the property of a class, but of 'the English people and...the artistic world'.[21] Bearman further adds that Marxist notions of the expropriation of 'the folk's' cultural property by 'bourgeois' collection and publication processes, which was fed back to them as their 'cultural heritage', fits the concept of 'invented tradition', as discussed by Hobsbawm, who cites A. L. Lloyd's work as one of his examples.[22]

Sharp was not the only collector to make editorial changes to the folk songs he collected, and folk song collectors often assumed that, because folk singers made changes to songs during the oral transmission process, they were entitled to do the same.[23] Collectors often did not recognise that singers made changes to materials from their own peer group, whereas collectors subjected songs to the 'cultural imperatives of their own society'.[24] Folk-rock performers interviewed expressed support for the work of early collectors and, with regard to their editorial policies, Simon Nicol maintained that 'you can't damage the inevitable, it's not anybody's business to put songs in aspic, you can't nail them down for ever', and that 'The people who say that Cecil Sharp was wrong...changing these songs, are wrong [themselves]. They're wrong because he changed it for the people, for his constituency.'[25] This view was common among performers interviewed and, while discussing aspects of variation in British folk music performance, several maintained that criticism of Sharp should be reconsidered. Martin Carthy rightly maintains that Sharp's alterations should be viewed in the context of the social environment of the early twentieth century and he believes that Sharp's aim was to promote aware-ness of what he and his peers regarded as a vanishing resource, which would have been rejected if published in the exact form in which it was collected. He goes further on the question of variation stating that the only way to damage a folk song is not to sing it. He regards folk songs as needing to be constantly reworked and suggests that there is permanence about folk music that is manifest as a continuity that cannot be damaged by variation.[26] Carthy's performance ethic has always been a constant process of updating performance repertoire, and this statement reflects his personal philosophy to the combination of performance and preservation. The statement obliquely raises the question of performance primarily for commercial gain. A (perhaps naïve) critique of Carthy's statement might link the commercial performance of folk songs to the potentially cor-rupting influence of a revivalist folk 'music industry'. Such a view is unrealistic in any sector of the creative arts, and, given the statements they made in interviews, I do not regard any of the performers I interviewed as performing solely for commer-cial gain.

Preserving tradition and heritage – a few critical views

Continuity, variation and selection in the adaptation of folk music for folk-rock performance raise issues parallel to those that are central in early music scholarship. While discussing early music, Raymond Leppard refers to the 'vexed question of authenticity' that has become 'a blinkered, faddish pursuit among performers, listeners and critics', adding that there is little understanding of ways in which authenticity may be of value.[27] Leppard maintains that nineteenth-century audiences would have regarded pre-1800 music as an 'imposition' on contemporary musical tastes and would have viewed its value as inferior when compared with the social, scientific and artistic developments of the period.[28] In contrast, Nicholas Kenyon describes modern early music performers who strive to recapture what they regard as 'insights into a past age' in order to convey past messages to contemporary audiences.[29] Robert Donington supports this description, although he proposes that there is also universal acceptance of a doctrine of historical authenticity among early music scholars that 'best serve[s] early music by matching our modern interpretation as closely as possible to what we know of the original interpretation'.[30] The aims of the Victorian and Edwardian folk song collectors were similar, in that they sought to preserve cultural artefacts from a past age that they regarded as a national legacy in danger of vanishing. Participants in the 'first' (Victorian and Edwardian) and 'second' (post-war) folk revivals in Britain often regarded folk songs collected by the Victorian and Edwardian collectors as source versions, imbued with authenticity. This is despite the fact that a vast number of folk songs had been printed and reprinted between the sixteenth and twentieth centuries, and had been subject to change and modification during the process of dissemination.[31]

Performer and audience perceptions of authenticity of source versions of folk songs become complicated by factors such as the number of versions of the same song that have been collected, the dates of collection, who collected them, and who sang them. This concept can also be applied to 'authentic' interpretation by singers, which is often as much a matter of personal taste as of performer view of authenticity. Daniel

Thompson discusses one possible distorting assumption in the study of early music performance – that audience interpretation of music is the same as it was centuries ago – and he rightly suggests that performance on modern instruments logically leads to quite different interpretations.[32] In the context of interpreting performance practice in early music, Gary Tomlinson suggests that the meaning of a musical work is not necessarily that which its creator or first audience invested in it, rather that the meaning is that which the current audience believes that its creator and original audience invested in the work.[33] Views such as these can equally be applied to the application of the notion of authenticity relating to what are regarded as source versions of folk songs.[34] Notated folk song anthologies published in the twentieth century from collections such as those of Sharp, Vaughan Williams, Lloyd and MacColl cite collection dates and singers' names as historical record, despite the fact that any version collected was a record of how a singer performed a folk song at a particular time and would have been subject to the transcribed interpretation of the collector. The question of perceived authenticity then becomes, as Howard Mayer Brown and Philip Brett have both put it, 'authentic to whom and authentic when?'[35]

My investigation into issues concerning authenticity in English folk-rock performance also examines notions of authenticity in rock music, which are similar to the 'hallowed distinctions' between rock and popular music.[36] The basis for these distinctions lies in the 'appropriation' of traditions to authenticate contemporary practice. During the rhythm and blues revival in the United Kingdom of the early 1960s, 'it became a matter of ideology to employ the "blues" within a thoroughly different social context, by venerating its originators', a concept that enabled artists of the period to appropriate the authenticity of those originators.[37] Similar distinctions can be made between folk music and rock music, although issues concerning perceived authenticity of folk songs most often relate to the source and the singer of a folk song. In terms of oral transmission, repeated performance by several singers inevitably changes a folk song, raising the question of what makes any particular performance 'authentic' and whether notions of authenticity relate to issues such as for how long the song has been sung in a particular way or from which folk performer it was collected. Further questions arise concerning perceptions of folk song authenticity, which rely on specific criteria, or folk descriptors, and that become factors in the validation of invented tradition. These criteria might include the age of a source version, from which collection it was taken or from which recording a folk song was learned and the reputation of the performer on that recording. Access to modern technologies enables 'those without history' to 'claim and construct history'.[38] This view may be applied to aspects of invented tradition in English folk-rock and its propagation through music industry practices, concepts that draw criticism from folk 'purists', who are often critical of what they regard as the 'perceived vacuousness and capitalism of pop music and its associated industry'.[39] Access to recordings of early folk music collections increased throughout the second half of the twentieth century, and English folk-rock performers used recordings such as these, as well as notated folk songs, as source versions for re-arrangement as new recordings from the late 1960s and early 1970s onwards. Promoted and distributed through the same media and distribution systems used in popular music, new folk song recordings ultimately become new source versions.

Benedict Anderson and Eric Hobsbawm both discuss the invention of historical elements such as 'tradition' as a means of validating notions of authenticity.[40] Anderson and Hobsbawm maintain that the manufacture of notions of 'tradition' and 'community' acts as a means of promoting aspects of antiquity in nationalist and preservationist nostalgia, although Hobsbawm's theory of invented tradition relates to an artificial distinction between 'custom' and 'tradition'. Hobsbawm defines 'invented tradition' as being 'a set of practices, normally governed by overtly or tacitly accepted rules and of a ritual or symbolic nature, which seek to inculcate certain values and norms of behaviour by repetition, which automatically implies continuity with the past'.[41] His theory of invented tradition is therefore as pertinent to folk revivalism as it is to discussion of customs, which are rooted in the past but are still subject to change and innovation, and notions of tradition that represent, as David Atkinson notes, an invariant connection with the past.[42]

In addition to the invention of nostalgic notions of tradition being promoted by folk music purists, establishment bodies in the United Kingdom have manufactured and promoted notions of 'cultural heritage' since the early twentieth century, and the UK music education curriculum has included folk music as a means of promoting national awareness throughout this period. While the teaching of folk music in UK primary and secondary schools is limited, English folk-rock, as well as other modern folk music styles, might be regarded by cultural and educational establishment bodies as a means of (re)establishing notions of tradition, community and heritage as part of a modern view of 'Britishness', albeit 'invented'. The issue of folk music preserved by links to perceived tradition as a means of validating notions of invented heritage has been a source of debate between folk music purists throughout the twentieth century. The extension of this discussion beyond folk and folk-rock performance to formal institutions in the UK, including the education establishment and the music industry, raises questions concerning the use of any kind of British folk music as a means of promoting national awareness and identity, as well as notions of national community branded as Britishness, rather than the 'Englishness' promoted during folk revivals earlier in the century. Global and national economics and ideologies consequently become connected to the mainstream promotion of what is regarded as traditional music and heritage.[43]

While notions of invented heritage and antiquity have been reflected in the promotion of English folk-rock since the 1970s, these perceptions have always been present in the folk music audience, and the 'imagination' of these elements encouraged notions of comradeship and fraternity in the first and second folk revivals.[44] There has been limited investigation concerning developments in modern folk music performed as English folk-rock and the presence of invented heritage and tradition following the second folk revival. Niall MacKinnon provides a comprehensive cultural overview of the British folk club scene during and after the second folk revival, and Boyes' analysis of twentieth-century folk revivalism in the United Kingdom examines issues surrounding the first and second folk revivals, although her work does not extend into change in folk music performance that followed the second folk revival. Boyes' description of a received history that supported an invented 'factual' symbolism in the structure of the folk revival movement is similar to the invented symbolism present in the English folk-rock movement, despite folk-rock's detachment from the second folk revival.[45] Both movements are reinforced by formal and informal institutions that exist within them and by the use of musical structures and lyrics collected by Victorian and Edwardian folk song collectors. Both movements also utilise notions of traditional English imagery – Morris dancers, or maypoles, for example – to promote revivalist notions of 'Englishness' and, in the case of more recent folk-rock music, 'Britishness'. This imagery enables folk-rock performers to transfer notions of historical myth and heritage from perceived traditional folk music to English folk-rock performance. The shared perceptions of invented authenticity in both purist and modernist standpoints provide connecting rather than conflicting views on modern British folk music performance. English folk-rock's post-punk identity has moved closer to revivalist aspects of invented tradition and notions of historical status in what I suggest is a new phase of revivalism in British folk music.

To illustrate the combination of commercialisation with aspects of revivalism in English folk-rock, I have drawn upon Tamara Livingston's useful model of descriptive characteristics of music revivals.[46] Several of what she refers to as 'basic ingredients' of music revivals are apparent in aspects of English folk-rock. Music revivals are based on information provided by 'revival informants and/or original sources', a concept illustrated by folk-rock performers interviewed who expressed admiration for the work of early folk song collectors, including Cecil Sharp. They also described a meticulous approach to their retention of melodies and texts contained in what they regarded as original source versions of folk songs – both notated and recorded – in their adaptations of these folk songs for folk-rock performance. From a commercial perspective, Livingston also includes the existence of 'revivalist activities' (such as organisations and festivals) as a central ingredient, as well as 'commercial enterprises catering to the revivalist market'.[47] Both of these characteristics are present in what I venture as a new phase in British folk revivalism, although connections to commercialisation are often contrary to folk revival ideology.[48] Commercial promotion of English folk-rock also enabled the establishment of links between the British folk music scene and that of world and roots music, providing folk performers with access to new audiences, often with diverse musical tastes. Aspects of tradition on both sides of a traditionalist/modernist debate demonstrate commonalities between both viewpoints and promote a contemporary perception of folk music that encompasses notions of invented tradition, nationalism and heritage, concepts that have their origins in twentieth-century folk revivalism in the United Kingdom.[49]

Tina Ramnarine provides a valuable overview of folk music revivalism in Finland in which there are several commonalities with the English folk-rock movement in the United Kingdom. Ramnarine describes Finnish 'new folk music' which is associated with tradition, the past and continuity, and in which folk musicians borrow and absorb new ideas and influences from other traditions.[50] Finnish contemporary folk musicians regard folk music as a process of continuity and change between the 'old' and the 'new', and between tradition and innovation in which change 'is negotiated in various complex ways'.[51] For these musicians, there is no issue of 'purism', and they prefer an individual approach to folk music performance – 'Before it was like that and now it is like this', as one of her informant's comments.[52] Ramnarine observes that folk revivalist transformation of traditional material simultaneously introduces new traditions, while reclaiming authentic perspectives that preserve old ones.[53] This process achieves a symbiotic relationship between old and new that has significant ramifications for the representation of a musical tradition as being 'folk'.[54] Ramnarine also describes how Bulgarian culture was subjected to control by the nation's communist government. The element of the 'new' was politically imposed by an ideology committed to changing and controlling all aspects of society and culture.[55] Whereas the United Kingdom government has no particular ideology that might be compared to those of the communist government in Bulgaria in the second half of the twentieth century, Ramnarine's description of Bulgarian individuals maintaining personal notions of tradition and modernity within a politically promoted arena can also be applied to the culture industry promotion of tradition and heritage in the UK. Ramnarine provides a convincing argument that can be recontextualised to suit the musical perceptions of English folk-rock performers. From a further perspective of commercialism in a culture industry context, Ramnarine notes that contemporary Finnish folk music representation has become increasingly interconnected with the world and popular music market, and that the record industry plays a vital role in its commercial success.[56] This view provides a useful link to a new music industry that has emerged within modern British folk music and, in particular, English folk-rock.

In the context of musical preservation, David Atkinson discusses changes made to folk songs by collectors and editors. He describes a process of 'textualisation' in verbal art as it becomes printed text and consequently acquires the appearance of 'permanence', 'stability' and 'authority'.[57] Notated texts of this kind are, however, subject to editorial alterations as well as errors. Atkinson rightly suggests that audio recordings also 'textualise' verbal art, and many twentieth-century folk and folk-rock recordings are now regarded by modern performers and audiences as also having 'permanence', 'stability' and 'authority'. Songs collected in notated and recorded formats consequently remain static as historical artefacts. Despite changes made to folk songs for performance in folk-rock contexts, the performers I interviewed still consider the work of the early collectors to have been vital to the preservation and continuation of British folk music throughout the twentieth century, and they regard folk music as durable and able to withstand 'spontaneous change'.[58] For example, Ashley Hutchings, a founder member of Fairport Convention, maintains that 'Given modern communications, the way forward is to have knowledge and a love of the music, a knowledge of the history of this [music], and then to move forward, to write, to rewrite, to compose. Using that basic knowledge, I don't feel we should be so rigid as the old collectors.'[59] While Hutchings' enthusiasm for new directions in folk music performance is evident in this statement, it is erroneous to suggest that any rigidity rests solely with the collectors. The regard in which the Victorian and Edwardian collectors are held has led to a rigid view among many twentieth- and twenty-first-century revivalists concerning how folk music should be performed, and this can be

regarded as stifling experimental creativity in folk music performance that may preserve its value and relevance in modern
social and cultural contexts. Nevertheless, the three dimensions
of continuity, variation and selection still provide a useful heu-
ristic illustration, which can be employed to describe a continuum in the contemporisation of English folk music as folk-rock,
ranging from preservation at one end to commercialisation at
the other.

Preserving folk performance

The initial amalgamation of folk music and rock music might be
regarded as part of a radical process in rock music that started in
the late 1960s and early 1970s, and this process is ongoing as
English folk-rock music continues to combine tradition and
transformation. In a fieldwork interview for this book, Boyes
discussed the question of variation in the adaptation of folk
songs for English folk-rock performance.[60] She stated, 'I'm not
sure that the early rock things actually did all that much, apart
from put electric instruments behind songs' and she suggested
that electric instruments simply provided an extra dimension to
the performance of folk music doing nothing more than accompany it. She also added:

> I think it depends on how well they're done. You can update or
> change anything badly, the fact that it's changed, I think, is
> neither here nor there. It's how well its done, it's like making a
> bad translation...the point of songs is the meaning and I don't
> just mean the literal meaning but what the songs mean to the
> people that sing them. If that's done well in whatever way, it
> doesn't matter if you accompany it with a xylophone, a nose flute,
> or a symphony orchestra, or indeed a rock backing.[61]

Boyes is also critical of what she regards as the British folk
music audience's lack of acceptance of innovation in folk music
styles, and maintains that, although this situation is changing,
there is still a reactionary faction. She suggested, 'It's becoming
much better than it was but people are still enormously hide-
bound by generic labels and we all lose by that.'[62] Boyes' views
on folk music performed in various instrumental settings reflects
change that has occurred since the initial amalgamation of folk

music and rock music in the late 1960s, despite what she refers
to as a 'reactionary faction' in the folk music audience. Macan
and Stump describe this amalgamation in cultural and historical
contexts whereas, in order to illustrate innovatory processes in
the amalgamation of folk music with rock music for performance in English folk-rock settings, I draw upon several studies
into the use of pulse in jazz, folk and rock music performance.
There are several theories on 'participatory discrepancies', or
minor rhythmic imperfections that jazz musicians refer to as
'feel' and 'groove', that were originally applied to analyses of
performances by American session drummers who sometimes
experienced difficulties when performing with a computer-
driven pulse, or 'click track'.[63] Computer analysis was also used
to derive quantifiable data on folk tunes by organising folk songs
ʋy melodic contour and numerical 'weightings'.[64] Digital instrument manufacturers have designed software systems aimed at
'humanising' computer-driven performance by the inclusion of
rhythmic adjustment, or slight 'imperfections', to the perfection
of mathematically maintained 'feel'.[65] I have expanded these
concepts to examine pulse differences between traditional folk
performance and folk-rock performance practices by electroni-
cally comparing recorded performances of folk songs in both
traditional unaccompanied settings and folk-rock music settings
by means of oscillographic diagrams produced by music programming software. In order to further investigate English
folk-rock performance, I have examined the use of metre in
the contexts of traditional folk performance and folk-rock performance. Folk-rock performers often perform folk songs in
the metrical structures notated by Victorian and Edwardian collectors in order to retain what they regard as the authenticity of
the source versions, and these adaptations of folk songs fit
Moore's description of the 'appropriation' of the blues style by
British rock musicians aiming to authenticate contemporary
practice.[66] Folk-rock band members interviewed for this study
maintain that it was the policy of each band to authentically
reproduce folk songs as close to source versions as possible, a
policy that included both harmonic structures and texts. I therefore explore the issue of change to texts by comparing 'source'
folk song lyrics with contemporary versions that have been
changed in order to make songs pertinent to modern audiences,

while retaining their original message and, thus, their perceived authenticity.

The development of English folk-rock as a stylistic component of the 1970s progressive rock movement was assisted by the UK record industry, which financed musical experimentation involving the amalgamation of rock music with other musical styles. Record companies at that time invested in bands that were successful at selling albums rather than singles, and progressive rock bands were given autonomy in their musical direction. Bicknell maintains that Fairport Convention's move towards the electrification of the traditional folk music of Britain was one variation in a number of musical experiments that took place with the financial support of the record companies.[67] The main significance of English folk-rock lies within the continuity of folk music change that followed the second folk revival. The initial combination of folk and rock music during the progressive rock movement can now be regarded as part of a trend in the development of both rock and folk styles that is culturally and historically separate from earlier twentieth-century folk revivalism. While performers interviewed were not necessarily part of any particular revival, information supplied by folk festival promoters, as well as my own observations while attending and performing at festivals, indicates that the English folk-rock movement has become a significant presence within the folk music scene. English folk-rock has arguably promoted awareness of folk music among new audiences, leading to what might be regarded as a new phase in British folk revivalism. Since the early 1970s, the transient nature of the English folk-rock movement has evolved into a new folk revival which fulfils Livingston's criteria for revivalism and which has, as Burt Feintuch puts it, transformed the subject of its efforts.[68]

Folk music in a commercial arena

Sales of folk music recordings are subject to the same commercial parameters as most other music styles in the twenty-first century. The music industry continues to experience the most dramatic changes since its inception in the early twentieth century, with recorded music sold as downloads and in CD and DVD formats at performances and through the retail industry.

How recorded music sales are measured, however, is often subject to a vague statistical process relating to the ways in which musical styles are described, and consequently the process relied on a subjective view of what folk music, or any other style, might be. This method does not take into account illegal or free downloads that have, to a certain extent, compromised the recording industry in recent years.

Descriptors used to identify popular music styles for the purpose of stylistic definition frequently changed during the importation of American popular music to the UK that occurred during the 1950s and early 1960s. From the early 1950s, the recording industry in the UK and in the United States gave 'top twenty' chart positions to records based on the number of sales each record achieved. These positions did not take the musical style of any hit record into account and meant that rock and roll records often shared the popular music charts with recordings by diverse popular music performers of the period, including folk singers. As the decade progressed, definitions of popular music became even more varied. There was a change in the classification of popular music in the UK sales charts during the late 1960s as the UK followed US trends in chart fragmentation by musical style.[69] Instead of one chart that represented the overall number of national record sales, charts representing different musical styles started to affect the statistics that governed success for artists and bands.

Despite the increase in the popularity of live folk music events, statistics from the music industry suggest that sales of folk music recordings remain small, possibly because of limitations in the British Phonographic Industry (BPI) method of statistical data collection. These sales statistics come mostly from sources such as major retail outlets, as opposed to specialist music outlets, performance events at which folk artists are able to sell their recordings, or mail order sales from performers' websites (see Table 1.1).

Popular music categories sharing the largest sales percentages – pop, rock, dance and rhythm and blues – are compared to sales percentages of musical styles that are, according to the BPI, regarded as minority tastes – country, jazz, reggae, blues and folk. The 1995 *BPI Statistical Handbook* was the first to feature separate listings for country music, folk music, blues, reggae and

Table 1.1 British Phonographic Industry percentage of record sales by musical style 1991–2000

Style	1991	1994	1997	2000
Pop	41.5	39.2	34.3	32.4
Rock	28.9	28.4	25.7	25.9
Dance	7.9	11.0	11.8	13.3
Rhythm and blues	n/a	5.7	7.7	8.5
Country	1.4	1.8	2.1	1.7
Jazz	1.1	1.6	1.2	1.0
Reggae	1.1	1.3	0.8	0.9
Blues	1.2	0.9	0.8	0.4
Folk	0.9	0.9	0.8	1.1

Note: The BPI statistics included here omit many of the styles that would only achieve minimal sales. Consequently, the statistics for each year do not add up to 100%.
Source: Statistics from the *British Phonographic Industry Statistical Handbook* (1995, 1998, 2001).

jazz.[70] Sales percentages listed in the handbooks published in 1995 (which includes information from 1991 to 1994), 1998 (1995 to 1997) and 2001 (1998 to 2000) indicate fluctuations in the sales of certain categories, but the trends between 1991 and 2000 remain similar. While the pop and rock music categories indicate the highest percentages of sales in each year, statistics indicate a gradual decline in both genres, although sales of rock music increased slightly in 2000. Sales of country music recordings increased by almost 1 per cent between 1991 and 1997 but fell in 2000. Reggae sales have also shown a decline, and a possible reason for this is the assimilation of reggae into the dance genre, which shows the largest percentage increase. Blues sales decreased but this might also be explained by the assimilation of electric blues into the rock genre (an example is the popularity of guitarist Eric Clapton, whose music is often classified as rock in non-specialised record outlets). The *1995 Statistical Handbook* also points out that rhythm and blues sales were included for the first time in the 1995 edition, an inclusion that could explain an under-representation in the separate pop and blues categories from that time onwards. BPI statistics of sales of folk

Table 1.2 British Phonographic Industry percentage of record sales by musical style 2001–2005

Style	2001	2002	2003	2004	2005
Rock	12.0	13.2	13.0	15.0	21.7
Pop	28.7	29.0	30.0	28.8	24.7
Urban	13.0	12.5	13.9	15.6	13.5
MOR	6.0	6.1	6.4	7.8	8.5
Dance	10.5	9.5	7.2	6.9	7.6
Others	16.8	19.1	18.4	15.6	15.5

Source: Statistics from British Phonographic Industry and the Official UK Chart Company – online resource (BPI Market Information Series, www.bpi.co.uk; accessed 26 July 2007).

recordings indicate that sales remained at a constantly low level between 1991 and 1997, but with a slight increase in 2000.

BPI statistics since 2001 have included 'rock', 'pop', 'urban', 'MOR' (middle of the road) and 'dance' – with further statistics on sales of sub-genres within both 'pop' and 'rock' – as principal listings in the 'Sales by type of music' figures. These sub-genres are 'mainstream pop', 'teen pop' and 'contemporary rock'. The BPI no longer provides information on rhythm and blues, country, jazz, reggae, blues and folk. There is a list, however, for 'others' that arguably includes these styles as one percentage. The overall statistics are shown in Table 1.2.

While the BPI is unspecific about the individual sales percentages of styles listed as 'others', it is significant that this group sells more recordings than each of the other genres, except mainstream pop music. The lack of specificity may also imply that the styles that are grouped together no longer have an individual impact on UK record sales that might warrant record company interest. The BPI's representation of popular music styles sales remains a problematic issue, and it is further discussed in chapter 2. In contrast to the above statistics, sales of English folk-rock recordings by Fairport Convention and Steeleye Span indicate that the fusion of folk music and rock music in the late 1960s and the 1970s may have increased folk music awareness among a broader audience. For example, Fairport Convention released twelve albums between 1968 and 1975, and each sold approximately twenty thousand copies. The band's album *Angel Delight* (1971) exceeded this and reached number twenty-six in the UK album chart. Steeleye Span released eight albums between 1970 and 1975. *Please to See the King* (1971) reached the top fifty in the UK album chart, and *Now We Are Six* (1974) reached the top twenty. The band released *All Around my Hat* in 1975, and the title track reached number three in the UK singles chart.

Reasons for the current growth in the popularity of the live performance of British folk music styles in the UK may be linked to aspects of festival marketing and promotion aimed at audiences with broad musical tastes. Change involving the presentation of British folk music in the context of multicultural events indicate that British folk revivalism has entered a 'third phase', with aspects of continuity being linked to aspects of commercial promotion. Issues of commercialisation linked to the promotion of rock music were often regarded as anathema to revivalists of the 'second' folk revival, which started in the late 1940s and went into decline due to decreasing folk club attendance during the late 1980s and the 1990s.[71] The reception of folk music amalgamated with other musical styles and presented at folk festivals, rather than in the more intimate environment of the folk clubs, raises questions concerning the age groups within the folk music audience, given that many folk festivals have increased the stylistic diversity of their artist rosters since the late 1970s.[72]

Between 1988 and 1993, audiences attending folk clubs were mostly aged between thirty and forty-nine years, and few young people were joining them.[73] Differences in individual taste, therefore, underlie differences between audience members who prefer traditional performance in a folk club setting and those who prefer the diversity of folk music styles presented in a festival setting. Music journalist Colin Irwin describes the change that took place in British folk music audiences and in folk music performance during the 1990s in relation to the growth in popularity of folk festivals (although his reference to a single decade is questionable).[74] His concept of a new generation of musicians delving into English and Celtic traditions 'with a wonderful disregard for notions of purity' would describe some of the amalgamations of folk music with other musical styles achieved by the folk-rock performers interviewed in fieldwork.[75] The issue of stylistic amalgamation also provides a link between the Sidmouth International Festival and the Cambridge Folk Festival, the two most highly attended folk festivals in the UK. Between 1996 and 2001, the Sidmouth festivals attracted in excess of sixty-five thousand people annually; the Cambridge Folk Festival has sold to capacity each year since 1994, with an audience of ten thousand people on site during each day of the four-day festival.[76] Despite differences in terms of the respective private-sector and public-sector promotion and funding of these festivals, they share a philosophy of promoting stylistic diversity reflecting change and continuity. Irwin's statement does not refer to discourse between traditionalist and modernist viewpoints concerning notions of authenticity in modern British folk music. Dave Laing and Richard Newman are dismissive of debate of this kind, suggesting that, if the traditionalist faction of the folk music audience had still existed in the early 1970s, they 'wouldn't have been seen dead at Cambridge'.[77] The folk-rock performers I interviewed take a different view and maintain that there has been an anti-folk-rock faction in the folk audience since folk music was first combined with other musical styles, especially rock music.[78] This view supports Boyes' comments on folk fans' lack of acceptance of innovation.

As well as continuity, variation occurs as British folk music styles are performed within the world music category. In 2001, the Sidmouth Folk Festival was renamed the Sidmouth International Festival of Folk Arts – a further example of folk events in the UK linking British folk music to world music performance.[79] The presentation of folk music and world music performers at UK folk-orientated festivals introduces audiences from several genres to new musical styles and further illustrates that boundaries between different folk music styles have become as blurred as those within the rock and pop music genres. Bohlman describes 'world music' as a 'global encounter' that is 'at once mediating and problematising the distance between Self and Other' in a process of 'domestication'.[80] The 'domestication' process is applicable to the convergence of folk music and rock music, a convergence that could be viewed as a means of negating perceptions of heritage and tradition as British folk music becomes 'exoticised' when combined with other popular music styles. This combination provides a paradox between English folk-rock as a contemporary means of preservation and its links to the popular music genre as part of the music industry, an industry that regards sales of recordings as the main criterion by which to measure success.

While audience perception of change in folk music performance is apparent in the reception of amalgamation of folk and popular music styles, conversely, influences from traditional folk music have been adopted in popular music performance since the 1970s. This has occurred, for example, in the music of Led Zeppelin and Jethro Tull, as well as Scottish bands such as Runrig and Big Country, and in Irish pop and rock music such as that of The Corrs and U2. The dimension of variation is therefore present in mainstream pop music influenced by folk music, just as it is in the folk-rock music of bands such as Fairport Convention and Steeleye Span, and, more recently, of Eliza Carthy, Bellowhead, The Imagined Village, Jim Moray, and Mumford and Sons. Diversity in interpretation of folk music in English folk-rock performance raises questions concerning how issues of authenticity are regarded by folk performers and by rock music performers whose backgrounds are outside folk music.[81] Folk and folk-rock performers interviewed proposed that folk music can be regarded as a product of popular culture that transforms as change occurs in cultural and social trends in order to remain pertinent to its audience. This view may reflect their musical origins in the commercial arena of rock music. Moreover, it supports my observation that change occurring in modern British folk music – through shifts in cultural and social trends – generates new variations in folk music styles and leads to increasing convergences between styles representing different cultures and ethnicities in the United Kingdom. Globalisation of British folk music within the boundaries of world and roots music provides folk and popular music audiences with new musical hybrids that are often criticised by folk purists on the grounds of 'inauthenticity', as described by performers I have interviewed. These hybrids include the amalgamation of British folk music with Jamaican reggae, with what is referred to as 'dance', with rock music and with folk music from cultures outside of the United Kingdom. An example of cross-cultural folk music hybridity is illustrated by recordings of performances of Anglo-Asian bhangra, particularly in Sheila Chandra's performance of 'A Sailor's Life'. In a preview of the CD *The Imagined Village* (2005), its combination of folk music with other popular musical styles from within the United Kingdom – including Martin Carthy and Paul Weller's performance of 'John Barleycorn', and Chris Wood, The Transglobal Underground and Johnny Kalsi's performance of 'Cold, Hailey, Rainy Night' – is described as 'English roots music in its broadest sense'.[82] Hybridity is, however, noteworthy in this research only from the point of view of 'boundaries that have been essentialised'.[83] Musical definitions, or boundaries, become problematic if their application fails to take account of change within a musical style, and the use of terms such as 'folk', 'traditional' or 'folk-rock' often alienates factions of the British folk music audience and elicits negative reactions to change.

Differences of opinion between folk music fans at either end of a purism–modernism continuum often relate to questions of personal taste, to what folk fans regard as essential descriptors of folk music and to different age groups. Issues of perceived authenticity in folk music therefore invite more debate than consensus, and the politics of difference do not always recognise performers who are in-between categories.[84] Hybridity in modern British folk music is a consequence of cultural, sociological and musicological factors that cross musical styles and performance practices, and change caused by these factors has enabled modern British folk music styles to become a multicultural music style that has influenced modern popular music performers since the early 1970s, while straddling the authentic/inauthentic debate. Hybridity in folk music may be defined as a composition of elements incongruous to a perceived traditional view of the style and I maintain that issues of authenticity do not depend on the organisation of these elements.

My interviews with folk and folk-rock performers suggest that many elements of folk songs were retained in order to establish perceptions of authenticity when these songs were used as source material for performance in an English folk-rock context. Folk songs adapted in this way provide new source versions of folk songs that become hybrids imbued with an invented authenticity. For example, Steeleye Span recorded 'The Gower Wassail' in 1971, although their usually comprehensive sleeve notes do not acknowledge that Phil Tanner recorded the song in

1947 except for a cryptic reference to his name under the title of the song. Folk musicologist A. L. Lloyd notes that in the first verse of Tanner's version, the fourth line is 'Some nutmeg and ginger, the best we could brew' whereas Steeleye Span's version has 'Some nutmeg and ginger, the best we could bake'.[85] There are several other textual differences between both versions and the significance of small changes such as these may lie with issues of perceived authenticity and with personal performance preference. 'The Gower Wassail' appears twice in an online collection of wassails, with both versions having almost the same text, once under its original title and once as 'The Steeleye Span Wassail', adding the appearance of permanence, stability and authority to Steeleye Span's version.[86] A similar process occurs in songs such as 'The Deserter', which Fairport Convention recorded in 1969. The text of this song, like many other historical songs, permits the performer to vary historical details to include wars currently being fought, or details of current monarchy in order to make it pertinent and authentic. In the case of 'The Deserter', Prince Albert arrives during the last verse to save a soldier from execution, situating the song around the time of the Crimean War. Songs that may be relocated into a contemporary context, while retaining their original message, provide renewal points for perceptions of authenticity that can be transferred and applied to new source versions. In this way, Steeleye Span's recording of 'The Gower Wassail' may have become the most popular and accessible version of the song and, consequently, a new source version – as has, in Bob Lewis' view, their version of 'The Spotted Cow'.[87] Similarly, Fairport Convention's recording of 'The Deserter' remains accessible as a war ballad for use in other chronological settings and could have been as pertinent to the First World War (with a change of monarch) as it was to the Crimean War.

A contemporary context for folk music

Hybridity in folk music, as it becomes amalgamated with diverse popular music styles, has continued so far for three decades and has been typified more recently by artists who have used modern Afro-American 'dance' rhythms and music programming technology to perform traditional British folk songs. Recordings of folk songs in new contexts, such as rock or folk-rock, encompass the principles of continuity, variation and selection and provide renewed points of origin for these songs as they become regarded by performers and audiences as new source versions. Continuity, variation and selection as descriptors in English folk-rock performance consequently sit at both extremes of the authenticity/inauthenticity continuum, as demonstrated by the style's 'permanence' and 'stability' and its potential for adaptation into contemporary contexts. The changing nature of popular music also places limits on the use of descriptions of folk music amalgamated with rock and other popular music styles and provides a problematic overview of folk music performed in new contexts.

This book recontextualises modern folk music performed as English folk-rock in terms of its location as a nationalising factor in a devolved community, in terms of innovative processes of change as folk and rock are amalgamated while maintaining notions of authenticity in both styles, and in terms of an emerging eclectic folk audience that attends a new folk club scene that has grown concurrently with an expanding world music-based festival circuit. Before we look at the background and musical practices involved in English folk-rock, however, we need to examine how a revised notion of Englishness itself has evolved in parallel to this musical style, a style which has assisted the re-conceptualisation of English national identity for generations of folk and rock fans. The next chapter therefore addresses how Englishness is identified within a hybrid musical style and within a folk-orientated culture industry. If Scotland, Ireland and Wales are able to enjoy national cultures and national musics, why does England have a problem with its own?

Notes

1 The other drummer who can be credited as one of the first English folk-rock drummers is Dave Mattacks, who joined Fairport Convention following the death of Martin Lamble in 1969.

2 Correspondence with various folk festival promoters, including Cambridge Folk Festival promoter, Eddie Barcan, and Steve Heap, who promoted the Sidmouth Folk Festival and the Sidmouth International Festival.

3 Eddie Barcan, email correspondence with author, September 2001 and October 2005; Steve Heap, email correspondence with author, 17 August 2001.

4 Philip V. Bohlman, *The Study of Folk Music in the Modern World* (Bloomington and Indianapolis: Indiana University Press, 1988), 131.

5 For information on previous artist rosters at Sidmouth and Cambridge, see Derek Schofield, *The First Week in August: Fifty Years of the Sidmouth Festival* (Matlock: Sidmouth International Festival, 2004), and Dave Laing and Richard Newman, *Thirty Years of the Cambridge Folk Festival* (Cambridge: Music Maker Books, 1994).

6 Michael S. Peluse, 'Not Your Grandfather's Music: Tsugaru Shamisen Blurs the Lines Between "Folk", "Traditional" and "Pop" ', *Asian Music* (Summer/Fall 2005), 59.

7 Peluse, 'Not Your Grandfather's Music, 59.

8 Peluse, 'Not Your Grandfather's Music, 76.

9 Peluse, 'Not Your Grandfather's Music, 76.

10 Britta Sweers, *Electric Folk: The Changing Face of English Traditional Music* (New York: Oxford University Press, 2005), 23.

11 Sweers, *Electric Folk*, 23.

12 Paul Stump, *The Music's All that Matters: A History of Progressive Rock* (London: Quartet Books, 1997), 148.

13 For example, members of Fairport Convention have always regarded themselves as a rock band that plays folk songs and not as an electric folk band. Simon Nicol, interview with author, December 1996.

14 Karl Dallas, Robin Denselow, David Laing and Robert Shelton, *The Electric Muse: The Story of Folk Into Rock* (London: Methuen Publishing, 1975).

15 Michael Brocken, *The British Folk Revival 1944–2002* (Aldershot: Ashgate, 2003).

16 Rob Young, *Electric Eden: Unearthing Britain's Visionary Music* (London: Faber, 2010).

17 Respectively, John Francmanis, 'National Music to National Redeemer: The Consolidation of a "Folk-Song" Construct in Edwardian England', *Popular Music* 21:1 (2002): 3, and A. H. Fox Strangways, 'English Folk Song', *Music and Letters* 5:4 (1924), 294.

18 Respectively, Boyes, *The Imagined Village*, 15, 47–8 and 66–9; David Harker, 'Cecil Sharp in Somerset: Some Conclusions', *Folk Music Journal* 2 (1972), 220–40; Harker, 'May Cecil Sharp Be Praised?', *History Workshop Journal* no. 14 (1982), 44–62; Harker, *Fakesong: The Manufacture of British 'Folksong' - 1700 to the Present Day*

(Milton Keynes: Open University Press, 1985), 172–97; A. L. Lloyd, *Folk Song in England* (London: Laurence and Wishart, 1967), 14 and 41–51; and Michael Pickering, 'Song and Social Context', in *Singer, Song and Scholar*, ed. Ian Russell (Sheffield: Sheffield Academic Press, 1986), 73–93.

19 C. J. Bearman, 'Who Were The Folk? The Demography of Cecil Sharp's Somerset Folk Singers', *The Historical Journal* 43:3 (2000): 753–6 and 773.

20 Respectively, Boyes, *The Imagined Village*, 15; Lloyd, *Folk Song in England*, 179; and Bearman, 'Who Were The Folk?', 773.

21 Bearman, 'Who Were The Folk?', 775.

22 Bearman, 'Who Were The Folk?', 773; Hobsbawm, 'Introduction: Inventing Traditions', 7.

23 Kenneth S. Goldstein, 'Bowdlerization and Expurgation: Academic and Folk', *Journal of American Folklore* 80 (1967), 374–86.

24 Goldstein, 'Bowdlerization and Expurgation', 384.

25 Respectively, Simon Nicol, interviews with author, December 1996 and August 2005; Martin Carthy, interviews with author, March 1997 and August 2005.

26 Carthy, interviews, 1997 and 2005.

27 Raymond Leppard, *Authenticity in Music* (London: Faber, 1988), 6.

28 Leppard, *Authenticity in Music*, 7.

29 Nicholas Kenyon, 'Introduction: Some Issues and Questions', in *Authenticity in Early Music*, ed. Nicholas Kenyon (Oxford: Oxford University Press, 1988), 18.

30 Robert Donington, *The Interpretation of Early Music* (London: Faber, 1974), 37.

31 David Atkinson, 'Folk Songs in Print: Text and Tradition', *Folk Music Journal* 8:4 (2004), 456.

32 Daniel N. Thompson, 'Aesthetics, Authenticities, and Appeals to Authority: The Editor as Author', *Current Musicology* 64 (2001), 10.

33 Gary Tomlinson, 'Authentic Meaning in Music', in *Authenticity in Early Music*, 115.

34 Folk singer Bob Lewis described his own performance philosophy to me thus: 'My preference is to sing unaccompanied as this enables me to concentrate on the words of the song or ballad with the tune being the means of emphasising and decorating the lyrics.' He added that he endeavours to change his style of delivery to suit the type of song he is singing, and his statements are therefore contrary to revivalist notions of perceived authenticity and the recreation of an 'exact' rendition of a folk song based on notated texts or earlier performances by other artists. (Bob Lewis, email correspondence with author, 28 January, 2002.)

35 Howard Mayer Brown, 'Pedantry or Liberation', in *Authenticity in Early Music*, 28; Philip Brett, 'Text, Context and the Early Music Editor', in *Authenticity in Early Music*, 110.

36 Allan F. Moore, 'Authenticity as Authentication', *Popular Music* 21:2 (2002), 210.

37 Moore, 'Authenticity as Authentication', 215.

38 Philip V. Bohlman, 'World Music at the "End of History"', *Ethnomusicology* 46:1 (Winter 2002), 26.

39 *The New Grove Dictionary of Music and Musicians*, 2nd ed., s.v. 'Folk Music'.

40 Respectively, Benedict Anderson, *Imagined Communities: Reflections on the Origin and Spread of Nationalism* (London and New York: Verso, 1991); and Hobsbawm, 'Introduction: Inventing Traditions'.

41 Hobsbawm, 'Introduction: Inventing Traditions', 1.

42 David Atkinson, 'Revival: Genuine or Spurious?', in *Folk Song: Tradition, Revival, and Re-Creation*, 158.

43 Julian Gerstin, 'Reputation in a Musical Scene: The Everyday Context of Connections between Music, Identity and Politics,' *Ethnomusicology* 42:3 (Autumn, 1998), 385.

44 MacKinnon, *The British Folk Scene*, 29.

45 Boyes, *The Imagined Village*, xii.

46 Livingston, 'Music Revivals', 69.

47 Livingston, 'Music Revivals', 69.

48 Boyes, *The Imagined Village*, 239.

49 Atkinson, 'Revival: Genuine or Spurious?', 144.

50 Tina K. Ramnarine, *Ilmatar's Inspirations: Nationalism, Globalization, and the Changing Soundscapes of Finnish Folk Music* (Chicago: University of Chicago Press, 2003), 14. (See also Mark Slobin, 'How the Fiddler Got on the Roof', in *Folk Music and Modern Sound*, edited by William Ferris and Mary L. Hart (Jackson: University Press of Mississippi, 1982), 21, who puts it that commercial amalgamation of folk music with popular music is part of a process of musical modernisation.)

51 Ramnarine, *Ilmatar's Inspirations*, 15.

52 Ramnarine, *Ilmatar's Inspirations*, 213.

53 Ramnarine, *Ilmatar's Inspirations*, 49.

54 Ramnarine, *Ilmatar's Inspirations*, 49.

55 Ramnarine, *Ilmatar's Inspirations*, 15.

56 Ramnarine, *Ilmatar's Inspirations*, 201.

57 Atkinson, 'Folk Songs in Print', 457–8.

58 Carthy, interviews, 1997 and 2005.

59 Ashley Hutchings, interview with author, May 1997.

60 Georgina Boyes, interview with author, August 1997. Boyes was keen to explain that she was not a performer but that she approached folk music from a cultural studies perspective.

61 Boyes, interview, 1997.

62 Boyes, interview, 1997.

63 Respectively, Charles Keil, 'Motion and Feeling Through Music', *Journal of Aesthetics and Art Criticism* 24:3 (1966), 337–49; David Epstein, *Beyond Orpheus: Studies in Musical Structure* (Cambridge, MA: MIT Press, 1979).

64 Respectively, Bertrand H. Bronson, *The Ballad as Song* (Berkeley: University of California Press, 1969) and Anne Dhu Shapiro, 'The Tune-Family Concept in British-American Folksong Scholarship' (PhD dissertation, Music Department, Harvard University, 1975).

65 J. A. Prögler, 'Searching for Swing: Participatory Discrepancies in the Jazz Rhythm Section', *Ethnomusicology* 39:2 (1995), 21–54.

66 Moore, 'Authenticity as Authentication', 215.

67 Ed Bicknell, interview with author, September 1997.

68 Burt Feintuch, 'Musical Revival as Musical Transformation', in *Transforming Tradition*, edited by Neil V. Rosenberg (Chicago: University of Illinois Press, 1993), 192.

69 Charlie Gillett, *The Sound Of The City* (London: Souvenir Press, 1983), 401 and 413.

70 Christopher Green, *BPI Statistical Handbook*, ed. Peter Scaping (Penryn: Troutbeck Press, 1995), 17.

71 MacKinnon, *The British Folk Scene*, 43; Paul Westwell, *Folk Music Report* (London: Executive Committee of the Musicians' Union, 1997), 2.

72 See appendix 1 for examples of diversity in artist rosters at the Cambridge Folk Festival and other United Kingdom music festivals between 1986 and 2002.

73 MacKinnon, *The British Folk Scene*, 43.

74 Colin Irwin, 'The New English Roots', in *World Music: The Rough Guide*, ed. Simon Broughton (London: Penguin, 1994) , 32–42.

75 Irwin, 'The New English Roots', 32.

76 Steve Heap, email correspondence with author, 17 August, 2001; Eddie Barcan, email correspondence with author, September 2001 and October 2005. It should be noted that there are also many smaller multicultural folk-orientated festivals promoted annually in the UK.

77 Laing and Newman, *Thirty Years of the Cambridge Folk Festival*, 38 and 43.

78 Simon Nicol, interviews with author, December 1996 and August 2005; Gerry Conway, interview with author, January 1997; Martin

Carthy, interviews with author, March 1997 and August 2005; Ashley Hutchings, correspondence with author, May 1997; Rick Kemp, interviews with author, between August 1997 and June 2005.

79 For example, in 2001 the Sidmouth Folk Festival included artists from Zimbabwe, Sicily, and Iraq; in 2003 the festival presented artists from Galicia, Australia, the United States of America, Korea, Ghana, India, Poland, and the Pacific Islands.

80 Bohlman, 'World Music at the "End of History"', 1 and 27.

81 See appendix 1 for artist rosters of festivals promoted in the United Kingdom since the late 1960s.

82 'Monocle,' *English Dance and Song* 67:2 (Summer 2005), 8 and 9.

83 Jan Nederveen Pieterse, *Globalization and Culture: Global Mélange* (Lanham, MD: Rowman and Littlefield, 2004), 86.

84 Nederveen Pieterse, *Globalization and Culture*, 85.

85 Respectively, Lloyd, *Folk Song in England*, 101, and Steeleye Span, *Please To See The King* (B and C Records 1029, 1971).

86 Atkinson, 'Folk Songs in Print', 457–8.

87 Bob Lewis, email correspondence with author, January 2002.

Selling England by the song   2

Whose culture is it?

Contemporary perceptions of Englishness, and in particular their location within notions of Britishness in the context of commercial and political relationships, have influenced the promotion of Englishness through English folk-rock from the late 1960s to the present day. The absence of a contemporary English identity distinct from right-wing political elements has reinforced negative and apathetic perceptions of English folk culture and tradition among the populist media. Negative perceptions such as these have to some extent been countered by audience reception of folk and popular music hybrids within a broad English folk-rock musical category that has become apparent since the decline of the progressive rock movement in the late 1970s. The emergence of a post-progressive rock-orientated English folk-rock style has enabled new folk music fusions to establish themselves in a populist performance medium that attracts a new folk audience. In this way, English folk-rock has facilitated an English cultural identity that is distinct from negative social and political connotations. A significant contemporary national identity for British folk music in general can be found in English folk-rock as it is presented in a homogenous mix of popular and world music styles. This new identity has attracted debate that will be discussed later in this chapter. From the perspective of national identity I argue that while devolution of the United Kingdom since the late 1990s has enabled the establishment of national assemblies for Scotland, Wales and Northern Ireland, the absence of an English national assembly has been problematic in the consolidation of a modern English identity that reclaims Englishness from recent links to xenophobia.

More recent fusions of folk and popular music styles remain influenced by the hegemony of the English folk-rock style established by Fairport Convention and Steeleye Span. By ending the progressive rock phase of their careers in the late 1970s and reuniting after a period away from band performance, both these bands – pioneers of the English folk-rock movement – needed to reinvent their musical identities in the early 1980s. These new identities, and their disassociation from the earlier progressive rock movement, enabled relocation to prominent and influential positions in what has become a new phase of British folk music revivalism within the English folk-rock category. This new revival is also situated in the world music genre and it enables new perceptions of English identity to be free of previous negative associations.

Connections between English folk-rock promotion and popular music industry business techniques have enabled a new phase in folk music revivalism that preserves notions of tradition and heritage, while embracing the commercial character of popular music. English folk-rock performers have enjoyed a commercial advantage given that the style has its origins in the mainstream popular music industry that has both avoided xenophobic associations and used standard music-industry business practice as a means of marketing, promotion and distribution. English folk-rock dissemination of promotional and recorded materials through the adoption of commercial business models, which are normally associated with the popular music industry, has since the 1970s provided a wider audience base than traditional folk music. Contemporary dissemination of British folk music, in various stylistic formats, exists within its own newly created culture industry and is often facilitated by a symbiotic relationship between folk and popular music styles, this relationship having also had a positive commercial influence on the reception of pop and rock during the intervening thirty years.

The English folk-rock performers I interviewed described a hostile reaction from some folk revivalists in the late 1960s and early 1970s to the amalgamation of folk music with rock music, as well as to folk-rock's connections to the popular music industry. These performers situate themselves in the rock genre of the period and not as part of any revivalist movement at the time. They express initial detachment from earlier notions of preservation and revivalism, although they acknowledge their own perceptions of English folk-rock, adopting a revivalist stance towards the end of the twentieth century. This view is also supported by my interviews with festival promoters, who describe an increase in audience attendance at world-music-orientated folk festivals in the UK since the mid-1990s.

I also focus on the use of British folk music in the UK primary and secondary music curricula as a means of potentially facilitating awareness of national identity. At the end of the twentieth century, primary and secondary music education aimed to provide a basic level of knowledge of the folk music of the various cultures present in the UK, as well as other music styles from what the curriculum vaguely referred to as 'the British Isles'. This teaching policy was broad enough to be interpreted to suit the ethnic origins of diverse groups of schoolchildren in the UK, as well as the personal skills of teachers, while avoiding references to British, or English, identity that might be perceived as negative. Contemporary popularity of English folk-rock presented at world-music-orientated folk festivals has assisted in redressing perceptions of the national origins of the style.

A culture industry perspective of English folk-rock

Prior to any discussion of commercial links between English folk-rock and contemporary British folk music revivalism, it is worth considering the scholarly debate that surrounds perceptions of Marxism in consumerist aspects of folk revivalism, as well as Adorno's term 'culture industry' in the context of folk music and English folk-rock. Scholarly debate in the second half of the twentieth century indicates diverse stances on the commoditisation of tradition and culture. The selling of national 'self', particularly from the perspective of the re-orientation of a contemporary English identity, is currently situated within broad notions of Britishness in a post-devolution United Kingdom. English folk-rock has established itself as a cultural commodity that also reinforces notions of tradition and national identity, and it both unites and separates politically devolved locations in the UK. These notions remain apparent in a new phase of revivalism within the English folk-rock movement. Folklore – and arguably folk music – is not representative of ancient tradition passed down unchanged from a pre-modern world. Instead, folklore can be aligned with the culture of the dominant class from which it draws 'the motifs which then become inserted into combinations with the previous traditions', a view reflective of amalgamations of folk music with other musical styles that are promoted through culture industry domination, and through links to notions of tradition and heritage.[1]

While I do not propose that British folk music and English folk-rock are hegemonic constructs, it is significant that the promotion of culture among the 'popular masses' is apparent in Adorno's cultural analyses. Popular culture exists within a dichotomy of subject and subjectivity in which subjectivity is increasingly overwhelmed and absorbed 'by the all-powerful machinery of the totally administered society' and in which 'the system is master and each individual is a manipulated cog'.[2] This description is also illustrative of hegemonic media control of the entertainment industry, which now includes a newly emerging and stylistically broad-based folk music industry.[3] In his consideration of Adorno's views on the commodification of culture, Simon Frith is critical of a broad analytical response to Adorno's pessimism that accepts the organisational account of mass cultural production, that ignores the complexities of Adorno's aesthetic theory, and that seeks the redeeming features of commodity culture in the act of consumption.[4] This view is out of step with a contemporary view of folk music that is presented in a global, world music context as denigrating to notions of its original traditions and culture. Frith observes, however, that 'If it is through consumption that contemporary culture is lived, then it is in the process of consumption that contemporary cultural value must be located.'[5] In terms of the cultural commodification of musics, musical styles such as jazz, folk, rap and rock are all, in one way or another, handling issues thrown up by their commodification. These issues relate to the position of the artist in the marketplace, the relations of class and community, the tensions between technology and tradition, the shaping of race and nation, and the distinction of the public and the private.[6] For Frith, none of these issues are confined to one social group or any one musical practice. Moreover, he convincingly argues that:

> The popular cultural studies line that popular consumer culture serves people's needs, and thus by denigrating it, we therefore denigrate those needs, misses the point. The issue is whether people's lives are adequate for human needs, for human potential. The political argument, in other words, concerns culture as reconciliation versus culture as transformation.[7]

This view is reflective of the debate surrounding political promotion of notions of national heritage and tradition – which include national folk musics – in the United Kingdom as a means of reinstating a state of unity following the dislocating effects of devolution.

Folk music journalist Roger Marriot is critical of music industry processes involved in the contemporary promotion of folk music, although he supports a view that commercialism is not an issue to modern British folk audiences, which are often situated within the audience for world music.[8] Marriot states that the commercialisation of modern folk music mainly relates to 'punters and performers', a phrase he uses as a description of the financial exchange that occurs between audience and performer. He states that 'the most visible part of the world of what is commonly called "folk" is dominated by festival organisers, promoters and entertainment agencies', as well as 'arts administrators who both solicit and dispense grants and subsidies', a statement that acknowledges the influence of commercialism and sources of government and private sponsorship on semi-professional and professional performers and promoters. Marriot aims to draw attention to what he perceives as a disparity between the maintenance of tradition by 'unpaid participants' and connections to what he regards as 'show-biz', arguably a reference to the performance status of established folk and folk-rock performers.

Ian Smith, Head of Music at the Scottish Arts Council and a founding member of the Musicians' Union Folk, Roots and Traditional Music Section, challenges Marriot's view. Smith maintains that commercial issues do not affect the maintenance of tradition, particularly in respect of old songs presented in contemporary contexts. He suggests that folk music is part of an industry that exists through songs as its most effective currency, and the trading and performance of folk songs do not make them cease to be traditional nor do they 'take the piss out of the culture'.[9] Smith regards folk music's links to commercial practices 'as taking it [folk music] to a new audience, most of whom are perfectly comfortable with it and not in any way intimidated by the way it's presented'.[10]

World music critic and journalist Colin Irwin observes that perceived tradition and commercial issues co-exist successfully in many areas of contemporary folk music performance, including amalgamations of folk and rock music that are performed by a new generation of folk performers.[11] While discussing recent developments in British folk music, Irwin refers to the latest incarnations of folk music fusion in the UK as 'Britfolk', and many of the artists he describes as part of a 'new folk uprising' cite members of the early English folk-rock bands as influences – views that are at odds with those of Marriot on the 'show-biz' nature of commercial success in folk music.[12] Irwin also observes that, while there may be a pattern of growth in folk music revivalism among newer folk performers, there also exists what he regards as a parallel growth in elitism that is 'in constant pursuit of obliqueness and obscurity with a pathological hatred of populism'.[13] He regards this folk music elitism as 'every bit as damaging to the public perception of the music as the old "hands–off" brigade', although, in what seems a contradiction, he describes television, radio and press promotion of new folk performers as 'hype', a term often used to describe media promotion of pop music performers. By being critical of media 'hype', Irwin thus aligns himself with those in the folk music scene that he criticises, and he places himself at odds with an enthusiastic review of a UK BBC4 television series, *Folk Britannia*. This review presented an overview of the current British folk music scene in an earlier edition of the journal in which Irwin often writes.[14] Dave Nunn, however, writes from a folk audience perspective in the 'Letters' page of *English Dance and Song* criticising media representation of folk music in the UK. He states that, while BBC4 television's broadcasts of *Folk Britannia* in early 2006 were to be generally commended, the programmer's suggestion that the second folk revival was 'hijacked in the late 1960s by Joe Boyd's drug crazed hippies' was erroneous.[15] He further adds that performers such as Fairport Convention and the Incredible String Band did not supplant the traditional scene but co-existed alongside it.

The views above indicate that, as a new phase in British folk revivalism emerges, there is a concomitant emergence of debate concerning issues of commercialisation in folk music that is similar to that which existed in both the first and second folk revivals. Current media promotion of the music that may stem from an elitist viewpoint adopts the use of 'hype' to serve its own promotional ends, despite arguable historical inaccuracies concerning connections between revivalism and the progressive rock movement. Whether 'show biz' and 'hype' are appropriate terms for media promotion in folk music contexts remains questionable, and this issue will be addressed later in this chapter.

Some English folk-rock history

Investigation of the transition in which the identities of Fairport Convention and Steeleye Span were reinvented in the 1980s suggests that both bands have retained audience popularity as leaders of a new English folk-rock movement. This movement has drawn upon contemporary notions of revivalism and new perceptions of Englishness following both bands' disassociation with the earlier progressive rock movement. What I regard as a growing area of revivalism therefore began in the period that followed the decline in the popularity of the progressive rock movement in the post-punk era of the late 1970s. As part of the progressive-rock counter-culture, English folk-rock was not part of the second British folk revival and remained detached from it, despite the number of folk fans that attended English folk-rock concerts (as described in fieldwork interviews with performers). In the mid-1970s, however, many rock music fans embraced the punk rock style that was the antithesis of the technical virtuosity and showmanship of progressive rock.

Many progressive bands were also unable to exist financially during the economic climate of the period, and record companies could not maintain the costs of supporting bands that often used elaborate stage settings and that needed large numbers of technical personnel to assist bands in performance.

Fairport Convention were one of the progressive bands that, while able to continue live performance due to the comparative simplicity of their stage settings, were unable to sell sufficient quantities of their recordings to maintain record company support from the mid-1970s onwards. Consequently, their record label, Phonogram, cancelled their recording contract in 1979 with four albums still remaining to be recorded. The band performed at a number of 'final' performances, notably at the Knebworth Festival with Led Zeppelin in August 1979. The most significant final performance was at Cropredy in Oxfordshire on the evening of their Knebworth concert. The band had first performed at Cropredy at a village fete in 1976 and they felt that, as many band members had lived in the surrounding area at various times, it would be an appropriate place to end the band's career. In 1980, Fairport Convention promoted a reunion concert in the village, which has since become an annual event, attracting an audience in excess of 20,000 each year.

Steeleye Span experienced difficulties similar to Fairport Convention in the late 1970s, despite having enjoyed commercial success in the popular music charts prior to this period. The band released the single *All Around My Hat* in 1975, a recording that was produced by Mike Batt. The single entered the top twenty of the United Kingdom record charts but the commercial success that the band achieved, together with their association with Batt, alienated both their folk and progressive rock audiences, while situating the band in the commercial mainstream.[16] Following the end of the band's progressive rock career in the late 1970s, Steeleye Span also reunited in the early 1980s and has toured and recorded, albeit with various line-ups, to the present day.

By reinventing their identities in the early 1980s, both Fairport Convention and Steeleye Span have remained influential in a new phase of British folk music revivalism that became apparent during the 1990s as British folk-music-informed performance became associated with the presentation of world music.

Also, by its association with commercial aspects of music promotion, English folk-rock remained distinct from earlier links to spheres of political influence that provided funding, albeit nominal, to folk music that it exploited as a means of promoting national awareness during the twentieth century.[17] Both Fairport Convention and Steeleye Span have maintained career longevity by openly embracing the commercial nature of music industry marketing, promotion and distribution processes and, in doing so, have also become central to a musical reinvention of notions of English and British national identity.[18]

English folk-rock/British world music

While discussion of musical values in an amalgamated stylistic marketplace can be situated in Adorno-orientated notions of musical aesthetics, perceptions of national identity in folk music are equally complex when links are made between this music and notions of Britishness and Englishness. This section explores theoretical discourses surrounding the terms 'nation' and 'identity' with specific references to Britishness and Englishness that are manifested in folk music. Promotion of an English, as opposed to British, national identity has been problematic since the early 1980s due to connections of Englishness with right-wing nationalism. While Scotland, Northern Ireland and Wales have long-established cultural identities outside their inclusion as components of the United Kingdom, perceptions of Englishness have often been regarded as connected to what folk singer Billy Bragg refers to as 'football hooligans, the skinheads and narrow-minded, xenophobic people'.[19] A letter to the editor of *English Dance and Song*, the EFDSS members' magazine, exemplifies Bragg's perception of English narrow-mindedness, and it is critical of the cover of the autumn 2000 issue omitting the word 'English', while abbreviating the title to *Dance and Song*. The criticism concerns the preservation of 'Englishness' in folk music and dance and what its author regards as the threat of their homogenisation with music and dance from other cultures. The author does not mention Scottish, Irish or Welsh folk music, an omission that may suggest that music from other parts of the British Isles is also a threat to Englishness. The letter is quoted in full:

Yes, approve of the re-vamped interior of the magazine; where is
ENGLISH on the cover? Couldn't believe it wasn't there. Smoked
out? Burned out? No, invisible from every angle. NOT GOOD
ENOUGH.

Since the introduction of see-through plastic covers, have felt it
was a good free advert to postal staff; ENGLISH Dance and Song.
Despite all the Society's efforts it is still a generally held belief that
'folk' starts on the other side of the channel. And that side don't
believe the English have any dances (our lack of national costume
not helping of course). I know, I've danced with groups 'over
there' and got very tired of replying, 'No, we are not German/
Swiss/Hungarian etc'.

We've lost our passport, are perilously close to losing our currency, yet again, and now our own ENGLISH Dance and Song has
truncated its title. PUT IT BACK.[20]

Absence of first person singular in the first two paragraphs
gives the letter a jingoistic, almost Dickensian character that is
reinforced by the use of 'over there', a veiled reference to Europe.
The perceived sense of loss of national identity makes the letter
more of a political, or perhaps even tribal, statement than a
musical one and demonstrates the potency of music as a symbol
of national identity.[21] An alternative view might be that this
letter parodies factions among the folk audience that regard the
preservation of English identity in British folk music as paramount.[22] The letter is illustrative of a broader perception of
English national identity that has been the subject of scholarly
debate throughout the second half of the twentieth century.
The question of English national identity becomes particularly
problematic in the debate on perceptions of Englishness located
within a devolved United Kingdom, although the problem
existed prior to the political events of the late twentieth century.

Government promotion of British folk music throughout the
twentieth century was based on notions of identity, tradition
and heritage, with folk songs representing statements of national
identity throughout the United Kingdom. Many aspects of tradition associated with folk music had their origins in the period
of the first folk revival during which revivalists, educators and
folk song collectors regarded British folk culture as 'a common
heritage to all' without which society could not exist, and they
called for the establishment of a national movement to reverse

the abandonment of this heritage.[23] Revivalists encouraged awareness of 'Englishness' and English culture, although they assumed that folk culture was a product of the lower classes, especially those regarded as uneducated and coming from isolated rural communities.[24] Restoration of a perceived musical heritage intended to re-kindle 'a love of nation' and national solidarity in the early twentieth century is therefore easily interpreted as a means of encouraging notions of 'Englishness', although promotion of English folk-rock in the late twentieth century remains distinct from aspects of nationalism, while enabling access to folk music in this setting to a more recent public forum.

Scholarly debate continued throughout the second half of the twentieth century concerning issues of identity in the United Kingdom in pre- and post-devolution periods. Simon Frith convincingly argues that the academic study of popular music is often limited to an assumption that sounds must 'reflect' or 'represent' the people and equates music experience with music identity. In his view, our response to music often draws us 'haphazardly' into emotional alliances with performers and with those performers' other fans.[25] These alliances often relate to perceptions of national identity, tradition and heritage.

British political endorsement of the teaching of folk songs was also intended to encourage notions of antiquity in nationalist and preservation-orientated nostalgia.[26] Notions of cultural nostalgia, however, often produce debate concerning the construction of personal versions of the past. English folk-rock has often adopted nostalgic perceptions of an idealised past to validate contemporary perceptions of authenticity since the early 1970s, despite initial detachment from aspects of folk revivalism. These perceptions remain influential in regard to how UK political and education establishments broadly perceive British folk music – including folk music amalgamated with popular music styles – as a contemporary means of encouraging awareness of national identity. Since the late 1960s, English folk-rock bands have recorded folk music from all of the British Isles, a stylistic policy that enabled them to remain detached from existing notions of Englishness that have often attracted negative connotations. More recently, this earlier detachment has situated English folk-rock as a significant representation of contemporary British folk music that contributes to a revised notion of Englishness located individually and collectively within the folk music of other parts of the British Isles, and without negative associations with nationalism.

Twentieth-century political promotion of British identity, tradition and heritage has included media broadcasts of British folk music since the 1940s, and a re-contextualised nostalgic past situates social history beyond official history providing idealised notions of heritage. A continuum links government endorsement of British folk music as a manufactured national heritage during the twentieth century to contemporary government funding and promotion of this music (often through education initiatives), which includes BBC television and radio broadcasts and the establishment of a new folk arts organisation – Folk Arts England – in the twenty-first century. Invented 'English' identity has been re-contextualised by government-assisted promotion of 'Britishness' as a means of unifying the diverse cultures present in the United Kingdom. This re-contextualisation reflects political perceptions of cultural diversity in the UK that are concomitant with the retention of national identity, particularly in Scotland, Northern Ireland and Wales where notions of individual identity are not problematic.[27]

In his definitive study of the deconstruction of Great Britain as a nation state, Tom Nairn describes the economic decline in the United Kingdom during the 1970s following the predictions of Enoch Powell, which were based on Powell's perceptions of the half-submerged nationalism of the English at the end of empire. Nairn provides a scathing observation of the surreal notions of English identity in Powell's perceptions of Englishness and describes Powell's 'Disney-like' English world as: 'a myth out of step with the reality of the English who are unlike their Celtic neighbours in that they are too vague and mixed-up to fit a national stereotype and too internally differentiated for the vulgar measurements of nationalism.'[28] This view of Englishness became more apparent during the 1990s, particularly in the period following 1997 as the UK approached the devolution process. Stuart Hall succinctly describes problematic issues discussed by Nairn that surround the establishment of national identity. Hall argues that a 'naturalist' approach to defining identity sees identification as 'a construction, a process never completed – always "in process" '.[29] Institutionalised teaching of perceptions of an invented past in folk music contexts aimed to stimulate awareness of national identity throughout the twentieth century. An imagined construct, however, only creates notional identity, tradition and heritage.

Teaching Englishness within a folk music construct

The teaching of folk music in the twenty-first century might be assisted by links to musical styles pertinent to the tastes of each school age-group. The introduction of folk music into a negative classroom environment, however, may prejudice ways in which it is perceived and prolong perceptions of irrelevance. When I attended school in the 1960s, I was often made to take part in country dancing, the music for which was often drawn from the repertoire of accordion music accompanied by a snare drum. As stated earlier, this representation of folk music was insipid and dull, and it did not draw me, or any of my friends, into the folk scene in our local area. My introduction to folk song came through a friend introducing me to the seminal English folk-rock album *Liege and Lief* (1969) by Fairport Convention, which in turn led me to the early recordings of Steeleye Span and ultimately to visits to Cecil Sharp House (the centre of the EFDSS), where I first became aware of a structured approach to learning about English folk music. It seemed appropriate, therefore, that any exploration into the EFDSS' input into contemporary folk music education should start with the organisation's education manager.

While English folk-rock may stimulate new perceptions of English identity among world music audiences, Diana Campbell-Jewitt (the National Education Manager of the EFDSS between 1995 and 2007), views English folk music from an educational perspective that is based on her experience as a teacher of history and literature, her publication of several resource books on folk dancing for schools, and her post-graduate work in cultural studies. She supports the inclusion of folk music and folk dancing in the primary and secondary curriculum, although she is critical of ways in which folk arts are regarded in British society. Campbell-Jewitt states that folk arts in the United Kingdom never made a successful transition from a rural setting to an urban setting and argues that 'people who see themselves as urban dwellers and sort of chic, the fashionable people in society, look down as being of higher status than the people who do folk arts and there is this assumption that, if you are into folk arts, you chew straw, you wear funny clothes, and you must have a strange rural accent'.[30] She also argues that there is no clear strand of English folk music in the current music curriculum that might define a sense of Englishness and that would enable comparisons to be made to the musics of other cultures and ethnicities that are present in it.[31] She commented, 'What you've got at the moment in England is an overwhelming institutional need to incorporate all the different nationalities [into the education curriculum] that we're being swamped with.' While this statement might be interpreted as a critical view of British post-colonialism, Campbell-Jewitt does not refer to immigration, but rather to the influx of musical styles to a contemporary curriculum that attempts to represent all ethnicities present in the UK.[32] She added that folk music performance from other countries seems more 'colourful and oddball' in comparison to English folk music, which does not have 'the kudos...the glamour that you get from other countries' traditions'.[33]

Political establishment endorsement of the teaching of English folk music in the UK primary and secondary school curricula exists as part of an educational framework that combines its use in dance and, to a lesser extent, in the teaching of notions of national identity and heritage. However, some critics assert that English folk music awareness at the end of the twentieth century had not moved forward since the work of Sharp.[34] Folk music has been taught in the British education system throughout most of the twentieth century, despite debate on how Sharp and others presented it. All of the English folk-rock performers interviewed for this book, however, commended Sharp's work and they all described the assembly of their initial repertoires as being a process of collecting songs from other performers, as well as from collections by Sharp, that had been part of the national curriculum at the time of their primary and secondary education.[35]

Folk music education remains a contentious issue a century after Sharp praised the inclusion of folk music in the Edwardian national curriculum. In the late 1970s, however, teachers questioned the teaching of folk music in primary and secondary schools. While discussing Morris dancing in the teaching of folk dancing to school children, educator Michael Pollard suggests that, as it is a reflection of primitive ritual, teachers should address issues surrounding it carefully:

> Morris, in so far as it has been involved in education, has become overlaid with various false notes – including the antiquarian interest of Victorian clergymen, the 'health and beauty' connotations of the revivalists of the 1920s, and the vulgarisations of television comedians. It has also become confused with that educational hybrid 'country dancing', which has always seemed to me the archetype of that process of bastardization through education.[36]

Pollard's view is equally applicable to the teaching of folk songs in schools. A lack of explanation of what folk music is, where it comes from and why it is an important cultural resource may prevent an enthusiastic reception among young audiences. Pollard's reference to a 'process of bastardization' echoes Georgina Boyes' description of the signifiers of folk music that were used to represent and sell 'Englishness' from the 1940s to the 1960s, such as Morris dancers, maypoles on the village green, orchestrated folk songs and British Rail posters.[37] Pollard's use of 'bastardization' can also be applied to combinations of elements of folk culture included in the twentieth-century music curriculum, such as the use of recordings of orchestrated folk songs as a medium for country dancing in schools without any explanation of their origins or the ways in which the music had been changed for the purposes of the curriculum. Folk songs used for country dancing at the time of the second folk revival were often taken from Sharp's arrangements and what educator Phil Everitt regards as 'the blandest arrangements that the [second] folk revival ever produced'.[38] Country dancing was taught in the 1950s and 1960s as a sporting activity – which led to the later funding connections between the EFDSS and the English Sports Council – rather than as a means of acquainting schoolchildren with elements of national awareness and folk culture. The removal of folk songs from their original, social and cultural contexts made them 'little more than curious oddities' to those who danced to them.[39] Schools were autonomous in the 1950s and, while British folk music was included in music teaching, the lack of a specific national music curriculum enabled teachers to include any musical styles they felt appropriate, and for which they had enthusiasm. Inclusion of country dancing in the music curriculum in the 1950s and 1960s can also be linked to the popularity of traditional folk music among teachers who had been influenced by the work of Sharp and by the broadcast of folk music recordings from the BBC during the second folk revival. Everitt also asserts that, in order to avoid 'the most insipid musical products of the folk revival', folk music awareness should be promoted through the use of recordings which make reference to other musical traditions, such as 'reggae, rock and aspects of world music', and through music which creates 'an immediate connection' with the musical tastes of children.[40] Teaching music in such a way would demonstrate the diversity of British folk music styles in comparison to other musical styles included in the national curriculum.

National folk-rock

While Scottish, Irish and Welsh folk and rock musics are often used as a means of stating national identity, Englishness represented in folk and rock music does not enjoy the same level of status and acclaim as the cultural identities of its UK neighbours. This section discusses perceptions of musical identity in Scotland, Ireland and Wales in comparison to that in England, which have changed since the process of devolution that occurred in the late twentieth century. The combination of English folk music with popular music styles in the UK may provide a solution to what David Arthur regards as a problem central to the reception of traditional performance of English folk music among new audiences outside the spheres of education and the folk club scene. Arthur, the editor of *English Dance and Song* between 1979 and 2001, regards English folk music as difficult to 'sell' and maintains that it sounds 'strange, odd, quaint, rough and scrappy' when compared to 'slick' Irish and Scottish folk music.[41] Arthur's statement is supported by folk record-company owner and folk music promoter Robb Johnson who criticises the use of the terms 'world', 'roots' and 'international' to describe British folk music festivals in the 1990s as an attempt to reclassify the folk genre, and as a means for folk performers to re-establish careers and professional identities:

> There are attempts (largely unsuccessful; if it didn't work for Sellafield...) to camouflage folk with different names like 'acoustic' or 'roots' music, or by subsuming it under the liberal umbrella of 'world music'. Some bands successfully half struggle out of the genre and then attempt to maintain trajectory by pretending they're not folk music at all. Coming the other way, musicians whose careers have gone a bit stagnant elsewhere go all unplugged at big folk festivals.[42]

Multicultural understanding among different cultures and ethnicities within the United Kingdom may be evident at musical events that feature cultural diversity, although scholarly debate remains concerning issues of perceived musical identity in Scotland, Ireland and Wales. While each of these nations has an established cultural identity distinct from its membership of the UK, English musical identity remains as problematic as its other cultural issues, particularly from the perspective of the United Kingdom having become an increasingly multi-ethnic society during the second half of the twenty-first century.

Stuart Hall argues that there are two kinds of identity – identity as being – which offers a sense of unity and commonality – and identity as becoming – a process of identification, which shows discontinuity with the past in our identity formation. Hall observes that 'Far from being eternally fixed in some essentialised past, [these two kinds of identity] are subject to the continuous "play" of history, culture and power' and that 'Cultural identities are the points of identification, the unstable points of identification or suture, which are made, within the discourses of history and culture – not an essence but a *positioning*.'[43] Martin Stokes provides a useful discussion on the position of music as a descriptor of national identity in the United Kingdom and an initial comparative analysis of the ethnic conflicts that took place in Europe in the last twenty years of the twentieth century, making particular reference to ethnic violence that has taken place in British cities in the second half of the twentieth century.[44] His inclusion of British ethnic conflict is particularly significant in post-devolution Britain where the politics of identity and difference have come to the fore, particularly in the case of a notional English identity that is problematic and embarrassing.

Stokes describes music as 'socially meaningful, not entirely but largely, because it provides means by which people recognise identities and places, and the boundaries which separate them' and he contends that the term 'ethnicity' allows us to turn from questions directed towards defining the 'essential and "authentic" traces of identity "in" music'.[45]

Peter Symon extends Stuart Hall's views in his own discussion of the use of Scottish folk music to articulate 'a significant sort of musical Scottishness'.[46] As it did in Ireland, nationalism became more pronounced in the twentieth century in Scotland, particularly in the mid-1960s following the discovery of oil in the North Sea on the east coast of Scotland, referred to as 'Scotland's oil'. Following this discovery, Scottish nationalism was further promoted by Scottish National Party's calls for devolution from the UK government, although there remained a tendency to relate any change in Scottish identity to cultural differences with England. Scottish nationalism was also evident in the Scottish folk revival during the 1970s, which was predominantly led by urban, cosmopolitan, middle-class revivalists.

In the 1970s, the revival drew not only on Scottish folk music, but also that of other regions of the United Kingdom and Ireland – particularly Irish jigs and reels – and on the commercial success of The Chieftains, which was regarded in Scotland as 'the instrumental breakthrough of the seventies'.[47] Scottish popular music gradually became situated within a broad Celtic periphery – predominantly Irish – although performer concerns now focused more on points of difference within a Celtic identity than on cultural distinctiveness from English popular music.[48] As Symon puts it, 'The meaning of the sounds produced by these musicians, in terms of how these give shape to personal, social, and national identities, is something which is mediated by the practices and organisation of a diverse range of institutions', and he adds, 'What sounded "Scottish" fifteen years ago...might probably sound "Celtic" to the global music market accustomed to the ethnic/vernacular, transcultured sounds arising from ten year's production by the "world music" industry.'[49]

Irish music has also become part of a global music market that perceives its Celtic overtones as part of a Scottish/Irish amalgamation existing beyond notions of separate Scottish and Irish identities. Noel McLaughlin and Martin McLoone argue that, in Ireland, music has always acted as 'a feature of "race", taking on properties for the coloniser that appeared to transcend the passage of time that remained fixed and unchanging'.[50] They describe the homogenisation and categorisation of Irish music as 'ethnic' by the Protestant Anglo-Irish Ascendancy in the eighteenth and nineteenth centuries and maintain that the music was later adopted by Irish nationalists as a response to negative stereotyping, a response reinforced today by continued government funding of bodies such as the Irish Folklore Commission, which was originally the Irish Folklore Institute. The current predominance of Irish rock music is also linked to a strong sense of national identity within an international arena.[51] With regard to the effect of rock music on perceptions of Irishness, McLaughlin and McLoone also argue that the new imperialising presence – which has replaced British colonialism – is global capitalism manifest in cultural terms by the US.[52]

Ireland is currently in a process of changing identity in which there is a potential for a culture of resistance that challenges the definition of identity imposed by the global. McLaughlin and McLoone maintain that local culture can also appear insular and stifling to such an extent that the cultural influences from the outside are to be welcomed as 'positively liberating and life enhancing'.[53] Clearly, then, this observation suggests a departure from notions of preservation of Irish traditions in music towards a globalised view of Irish music located in other musical contexts, and it reflects similar departures that have occurred within British folk music. As with Scottish music, Irish music continues to be framed within the hegemony of both national and international expectations of what Irish music should be. This aspect of Irish music supports notions of a regionalised popular music culture that operates in tension with, and is even critical of, dominant notions of national identity, while excluded and marginalised 'by those agencies [the culture industry], internal and external, which act as the arbiters of what gets made, distributed and valorised'.[54]

In his discussion on the use of the Welsh language in popular music, Meic Llewellyn suggests that the first 'explosion' of modern popular culture in Wales began in the 1960s.[55] This phenomenon was closely associated with the rapid development of the Welsh Language Society, which has remained 'the dominant force in the provision and stimulation of live rock music in Welsh-speaking Wales' – unlike the global influences that have been adapted in Scottish and Irish music.[56] It is necessary to understand differences in understanding between the Welsh notion of 'traditional' and the English cultural conventions within the Anglo-American world in which 'ideas about "folk music" have become associated with a number of social and musical attitudes that do not translate easily into Welsh terms'.[57] Llewellyn supports both Simon Frith's and Richard Middleton's arguments that the existence of 'folk' is a dubious concept and that, if folk music were to exist, it would simply be a bourgeois nationalist construct serving to 'protect the ruling class from the threat and suffering of the proletariats by first exoticising them and then absorbing their cultures into their own'.[58] Consequently, Llewellyn argues that a perceived distinction between folk and other types of music does not register among Welsh musicians and audiences.

Welsh-language popular music has been promoted and disseminated by an emerging Welsh popular music industry and by certain national television and radio broadcasters. Llewellyn, however, notes a tendency by some Welsh media to 'ape transatlantic patterns and to introduce and popularise as "trendy" an Anglo-American slang' as well as 'government departments and commercial institutions' being reluctant to pay more than lip service to bilingualism.[59] Moreover, Llewellyn observes that the most successful Welsh pop artists – who once sang exclusively in Welsh – now appeal to audiences both within and outside Wales and retain close ties with Wales and the language movement by performing at the National Eisteddfod and other Welsh-speaking events. Nevertheless, most sing predominantly in English, are signed to Anglo-American record companies, and are marketed as global commodities.[60] Simon Brooks notes 'a powerlessness' in allocating funding to national youth culture in Wales, as well as a lack of 'proper' capitalist enterprise, that makes it inevitable that Welsh 'talents' have no choice but to 'service English culture rather than the culture of Wales'.[61] Llewellyn summarises the Welsh national and musical identity discussion as follows:

There can be no doubt...that the crossroads currently being negotiated by musicians and their audiences within small societies are particularly complex. The landscape around them [is] mutating and transmogrifying to a previously unguessed-at extent. Here in Wales, new generations are returning to Welsh culture and the Welsh language in areas that for decades have been Anglophone. The penetration of fast capital and global culture is impacting on language and taste, social patterns and long established ideologies. Debates about political autonomy and national identity have been sharpened, and many detect a scent of freedom and new beginnings associated with the advent of a Welsh assembly – however constrained – within a British constitution that at last seems capable of releasing small nations from the suffocating embrace of imperial neighbours.[62]

While Llewellyn's comments suggest a sometimes extreme nationalistic standpoint on the artistic exchange that occurs between England and Wales, they also demonstrate that, as with the cases of Ireland and Scotland, there exists in Wales a continuing struggle for national and artistic identity away from connections to an English hegemony – and consequently an American hegemony – and away from perceived notions of a unifying Britishness.

But what about Englishness?

In his discussion on globalism, Stuart Hall suggests that globalisation in the United Kingdom, and particularly in England, is an historical process forged from economic growth and perceptions of empire into which English identity not only placed the colonised 'other' but into which it also placed '*everybody*' [sic] else.[63] To be English is to know your self in relation to others – 'to know what you are and what they are not' – and Hall posits that, in this respect, notions of identity become a structured representation in which the positive is achieved through the narrow eye of the negative.[64] Cultural and political ambivalence concerning notions of Englishness, and/or Britishness, have origins in what Bernard Crick describes as 'a country with no agreed colloquial name'.[65] Crick discusses the confusing titles, and consequent confusion in national identity that exists among a nation that at once refers to itself as Britain, England and the United

Kingdom. Crick notes that non-abusive discussions of English-ness are rare and that this omission is due to an English propen-sity to mistake patriotism for nationalism and to forget that the United Kingdom is a multi-national state. He also states that this confusion is a result of 'a legitimate, if paradoxically under-expressed, Englishness with Britishness (as Englishness for all)'.[66] Crick also points out that England remains the only country in the European community without its own written constitution or Bill of Rights.

For England, therefore, the absence of an independent Bill of Rights and the problematic question of re-branding its status as a member state within the UK remove an easily accessible repo-sitioning of national identity distinct from previous negative connotations. In his comprehensive commentary on the devo-lution of Britain, Michael Gardiner proposes that 'England has a longer history of direct connection with the land in demo-cratic local systems – a history becoming divergent when images of a countryside home were put into propaganda use in World War I.'[67] Gardiner convincingly describes a positive culture of Britishness that existed in the United Kingdom during the 1960s at which time the 'toe-curlingly embarrassing' term 'Cool Bri-tannia' became widespread with its implied reference, through popular culture, to Victorian and Edwardian notions of empire.[68] With its notions of *Rule Britannia* still inherent, the slogan was taken up again as part of the 'New Britain' propaganda that sur-rounded the Labour government elected in 1997. Gardiner points out, however, that notions of an 'integrative young Britain' were deployed against more divisive and ground-level youth cultures, many of which already existed within local cul-tural diversity that had become detached from Britain as a whole and which were scathing of the government's unifying initia-tives.[69] This youth culture regarded itself as more English than British, 'less based on imperial "race" than inclusive place', argu-ably a further reinforcement of the negativity that has often surrounded perceptions of Englishness.[70]

Scholarly discourse therefore indicates that, while Scotland and Ireland have long-established popular cultures that are able to embrace more recent global influences without loss of national or cultural identity, perceptions of popular culture in Wales reflect an isolationist stance that regards outside influence as denigrating. Moreover, despite devolution that has enabled most components of the United Kingdom to reinforce singular identities, aided by each having a separate governing assembly, English cultural identity remains linked to aspects of imperialism and colonialism, and, more recently, to xenophobia.

Rebranding Britishness

Given that Scotland, Ireland and Wales are comfortable with their established cultural identities, it would seem that England is still a long way from repositioning its own within a framework of its traditional music. While folk music in popular music settings may attract audiences from multicultural backgrounds, Diana Campbell-Jewitt is critical of popular media misrepresentations of English folk music and folk traditions. As an example, she cites a UK television programme about an English serial killer that depicted his early life in a village in Gloucestershire while showing slow-motion images of maypole dancing. Campbell-Jewitt feels that these depictions of English rural life insinuated sinister connections between the killer's upbringing and English folk culture.[71] Folk musician Pete Castle supports Campbell-Jewitt's views, maintaining that the lack of awareness of the traditional music of the British Isles is most apparent in England, and he suggests that Ireland, Scotland and Wales 'never became quite as urbanised and their living traditions were able to survive into the age of recordings'.[72] This latter statement is debatable given that Ireland, Scotland and Wales all have large areas of urbanisation, which have not prevented the continuation of folk traditions, including the preservation of traditional music. A more plausible reason for the awareness of folk culture of each of these countries is that folk music and folk culture are promoted as a national resource and heritage. As an example, heritage promotion in Scotland can be demonstrated by an initiative described to me by Bob Pegg, a folk singer and scholar, who worked as an educational music project worker in the Ross and Cromarty region of Scotland in the 1990s. Pegg maintains that Scottish folk music is 'becoming more and more important as a part of Scottish national culture' and that it is often regarded as Celtic music, despite a lack of awareness of its origins among many of its younger performers who perform in folk-rock styles.[73]

Pegg conducted what he describes as 'music and story telling things', and the project was promoted and financially supported by funding from the Ross and Cromarty education authority.

Government policies in the Republic of Ireland during the 1960s encouraged foreign investment, which reversed the decline in the Irish economy.[74] This investment enabled new prosperity that altered the way in which Irish folk music was perceived and practised in the Republic, as well as in Northern Ireland. The Comhaltas Ceoltoiri Eireann (The Irish Musicians Society) was formed in the 1950s and its membership grew during the mid-1960s with audiences of 50,000 people attending the annual traditional music festival, *Flea Ceoil*. During the late 1960s, Irish bands such as The Dubliners achieved success in the music charts in Ireland and the United Kingdom and The Chieftains recorded albums of Irish instrumental folk music on traditional Irish instruments achieving international success. In a fieldwork interview, Ian Smith, Head of Music at the Scottish Arts Council, maintained that change in Irish politics since 1998 has enabled establishment of artistic links between both the Republic of Ireland and Northern Ireland that now present both countries as an artistically unified whole.[75] A unified view of Irish folk music, distinct from any reference to political location, has been promoted more recently by the international popularity of stage shows such as *Riverdance* and *Lord of the Dance*, as well as by Irish folk-influenced rock artists and bands.

The Arts Council of Wales National Lottery Unit provides grants for various folk music events such as Welsh harp festivals and the National Eisteddfod, one of the largest folk festivals in the world.[76] Welsh folk culture, music and arts are promoted each year in the National Eisteddfod and further funding is available to performers and promoters of folk music in Wales.

Scottish, Irish and Welsh folk traditions promoted and funded by respective government institutions have therefore enabled these countries to maintain individual folk cultures as a means of preserving national identities at the end of the twentieth century, as each country entered a process of devolution. Despite UK government promotion of British 'heritage', there is ambiguity in the way English people regard their own cultural identity that is, as Billy Bragg suggests, linked to the adoption of notions of English identity by right-wing nationalists.[77] Billy Bragg, a

British folk singer whose reputation as a social critic was established in the 1980s and whose musical roots lay in the punk
movement of the 1970s, has argued that there exists a patriotism
among English people with which they were brought up, but
that is no longer observed.[78] Bragg observes that a central reason
for this is the image of English football hooligans 'rampaging
through foreign cities chanting [their] country's name' with the
result that English people came to a conclusion that, if these
people were patriots, then patriotism was untenable.[79] Bragg
also notes that the success of former Prime Minister Margaret
Thatcher during the 1980s alienated 'England's smaller neighbours' and strengthened the case for devolution.[80] The notion
of English identity during the period following devolution was
further weakened by the 2001 national census, that gave the
choice of 'British, Scottish, Irish or other' as options for ethnic
identity. Perceived English identity was strengthened, however,
in 2003 following the England victory in the rugby world cup.
Following this victory, the flag of St George became popular at
sporting events in which English teams played, such as the European Football Championships in 2004, and in the aftermath of
the English Ashes series victories. Nevertheless, for Bragg, devolution gave 'new confidence' to Scotland and Wales, 'while
casting doubt on the future of the UK' and England's position
within it. Bragg argues that the English flag has become 'a
symbol of our liberation' from the stereotype of xenophobia
achieved without 'prompting from political parties or national
institutions', and that the English have decided to 'rehabilitate
their flag and its meaning'.[81]

While the flag of St George is often used as a sporting symbol
at many televised events, its use as a banner for the British
National Party since 1982 (and the more recent English Defence
League), as well as its connections to football hooliganism, has
prevented its use as a symbol of Englishness in the same way as
the Saltire and the Red Dragon represent Scotland and Wales
respectively. In an online debate on the BBC News website in
2001, readers were asked to comment on their views concerning
whether the English should be patriotic. While responses to
this question do not represent a rigorous statistical survey, the
majority of the respondents, 67 per cent, thought that the
English should be patriotic, although 6 per cent stated that they

preferred to be regarded as British as well as English.[82] Nine per cent of respondents favoured multiculturalism. In 2002, the same site posed a similar question concerning support for St George's Day becoming an official national holiday in England. Again, the majority of respondents, 75 per cent, supported the concept while 8 per cent preferred to be regarded as British and were opposed to another national holiday.[83] Ten per cent of respondents expressed a preference for multiculturalism, a view-point referred to by Marxist journalist Paul McGarr as 'fluffy popular nationalism', indicating that multiculturalism is as unappealing to the far left as it is to the far right.[84] Significantly, a third of all respondents from both debates whose comments were posted on the site expressed dissatisfaction with what they perceived as a missed opportunity to establish an English national assembly, and a re-branded English identity, during the devolution of the United Kingdom in the late twentieth century. Respondents blamed the Labour government for establishing national assemblies, and consequently reinforcing notions of separate individual national identities, for Scotland, Northern Ireland and Wales, while omitting to do so for England. The United Kingdom entered the process of devolution in 1997 as the Labour party sought to re-brand both Britain and England, and this was partly achieved by the retention of nationalist elements familiar to the British public, such as the promotion of notions heritage and folk culture, in each area of the country.

In 2001, Bragg suggested that the re-establishment of aware-ness of English folk culture might be achieved by an 'English folklore centre', an enterprise that would amalgamate BBC folk music recordings with the National Sound Archive and the Vaughan Williams Memorial Library on digital recordings that would then be made available to the public at a central loca-tion.[85] Government initiatives already aimed to facilitate cul-tural commoditisation in the United Kingdom at the end of the twentieth century. Aspects of national identity linked to arte-facts of English culture were to be collected as an historical resource and made accessible to everyone in the British Isles.[86] In an interview with Bragg, Chris Smith, the Labour Secretary of State for Culture, Media and Sport from 1997 to 2001, explained that the government had a proposal of this kind at the beginning of the twenty-first century and was in the process of establishing what he referred to as 'Culture Online'.[87] Smith proposed that this internet facility would enable access to 'all the great collections and the creative activities happening in this country' and referred to it as 'a memory bank of how people have grown up' that would record 'how the lives of ordinary people have changed over the last 80 to 100 years', while promoting awareness of various cultures present in the United Kingdom.[88] Culture Online, supported by the Department for Culture, Media and Sport, became accessible to the public in 2002. Its stated purpose is to provide interactive resources designed to encourage participation in culture through the 'innovative use of technology'. Among the resource's published aims is access to the arts, to cultural institutions, and to new technologies. The resource does not provide specific access to English folk culture and folk music due to its broad-based, multicultural nature.

Ed Vulliamy, a former arts journalist at *The Guardian* newspaper who has recently contributed political commentary to the *Observer* newspaper, is critical of UK government initiatives such as Culture Online, referring to them as the 'domain of National Heritage'. Vulliamy maintains that the broadness of their subject matter does not address a lack of public awareness of English folk song and English culture.[89] A new folk music revival in the United Kingdom may therefore be compromised by the broadness of initiatives such as Culture Online, as well as by formal validation and support from the political establishment that may be viewed by contemporary revivalists as politically sanctioned promotion of a new form of British nationalism.

A short history of politics, money and folk music

Various political initiatives towards the end of the twentieth century continued to endorse folk music as a means of promoting cultural awareness in the UK. Conservative and Labour governments regarded folk music as a national resource and promoted aspects of folk tradition, such as folk songs and folklore, through English Heritage and the English Sports Council. English Heritage was established by the National Heritage Act in 1983 and it later became a part of the Department of National Heritage, which was established by a Conservative government in 1992. The following Labour government changed its title to the Department for Culture, Media and Sport in 1997. This department provides limited financial support to the EFDSS through the Arts Council of England, although its occasional donations of between £4,000 and £15,000 are primarily for the maintenance of Cecil Sharp House, in which is housed the Vaughan Williams Memorial Library. The EFDSS also receives an annual grant from Sports England as a contribution towards the provision of workshops for schoolteachers known as Community Sports Leader Award training, which is delivered in collaboration with the Central Council of Physical Recreation.

The Sports Council announced in 2005 that it planned to cease funding the EFDSS, although funding was made available in 2006 and 2007 (more recent funding has come from the Heritage Lottery Fund). The EFDSS has faced decreasing government funding since 1986 and activities that originally generated other funding opportunities, such as festival promotion, have now become commercial enterprises managed outside the Society.[90] Folk music as an inter-cultural and musically multi-linguistic art form may be apparent at performer and audience level but David Arthur – the editor of the EFDSS magazine, *English Dance and Song*, between 1979 and 2001 – informed me of his view that the Society missed the opportunity to become a festival promoter in the United Kingdom and that 'a lack of vision' on the part of the Society lost control of the Sidmouth Folk Festival.[91] The EFDSS gave up control of the festival in 1986 due to a financial crisis that prevented the Society from investing in its promotion.[92] Further investment might have put the Vaughan Williams Memorial Library at risk and could have brought the Society to bankruptcy, especially if the festival had been affected by bad weather.[93]

Arthur remains critical of the Society's managerial policies, and his views are contrary to those concerning revivalist criticism of commercial issues in folk revivals.[94] While Arthur adds that he does not wish to denigrate the quality, variety and facilities provided by Steve Heap, the director of the Sidmouth festival from 1986 to 2004, he claims that 'this, sadly, is the history of the Society. Over the years they have given up the responsibility for areas of folk music for which [the Society] is suited to take a lead.'[95] Arthur suggests that there is a reactionary element within the managerial structure of the EFDSS opposed to event promotion involving what they might regard as commercialisation of folk music. Arthur maintains that the Society should 'go out on a limb and employ a staff of professionals and let them get on with making it financially and artistically viable' in terms of promotion of festivals and folk clubs.[96] By using the term 'professionals', he refers to music industry personnel such as managers, promoters and agents who would manage the Society as a commercial entity. These aspects of the music industry are already present in the promotion of many folk festivals and in most aspects of the emerging folk music recording industry.

In May 2006, the English Folk Dance and Song Society launched VWML [Vaughan Williams Memorial Library] Online, a web-based library resource that provides access to aspects of British folk culture and to British-based cultures in other lands, in particular North America and Ireland. VWML Online provides access to a multi-media resource that contains, among other ephemera, books, manuscripts, broadsides, prints, phonograph cylinders, tapes and cassettes amassed by collectors such as Cecil Sharp, Ralph Vaughan Williams, Lucy Broadwood, Frank Kidson, George Butterworth, the Hammond brothers and Maud Karpeles, as well as the BBC Folk Music Archive. Richard Butterworth, an academic at Middlesex University, developed VWML Online as a volunteer project and the resource was not assisted by government funding.[97] Malcolm Taylor, the VWML librarian, supports Bragg's view that promotion of British, and English, folk customs and music through a resource such as this should aim to 're-appropriate those things that make us embarrassed'.[98] In a fieldwork interview, Taylor suggested to me that traditional music styles from other cultures in the UK can exist 'side by side' and that their presence as components of new British folk music does not weaken perceptions of Englishness, adding 'it's only when you juxtapose English culture with [diverse] culture within Britain ... that you really understand the [English] culture anyway, that you really start to understand its value'.[99]

In his 1998 discussion on possible reforms that could be made to the society, Roger Marriot argued that greater funding is necessary to ensure that the Vaughan Williams Memorial Library remains secure, although he maintains that a more realistic proposal would be its relocation to a university library.[100] Marriot also maintained that the Society is moribund and that a 'fresh organization built on traditional arts' needs to be created.

In contrast to limited funding provided to the EFDSS, the Arts Council of England provided £400,000 to Folk Arts England in 2005. This organisation was founded in 2003 by Steve Heap, who also runs the Association of Festival Organisers (AFO). In keeping with the Labour government's policy of funding specific projects in preference to regular donations to organisations, the AFO submitted an initiative to set up Folk Arts Network – later renamed Folk Arts England – with Heap as director with a view to supporting folk activities in England. This organisation may therefore reflect political commitment to the support of promotion and preservation of folk culture, although it effectively makes the EFDSS redundant as all Arts Council funding for projects related to folk culture are now promoted through Folk Arts England, and the EFDSS is a member of that organisation.[101] An alternative view of government support for Folk Arts England as a new initiative promoting folk music is that folk fans may perceive the EFDSS as an organisation that has been in gradual decline since the 1970s, and that it is often regarded by folk performers as aloof and out of touch with grass-roots performers and audiences.

Despite low levels of funding allocated to the EFDSS, as well as to the other folk music organisations and folk music events promoted throughout the UK, perceived connections between British folk culture and political promotion of cultural heritage are further reinforced by the level of financial assistance provided to Folk Arts England. With regard to government support, Malcolm Taylor maintains that the 'current upsurge' of interest in British folk music should be reflected in government funding that would facilitate the Society's prime purposes – to be a folk club and a library resource – although he admits that the Society's charity status and public perceptions of the Society as a national institution has often attracted criticism through the Society's association with the government.[102] Despite potential support from a new funding body, an emerging revival may therefore be regarded by folk performers and folk fans as a further politically assisted initiative aimed at creating re-branded tradition and heritage.

The culture industry and English folk-rock

In a preview for the Cropredy Festival that was promoted by Fairport Convention in 1995, Ed Vulliamy discusses political connections to folk music in the promotion of notions of heritage. He describes the modern folk music audience as the 'new folk' seeking an 'Englishness' that is not part of 'the supposed patriotic establishment which these new voices from below accuse of crushing, rather than celebrating, England, her land and her people'.[103] Vulliamy maintains that the new folk music audience that attends folk-orientated rock and world music festivals, such as Cropredy, is in search of an alternative to the 'domain of National Heritage' and the 'love-of-country' aspects adopted by the Conservative Party in the 1980s and 1990s, which still played Blake and Parry's *Jerusalem* at conferences. Vulliamy posits with almost Blakean rhetoric that the 'new folk' is neither left nor right in terms of its political allegiances but that it is 'the voice of the new politics, in a language of earth, land and liberty in England, tying history to the present' and that this sentiment is echoed in the music of many of the English folk-rock bands of the 1990s, such as The Levellers and The Oysterband.

The popularity of Fairport Convention among a new folk/world music audience suggested by Vulliamy is described in the following preview of the Cropredy Festival to be held on Friday the 8th and Saturday the 9th of August 1997:

Cropredy was advertised some years back as 'the only festival that guarantees good beer and clean toilets'. Sensational as these claims may sound, they are not the only peculiarity. The festival is hosted by Fairport Convention, which this year celebrates its 30th anniversary. Fairport are like a downsized, folky English version of the Grateful Dead (with a penchant for real ale rather than hard drugs). They have a devoted following and almost cult status outside the loop of passing vogues. Led by the now deceased Sandy Denny, the band was the hallmark of the English folk-rock underground back in the sixties and are now a seminal part of the Pogue-ish, Leveller-ish folk revival. Cropredy is a very English,

Blakean, pre-industrial affair in a Cotswold meadow by Cropredy
Bridge on the Cherwell, site of a civil war battle. Hundreds of fans
arrive by narrowboat and converted Telecom vans, these days
others purr in by BMW.[104]

This favourable preview (albeit with much of the wording
taken from Vulliamy's descriptions of the festival and its audience in his article published two years earlier) came from a series
of previews that included those of performances by bands at
several other festivals that were, at that time, enjoying greater
popularity than Fairport Convention. It is also further evidence
of a blurring of musical boundaries between rock and folk music
that is part of a larger movement towards the deconstruction of
differences between pop and rock and the historical connections being made between rock and folk music.

Vulliamy's reference to Fairport Convention's promotion of
the Cropredy Festival – and the running of their record label,
Woodworm Records (known as 'Matty Grooves' since 2004) – as
a 'scaled down version of the autonomy established by the
Grateful Dead', however, incorrectly imbues the band's commercial autonomy with political motivation. Vulliamy posits
that the Grateful Dead's music was a form of 'absolution' for the
existence of Reaganite America.[105] Fairport Convention's music
during the 1980s represented an English culture that was distinct from Thatcherism or right-wing Conservatism.[106] Furthermore, while Fairport Convention's music might be regarded as
an antidote to Conservative political policies – for example their
songs such as 'Wat Tyler' (1985) and 'Here's To Tom Paine' (1997)
are both protest songs – an alternative view might be that Fairport Convention was formed in the late 1960s as a rock band in
the style of American acid rock groups such as Jefferson Air-
plane, and were thus part of the acid or psychedelic rock movement. Fairport Convention's inclusion as part of this movement
is also illustrated by Ashley Hutchings' statement that the band's
record company regarded them as 'freaks', a term often used to
describe hippies in the progressive rock counter-culture.[107]

By the mid-1980s, the band had become commercially established and promoted its own festivals and tours, presenting a
problematic stance in the analysis of views held by Vulliamy.
The policies of Thatcherism, which were based on the increased
financial wealth of the middle and upper classes in the United

Kingdom and which encouraged entrepreneurial ventures, would have been contrary to the hippy philosophy that rejected accepted social and political values. Fairport Convention have been able to remain detached from political links Vulliamy discussed and have remained close to the original communal ties to their early audiences. They have also gained commercial autonomy on their own terms within the hegemony of the music industry.

Vulliamy does not define what he regards as 'the language of earth, land and liberty in England', nor does he explain what the 'new politics' might be. Moreover, his views on 'tying history to the present' are similar to the philosophies of the first and second folk revivals. He does not mention that extreme political elements were inherent in both revivals as revivalists became disenchanted with the perceived exclusivity of the EFDSS that failed, as Georgina Boyes suggests, 'to create a popular movement at a time of heightened social awareness'.[108] Vulliamy's descriptions of a Utopian notion of 'Englishness' is at odds with his own Blakean pretence, as is his suggestion of the 'new folk's' call for a return to notions of a lost England and the re-invention of its lost traditions. Similarly, Vulliamy's suggestion of the existence of a 'new folk' seeking a reinvented 'Englishness', and promoting folk music as they reinvent 'tradition', implies that members of a new revival may perceive problems in the existing social order as being rectified by the re-imposition of 'traditional' values, a sentiment echoed in late twentieth-century Conservatism.

A new phase of folk revivalism that embraces English folk culture, may enable the re-branding of English identity among audiences attending folk-orientated world music events, which are not linked to the aspects of nationalism often inherent in the institutionalised promotion of folk music. Re-branded English identity may emerge once reclaimed from negative connotations and it can exist individually and collectively located within the United Kingdom community. Malcolm Taylor and Niall MacKinnon both acknowledge that folk clubs no longer attract large audiences, and this issue will be discussed further in chapter 4.[109] The success of world music events lies partly in the diversity of their artist rosters, which combine international folk music styles with folk styles from the British Isles. This success is particularly apparent in the audience reception of English folk-rock and other folk music amalgamations, despite separateness that once existed between English folk-rock and traditional folk music at the end of the second folk revival, and the commercial issues that have facilitated the emergence of the revivalist folk music industry.

The new folk festival scene and an emerging folk industry

Growth in popularity of English folk-rock can be linked to commercial marketing and promotion components within the expanding world music festival market. A consequence of these commercial links is that English folk-rock, as well as several other British folk music styles, is often perceived by festival audiences with diverse musical tastes as one stylistic component within the world music arena. Although there were few large folk music festivals promoted in Britain until the mid-1950s, investigation into the origins of commercially promoted folk-festivals in the United Kingdom and the United States of America illustrates that those promoted in the UK were often more successful, and more stylistically varied, than those promoted in the US. Early twentieth-century folk revivalism in the US had been assisted by commercially sponsored folk festivals that were often regarded as a means of celebrating regional, ethnic and national identity, and as public relations events. During the 1930s, however, the Great Depression stimulated social consciousness to an extent where folk music became linked to the 'expression of the American masses' by socialists and liberal populists.[110] By the 1950s, many folk performers in both the US and the UK also performed in the mainstream popular music arena, a change in musical status that provided a moral dilemma for successful British folk singers seeking to preserve their non-professional image and, as Neil Rosenberg has it, folk performers often became 'professionalized with an ethos of non-professionalism'.[111]

During the early 1960s, the UK media presented British and American folk music as 'respectable' alternatives to pop music. Many American folk artists had, however, experienced the inquisition of the House Un-American Activities Committee and, given the social climate of the Cold War during the late

1950s and the left-wing sympathies of many folk singers, it is unsurprising that American folk festivals were often financial failures, despite the increasingly commercial nature of their promotion.[112] This was in contrast to folk festivals promoted in the UK from the mid-1950s, which were a forum for both British and American folk singers.[113] The romantic idealism of folk revivalism had, however, become unfashionable by this time as revivalism in the US, and to an extent in the UK, was in decline, and the commercial nature of the popular music industry had become stylistically all encompassing. Many successful folk singers in the US considered themselves (and were considered by the industry) as professionals in the same way as other popular music artists. Bob Dylan's music had become 'ratified by the commercial establishment' and his reputation was enabled by the same economic constraints that established the hippy movement.[114]

From 1969 onwards, festivals such as Woodstock established stylistic diversity at US and UK music festivals that attracted audiences with diverse tastes. Following trends in the United States, rock music festivals promoted in the United Kingdom during the 1970s also became less defined by the musical style of the artists they presented. UK popular music events, often known as rock festivals, became a platform for diversity. These events demonstrated a growth in eclecticism in the musical tastes of audiences, and in the performance styles of artists. Government institutions in the United Kingdom promoted national awareness, thus aiding revivalism, throughout the twentieth century by imposing notions of tradition and heritage, and by promoting social continuity through awareness of folk culture. Whereas the promotion of folk-only festivals in the UK that took place from the mid-1950s was often linked to local government institutions, most contemporary UK folk festivals remain relatively autonomous and compete with other music festivals presenting several musical styles at the same event.[115] There are many annual UK folk festivals that promote a variety of British folk music styles and folk-influenced music, but I focus on Cambridge and Sidmouth because these are two of the largest folk-oriented festivals in the UK and they have demonstrated audience growth annually throughout the late 1990s and into the twenty-first century as they have consolidated world music identities.[116] I also focus on Cambridge and Sidmouth because of the cosmopolitan nature of their artist rosters, particularly the Cambridge festival's inclusion of British folk music performers alongside popular and rock music artists and the Sidmouth festival's long tradition of including artists from other countries.[117] Both of these festivals have been promoted for approximately forty years, although stylistic variation within their artist rosters has been recent in comparison with UK rock festivals.

Cambridge City Council's involvement in the Cambridge Folk Festival has continued to include funding and promotion since the mid-1960s, and decisions concerning the selection and booking of artists for each festival are made by the Marketing and Promotions Section, a part of the Arts and Entertainment Department at the Council. Eddie Barcan, the Cambridge Folk Festival promoter, is a Cambridge council employee working for its Marketing and Promotions Section. He no longer regards the festival as a 'traditional folk festival', and the event is now promoted as an 'eclectic mix of music' with 'a wide definition of what might be considered folk'.[118] The festival has been a three-stage event since the late 1970s, with performances occurring consecutively on all three.

Folk festivals promoted in the United Kingdom during the 1950s and 1960s were single-stage events and did not include stylistic diversification until the early 1980s.[119] Rock festivals promoted between the 1970s and 1990s that presented stylistically diverse artist rosters, utilised performance diversity as a means of marketing and promotion, and arguably influenced the presentation of folk festivals. Significantly, one of the stages at the Cambridge festival is known as the Club Tent, in which established traditional folk artists and floor singers perform for up to five hundred people. The tent has its own bar area and it is intended to recreate a folk club atmosphere within the confines of the main event, which the council regards as an international festival.[120] The commercial nature of the festival's promotion is further illustrated by the use of a dedicated website to sell tickets for the festival on the internet, and the council has a mailing database containing twenty-four thousand names and addresses. The festival is recorded for radio and is presented on the BBC4 television channel. There is also a musical archive of the festival dating back to the 1970s and the Cambridge council, in conjunction with the BBC, has released some of these recordings as commercial CDs. The Marketing and Promotions Section of the council won a UK government 'Chartermark' for excellence in 1990 and a bronze medal for festival production at the 1999 *Time Out* magazine 'Live!' awards, further factors illustrating music industry links to aspects of the festival's promotion.[121]

The Sidmouth Folk Festival is the largest folk festival in the United Kingdom. It was first promoted in 1955 by the EDFSS as a result of a proposal that the south west area organiser might approach the Sidmouth Town Council for permission to hold a festival there.[122] The application was successful and the early Sidmouth Folk Song Festivals – as they were then called – combined folk music performance with folk dance events that were broadcast by the BBC as part of its *Country Dancing* series. The festival was renamed the Sidmouth Folk Festival in 1962 and, in that year, the festival promoted a venue called The Folk Song Loft, an initiative intended to recreate the intimate atmosphere of a folk club by similar means to the later promotion of the Club Tent at the Cambridge Folk Festival. During the early 1960s, international folk artists were included in the festival's artist roster, and this policy was further consolidated in the 1970s and has continued to the present. In its early years, the Sidmouth Folk Festival was not artist-orientated and was intended to be a forum for non-professional singers, although a small number of professional singers were presented each year. Festival promotion was taken over by Mrs Casey Music in 1987, under the directorship of Steve Heap and John Heydon, due to a financial crisis at the EFDSS.

Derek Schofield aptly describes the festival as having a 'catholicism' that has allowed the festival to become 'a series of overlapping festivals' and, in order to provide more performance space, the festival has, since the early 1970s, adopted the use of large marquees in the Bowd and Bulverton areas outside Sidmouth for late-night performances.[123] This development illustrates the festival's gradual change of identity as it became more diverse in its artist roster, presenting British folk music in a world music context that is demonstrated by the inclusion of musical styles as diverse as Russian gypsy music, salsa and Appalachian dance music. In contrast to Cambridge City Council's involvement in the Cambridge Folk Festival, Sidmouth Town Council only provides a small grant towards children's events at the festival. The promotion, choice of artists and funding of the event remained the responsibility of Mrs Casey Music until 2004, when it was renamed Sidmouth Folk Week and was promoted by Sidmouth Folkweek Productions Limited with sponsorship from Hobgoblin Music, *fRoots* magazine and the Association of Festival Organisers. This non-political financial independence identifies the Sidmouth festival as a private, commercial venture run in a similar way to many rock and pop festivals that depend on profit for future promotions.

The Sidmouth Folk Festival has been described as 'the grand-daddy of all folk festivals pioneering world music of all shapes and sizes, with a particular favouritism towards Celtic folk'.[124] In his description of British folk music styles presented as world music, Colin Irwin posits that there is a change in perceptions of folk music:

> Not long ago, confessing even a passing affection was about as un-hip as being a train spotter. Folk's image of incest ballads sung with fingers planted firmly in the ear, singer-songwriters parading their hopeless love affairs and, of course, the dreaded Morris dancers didn't exactly denote credibility and relevance. Over the past decade, there has been a sea change, as a new generation of musicians delved into English (and Celtic) traditions, knocked them around with a wonderful disregard for notions of purity, and came out with what the labels and press started calling 'roots'.[125]

Irwin's statement that a new generation of musicians delved into English and Celtic traditions 'with a wonderful disregard for notions of purity' is an apt description of the amalgamation of folk music with other musical styles, particularly English folk-rock. This issue links the Sidmouth Folk Festival to the Cambridge Folk Festival. I attended both of these festivals between 1996 and 1999, and my lasting impressions of each were differences between the commercially sponsored Cambridge Festival, the atmosphere of which was more akin to a rock festival, and the Sidmouth Festival, which, despite being well organised and promoted in conjunction with local businesses, retained many of the intimate aspects of the folk club scene. Despite the difference between the private and public sector promotion and funding of the respective festivals, there is a shared philosophy of stylistic diversity reflecting change in modern folk music, as both are promoted from a commercial perspective. Irwin's statement does not, however, acknowledge the discourse among folk fans concerning perceptions of authenticity in folk music that has continued since folk music was first amalgamated with rock music in the late 1960s.

The renaming of the Sidmouth Folk Festival as the Sidmouth International Festival of Folk Arts in 2001 is an example of the globalisation of musical styles at folk festivals presenting British folk music styles in world music contexts.[126] The inclusion of British folk music at world music events also introduces members of the folk festival audience to new styles within the world music category, a category that encompasses English folk-rock and that causes boundaries between different styles of folk music to become as blurred as those existing within rock music. World music festivals – which enable audiences to experience multiple musical styles performed within a relatively short time span – encourage musical multiculturalism. They also encourage audience association of musical styles with the event at which they are performed as a means of generating stylistic interrelationship. Growth in audience attendance at folk festivals promoted as world music festivals since the mid-1990s supports a rise in the popularity of British folk music styles, including English folk-rock, presented at these events. Increased audience volume consequently indicates that diversity of musical styles at world music festivals provides audiences with a global encounter in which notions of preservation and change in folk music co-exist.

The Sidmouth and Cambridge festivals are also arguably part of the 'commodification' of folk music. As Philip Bohlman has it, revivalism and 'contemporary institutions' in folk music are inseparable, and the use of modern technology and music distribution networks enables recordings of past traditions to become new ones in the present.[127] In a similar way, the term 'contemporary institutions' can also be applied to aspects of the music industry present in folk music, such as record companies, promoters, agents and marketing networks. Many folk performers and promoters in the UK generate direct revenues through links to aspects of the popular music industry by a process of commodification of folk music that includes commercial business practices used in the music's promotion, marketing and distribution. They also receive indirect revenues from limited government funding mechanisms aimed at endorsing the promotion of folk culture. Business practices adopted by these performers and promoters therefore situate folk music performance at large events, such as festivals, within the hegemony of the commercial sector, although new government funding initiatives may also provide support for smaller folk music projects enabling renewed growth in a localised folk club scene in the UK. Folk Arts England, an organisation established to promote folk arts projects in the UK, may be well placed to act as a link between the commercial arena of folk music promotion and the support and promotion of the comparatively small folk club scene.

Art for art's sake/money for folk's sake

The emergence of a revived folk festival scene, and its concomitant folk industry, runs counter to a decline in the traditional folk club scene, as noted by Niall MacKinnon. MacKinnon's research between 1978 and 1987 indicated an increase in the number of folk clubs during that period, although attendance went into decline in the early 1990s.[128] Increases in folk club attendance are no longer apparent, although there is still a network of 'informal' sessions occurring regularly in pubs.[129] Decline in audience attendance at folk clubs can be partly linked to generational and commercial issues given that, during the 1980s, many folk clubs had an average financial turnover of between £150 and £3,380 with many charging an entrance fee of between 35p and £1.50.[130] This is in contrast to the Sidmouth festival, which has attracted in excess of 65,000 people each year since 1996 and has shown an increase in audience attendance of between 5 per cent and 10 per cent annually.[131] The Cambridge Folk Festival sells out each year and it has a capacity audience of 10,000 people on site during each day of the four-day festival.[132] Its financial turnover in 2001 'approached £730,000' despite the non-profit-making policy of the Cambridge City Council, which purposely keeps ticket prices low.[133] The festival was first established in 1964 as part of a council initiative to promote three festivals – the other two being jazz and drama – and the council provided an initial budget of £1,500.[134] The budget provided by the council for the promotion of the renamed Charles Wells Cambridge Folk Festival in the 1990s had increased to approximately £350,000, although at time of writing the festival is promoted and funded by the council with sponsorship from the Charles Wells Brewery, BBC Radio, the Musicians' Union, *Mojo* magazine and The Performing Right Society.[135]

It has always been Cambridge Folk Festival policy to include artists who reflect change in the folk music scene since the festival was first promoted and, since the mid-1980s, the festival artist roster has become increasingly diverse in a similar way to those at rock festivals.[136] The Cambridge Folk Festival also competes for audiences during the summer season with the Glastonbury Festival of Contemporary Performing Arts, which presents world music performers within a broad rock music context. This festival had an annual turnover of approximately £8 million during the late 1990s, and its gross profit in 2005 was approximately £19 million when it attracted an audience of 150,000.[137]

The emergence of many folk festivals from a process of reinvention as multi-cultural events adds to a confusing mix of titular musical boundaries apparent among many UK festivals. While commercial success is evident in folk festivals reinvented as world music festivals, stylistic diversity in their artist rosters has been recent in comparison to other UK music festivals such as Glastonbury, which has always attracted an audience large enough to enable the presentation of established artists from a variety of musical styles. The inclusion of performance areas intended to recreate the atmosphere of a folk club at both the Cambridge and Sidmouth Folk Festivals reflects a new identity distinct from their original image as traditional folk festivals. This inclusion could, however, be regarded as a means of continuing, and re-authenticating, the festivals' folk identities. It is also significant that database technology and the internet are used to promote the Cambridge and Sidmouth festivals, as well as many others in the UK, given their origins in the regionalised British folk clubs that have always relied on localised support. As the music becomes further associated with other musical styles and events outside the folk club sphere, commercial methods of promotion of world music events make British folk music styles accessible to new audiences unfamiliar with notions of tradition and heritage, posing a range of issues that will be addressed in this section. On the other hand, a homogeneous mix of styles within the context of folk music could be detrimental to the maintenance of its original identity, although this view is not evident among performers interviewed for this project.

World music promotion of folk music fusions may be relatively recent, but links to commercial promotion in English folk-rock have been apparent for over thirty years due to the nature of its association with the popular music industry. As stated in chapter 1, commercial availability of English folk-rock recordings by Fairport Convention and Steeleye Span indicate that the fusion of folk music and rock music in the late 1960s and the 1970s may have stimulated curiosity about folk music among a broader audience than the folk club settings of the period. More recent English folk-rock promotion, and distribution, assisted by the application of popular music industry business practices, has assisted in the creation of an emerging folk music industry, with many folk and English folk-rock artists releasing recordings on their own or specialist record labels that are distributed by mail order or through performers' websites.

An emerging folk music industry does not solely revolve around increased availability of old and new recordings. It also involves a large performance network, agencies dedicated to the promotion of folk music performance, musical instrument manufacturers specialising in the construction of new instruments based on traditional designs, and publishers who specialise in folk music and folk-music-related material. Many styles of traditional folk music now have a 'market value', and a common feature of revivals is the growth of a marketing network.[138] This network serves the revival with news, promotion of live events, pedagogical publications, recordings and supplies for musicians. Commercial issues are often a source of embarrassment to revivalists given their distrust of commerciality, a concept that is not part of the history of revivals.[139] Audience attendance statistics gleaned from folk festival promoters support a view that there is a growing industry in folk music promotion and distribution as commercially promoted folk festivals are promoted in similar ways to rock festivals.[140] Folk festivals promoted since the mid-1990s and advertised as world or international music events may have demonstrated audience growth, although, as stated in chapter 1, this is not reflected in music industry sales statistics of recordings that suggest that folk music only appeals to a minority audience. Confusion concerning the identity of contemporary folk music, and issues surrounding any analysis of its commercial success, may be a reflection of increasing stylistic diversity in artist rosters at folk and world music festivals in the second half of the twentieth century.

Growth in the folk music audience since the mid-1990s can be linked to the diversity of the fusions of folk and popular music that have become available from the 1980s onwards, and British folk audiences are often situated in the audience for world music in which stylistic diversity is not an issue. English folk-rock has achieved popularity through its amalgamation with popular music styles, especially in live performance contexts, yet music industry sales statistics of all folk recordings do not reflect this. All of the folk performers interviewed for this study sell many of their albums by mail order, having set up websites and having established a database of audience information. They also sell their recorded media at live events, such as festivals that often have a merchandising area for the purpose of artist promotion, and these sales figures do not register with the BPI. As previously stated, BPI statistical data suggests that folk music remained a minority taste and that its sales did not increase during the 1990s in line with audience attendance at festival events. These statistics consequently provide a confusing account of contemporary record sales, given that definitions of popular music styles constantly change as they merge creating new styles that may only be popular for a short time before stylistic metamorphosis re-occurs.

Statistical analyses from the BPI provide a misleading picture of the contemporary popularity of British folk music and its performers, although promoters and the Musicians' Union regard folk music in the UK as a growth industry. Live events are well attended, audience attendance has increased since the mid-1990s, recordings and other related merchandise are sold through various media outlets and opportunities for employment exist in a range of folk-music-related areas, criteria that define contemporary revivalism.[141] In contrast to folk music's

misrepresentation in BPI sales statistics, the Musicians' Union
has taken the view that it should represent the interests of folk
musicians active in both the folk festival and in the folk club
spheres. The Union has long-established instrumental sections
with their own sub-committees for orchestral musicians, composers, musicians in theatre productions, jazz musicians and
session musicians involved in a variety of musical genres. At a
Union conference in 1995, many members who were involved
in folk music performance expressed the view that the Union
did little for them and that it did not identify with their musical
sector.[142] The Executive Committee of the Union consequently
approved the compilation of a report into folk music activity in
the UK, choosing as samples south Wales and the south west of
England. This report provided information that confirmed that
an active community of folk performers and dancers existed in
both areas. The Musicians' Union 27th Biennial Delegate Conference in 1996 appointed a full-time official to monitor the
continuing growth of folk music's popularity in the UK, the
number of its performers and the size of its audience, as well as
to set up the Folk, Roots and Traditional Music section of the
Union. Folk music performers and promoters such as Martin
Carthy, Steve Heap and Eddie Barcan supported this initiative.
Since 1996, the section has established links with the Performing Right Society, which distributes royalties to folk performers
through its Specialist Music Group, and it provides members'
recordings to BBC Radio 2 and Radio 3 and to Music Choice
Europe, part of a 'themed' channel initiative by the Sky Digital
Network.[143] The emerging folk music industry is, therefore,
partly enabled by the Folk, Roots and Traditional Music Section.

Ian Smith, the Head of Music at the Scottish Arts Council, told
me that he became secretary to the Section in 1996 and, since
that time, performing members have established their own
record labels and distribution companies that have access to
partner distribution companies – which, Smith observes, work
in similar ways to European wine cooperatives. Performers also
have their own websites and download facilities and, in Smith's
view, are 'more sorted than their contemporary [rock] music
colleagues'.[144] Musicians' Union initiatives towards supporting
and encouraging folk musicians to become commercially self-
sufficient and to embrace music industry business practice has

enabled a widespread national growth of professional and semi-professional folk music performance in several folk music styles that have, as Smith observes, established synergies with jazz performance and world music performance. The success of the Musicians' Union folk and traditional music initiative, and the recent government-assisted establishment of Folk Arts England, therefore challenges the BPI view that folk music performance is a minority pursuit that is unsupported by a significant audience, and that is consequently not reflected in its statistical analyses of sales of recordings.[145]

While folk performers are currently able to draw upon various areas of support offered by Folk Arts England, the EFDSS and the Musicians' Union, folk music performance at events other than festivals and established concert venues has recently become problematic. In 2005, the UK government revised its licensing laws concerning Public Entertainment Licensing. The process of change began in 2002 when Kim Howells, a junior Minister at the Department for Culture, Media and Sport, proposed changes to entertainment licensing laws linked to the sale of alcohol. James Purnell, the Labour Minister for Licensing, further supported the bill as it passed into law in 2003. The reform is aimed at addressing noise problems that the government perceives as being caused by live music-making, although the UK Noise Association, an organisation that assisted the Musicians' Union in its opposition to this reform, states that most noise complaints come from the amplification of recorded music.[146] Purnell argues that the act is primarily intended to address problems relating to alcohol abuse and violence, although, in a BBC Radio 4 interview, he neglected to relate noise and violence to live music-making.[147] The 2003 law is able to regulate performances as diverse as those by string quartets, jazz bands, folk performers, theatre productions and carol concerts. The new law also prevents unaccompanied solo performers from performing in public venues that sell alcohol, unless the licensee has applied for a new licence that requires completion of a twenty-six-page document – which is accompanied by a sixty-page explanatory booklet – and paid a licence fee that relates to size of premises rather than amounts of alcohol sold.

Many phone respondents to Purnell's BBC radio interview felt that the application document had no relevance to their situations. These respondents were involved in diverse events, such as occasional social club meetings or small theatre productions, while others were involved in activities that included use of village halls for wedding receptions. All of these events involved the sale, or distribution, of alcohol. Several respondents commented on the cost of the licence, as well as the cost of other documents required for licence application submission – such as building plans and the cost of advertising a change of licence in the local press. There was also the cost of a two-day training course on completing the form that the government was offering. One example put to Purnell concerned the cost of a licence to a parent/teacher society that had previously paid £16 to sell alcoholic drinks at fund-raising events. The new licence, based on the size of the school, was to be £635. When asked about the rise in licensing costs for the school, Purnell commented that the government had aimed to base costs of individual licences on ratable value of premises rather than on the amount of alcohol sold on the grounds that 'administering the system ends up being so expensive that everyone overall has to pay more'. Purnell added 'that does mean in some cases that you get rough justice'.[148]

The Musicians' Union argument against the imposition of the bill is that it would negatively affect performance opportunities for musicians who perform in small venues whose management may consider the cost of a new licence, compared to the limited income from live music events, to be untenable. Given that the live entertainment section of the previous licensing law applied to ensembles of three members and above, solo performers and duos were unaffected and could perform in licensed venues with no entertainment licence. Many folk performers in the folk club circuit perform as solo artists or in small ensembles. The new licensing system therefore proved problematic, particularly for those who perform in clubs in which floor singers are encouraged to sing and which do not rely financially on entry charges.

Martin Carthy maintains that the new bill was a government-based financial exercise and that no consultation was conducted with the folk club community.[149] He adds that when Howells was informed of the financial contribution music performance makes to the economy 'he was thunderstruck', although this did not deter him from ensuring that the bill became law. Carthy also regards the bill as an 'attack on people, on people's music' that will prevent a new generation of musicians from gaining performance experience, and at the time of the interview Carthy noted that some major breweries were already banning music in their pubs. Simon Nicol supports Carthy's view, stating that the damage the bill will cause to generations of amateur, semi-professional and professional musicians is incalculable.[150] Nicol describes the 2003 law as based on government misunderstanding of live music performance that has been erroneously linked to noise pollution – adding that the legislation has not affected amplified recorded music and that loud karaoke sessions still take place in venues unavailable to live folk musicians. Nicol also predicts that in future years there will be no live music infrastructure that will provide performance opportunities for young musicians, or for that matter older ones.[151]

Consecutive UK governments have acknowledged the importance of folk music in the promotion of national heritage awareness by financial contributions made through various government funding mechanisms. In contrast, an area that is of immediate benefit to the promotion of folk music in the UK – opportunities for its live performance – has narrowed considerably as a consequence of the Public Entertainment Licence Act. This dichotomy of purpose illustrates a lack of informed decision-making and a further misrepresentation of the nature of folk music performance on the part of the political establishment. Political support of folk culture in one government department is undermined by depletion of performance opportunities for folk music caused by another. The origins of English folk-rock performance lie in the events promoted in rock clubs and student unions in the late 1960s and early 1970s, and more recent folk-rock performance has often taken place in venues established for the purpose of popular music performance, or at various rock and world music festivals. While these venues and events need the performance licence to continue trading, many other performance opportunities for solo and duo performers previously existed at venues unlicensed for public entertainment. The danger was that these venues might not continue to promote folk music, or any other live music, following the Public Entertainment Licensing Act becoming law. In consequence, the UK government was putting the new phase of folk revivalism in jeopardy by preventing promotion of performance opportunities at grass-roots level.

So where is Englishness positioned within English folk-rock?

Despite increases in audience attendance at UK world music festivals presenting folk music of the British Isles, the debate concerning English folk culture linked to earlier perceptions of English cultural identity continues. Folk music is driven by a commercially and politically motivated culture industry, yet negative associations in the twenty-first century still prevent relocation and re-branding of English folk music as a notional national heritage that could be endorsed in similar ways to Scottish and Irish folk music, and thus re-contextualise English identity. Reinforcement of notions of 'Englishness' or 'Britishness' may be less important than the promotion of 'Englishness' situated among the various folk cultures present in the UK, a diverse range of music styles that have often been amalgamated with traditional British folk music.

If 'British' folk music were to be marketed in terms of its regional origins, audience perceptions of English, Irish and Scottish folk music would be reinforced as separate entities instead of being acknowledged as diverse variations of globalised folk music in the British Isles. Globalisation in modern folk music can be regarded as positive, given the market expansion that has occurred as British folk music has become amalgamated with other musical styles, while retaining its identity, both national and regional. The stylistic differences between artists performing at world music festivals, and their often-capacity attendances, indicates that concerns about the globalisation of British folk music among many folk fans are unfounded. Growth in folk festival attendance is an example of the interrelation of regionality with musical multi-lingualism and inter-culturalism, and it further reflects diversity in the musical tastes and cultural backgrounds of modern folk audiences, as well as modern folk performers.

Whether English music is difficult to 'sell' and whether it sounds 'strange, odd, quaint, rough and scrappy' when compared to 'slick' Irish and Scottish music is a subjective issue, given the scepticism that exists concerning a cultural mix that might amalgamate folk music from the different cultures present in the United Kingdom. Terms such as 'world', 'folk', 'roots' and 'international', which are often used to advertise music festivals, illustrate stylistic expansion and a further blurring of the boundaries that previously separated folk from other performance styles. Promotion of this kind may be perceived by some folk fans as culture-industry commodification of folk music that leads to further globalised viewpoints, and it supports the warnings of some critics that folk music of the British Isles will ultimately become a bland and unsatisfying musical 'soup'.[152]

In the mid-twentieth century, British folk music was limited to small groups of enthusiasts and it existed in regional frameworks with an emphasis on locality and the familiarity of relationships.[153] Contemporary regional folk traditions in the United Kingdom interrelate with musical diversity and multiculturalism, in a similar way to many of the folk festivals promoted in Europe.[154] The broad use of terms such as 'world' and 'international' to describe stylistically varied folk-orientated festivals has introduced change in the perceptions of promoters, performers and folk audiences towards eclectic notions of what folk music might have become. Global concepts of cultural diversity and relativism support preservation of individual traditions in folk music, as well as the uniqueness and self-reference of musical ethnicities within it. In this way, audience perception and reception of traditional British folk music and English folk-rock styles presented as British world music may reflect what Max Peter Baumann describes as 'particularism' versus 'homogenization' – terms that might be interpreted as folk fans opposing change versus folk fans that embrace it – although modernism exists within particularism and homogeneity exists within invented traditions present in British folk music.[155]

The world music festival in the late twentieth and early twenty-first centuries creates its own musical context as audiences experience concepts that are often musically varied and foreign to their musical tastes. Perceptions of authenticity and tradition in folk music performance are consequently no longer central issues to world music festival audiences. Modern revivalism is often centred on calendars of festival promotion, and each revival promotes 'selected cultural goods in ways representing the modern needs of those sponsoring the revival'.[156] This aspect of culture industry commercialism provides the most discernible link between audience and performer perceptions of tradition and heritage in British folk music and a new phase of folk revivalism situated in the world music arena.

Notions of authenticity in folk music and opposition to what was regarded as commerciality were, nevertheless, central to twentieth-century British folk revivalism, and the 'Ghost of Electricity' – a synonym for folk music performed on electrified instruments – remains a source of debate between factions of the folk music audience in the UK.[157] Nonetheless, English folk-rock remains a significant identity for modern British folk music, and it has utilised aspects of commerciality within a culture industry framework, while remaining detached from aspects that were once anathema to folk fans.

Notes

1 Kate Crehan, *Gramsci, Culture and Anthropology* (Los Angeles: University of California Press, 2002), 54–5. (See also Hobsbawm and Ranger, *The Invention of Tradition*.)

2 Robert W. Witkin, *Adorno on Popular Culture* (London: Routledge, 2003), 99.

3 See also Max Paddison, *Adorno's Aesthetics of Music* (Cambridge: Cambridge University Press, 1993), 26; J. M. Bernstein, 'Introduction', in *The Culture Industry-Selected Essays on Mass Culture*, ed. J. M. Bernstein (London and New York: Routledge, 1991), 20; Deborah Cook, *The Culture Industry Revisited* (Lanham, MD: Rowman and Littlefield, 1996), 103.

4 Simon Frith, *Performing Rites* (Oxford: Oxford University Press, 1998), 13. Mike Featherstone shares this view, stating that 'If it is possible to claim the operation of a "capital logic" deriving from production, it may also be possible to claim a "consumption logic", which points to the socially structured ways in which goods are used to demarcate social relationships' (Featherstone, *Undoing Culture: Globalization, Postmodernism and Identity* (London: Sage, 1995), 16). (See Paddison, *Adorno's Aesthetics of Music*, 9 for Adorno's views on folk music as art music.)

5 Frith, *Performing Rites*, 13.

6 Frith, *Performing Rites*, 45–6.

7 Frith, *Performing Rites*, 20.

8 Roger Marriot, 'The EFDSS: A Future', *The Living Tradition*, 27 (June/July 1998), www.folkmusic.net/htmfilesinart424.htm (accessed 25 July 2006).

9 Ian Smith, interview with author, August 2005.

10 Smith, interview, 2005.

11 Colin Irwin, 'The New Folk Uprising', *fROOTS* 27:11 (2006), 27.

12 Irwin, 'The New Folk Uprising', 27.

13 Irwin, 'The New Folk Uprising', 25.

14 Ian Anderson, 'A Weekend of Britfolk', *fROOTS* 27:10 (2006), 34–7. Anderson's article was a review of *Folk Britannia* held at the Barbican Centre in London in February 2006 and broadcast on BBC4 Television.

15 Dave Nunn, 'Folk Britannia', *English Dance and Song* 68:2 (Summer 2006), 25. Joe Boyd was the producer of both Fairport Convention and The Incredible String Band in the late 1960s and early 1970s.

16 Audience criticism concerned Batt's association with popular music as, among other projects, he had composed and produced the music for *The Wombles*, a children's television series during the 1970s.

17 Patrick Humphries refers to Fairport Convention as 'founders of the English folk-rock Movement', maintaining that the band became pioneers of this 'movement' following the release of *Liege and Lief* in 1969. (Humphries, *Fairport Convention – The Classic Years* (London: Virgin Books, 1997), 131). Band members state in interviews for this study, however, that Fairport Convention at that time was a rock band.

18 Email correspondence with folk festival promoters Eddie Barcan and Steve Heap, 2001–05.

19 Billy Bragg, 'That England', *fROOTS* 22:11 (2001), 31.

20 Muriel Eden, 'Letters', *English Dance and Song* 62:4 (Winter 2000), 24.

21 See Marina De Chiara, 'A Tribe Called Europe', in *The Post Colonial Question: Common Skies, Divided Horizons* (London: Routledge, 1996); see also. Caryl Phillips, *The European Tribe* (London: Faber and Faber, 1987).

22 This view could explain the use of Eden as a surname, given the comparison made between England and the Garden of Eden in Shakespeare's *Richard the Second*, Act II, Scene 1.

23 Boyes, *The Imagined Village*, 35–6.

24 Richard Sykes, 'The Evolution of Englishness in the English Folksong Revival 1890–1914', *Folk Music Journal* 6:4 (1993): 446–90, here 449–51.

25 Simon Frith, 'Music and Identity', in *Questions of Cultural Identity*, ed. Stuart Hall and Paul du Gay (London: Sage, 1996), 109 and 121.

26 Hobsbawm, 'Introduction: Inventing Traditions', 2–3.

27 See Bragg,'That England' and Paul Davenport, 'Five Men and an Idea', *English Dance and Song* 66:3 (Autumn 2004): 17.

28 Nairn states that Powell saw public perceptions of 'old-Englishness' re-emerging 'by tower and spire' and 'in old country churches as the Saxon ploughs his fields and the sun sets to strains by Vaughan Williams' (Tom Nairn, *The Break-Up of Britain: Crisis and Neo-Nationalism* (London: New Left Review Editions, 1977), 262 and 292).

29 Stuart Hall, 'Introduction: Who Needs Identity?', in *Questions of Cultural Identity*, ed. Stuart Hall and Paul du Gay (London: Sage, 1996), 2–3.

30 Diana Campbell-Jewitt, interview with author, August 2003.

31 Campbell-Jewitt, interview, 2003.

32 As a contemporary music lecturer in the UK during the late 1990s, I often ran seminars and training workshops in popular music assessment for secondary school music teachers whose prior experience had only been in the assessment of Western art music. The relatively recent inclusion of popular music, as well as many world music styles, in the curriculum had presented assessment problems for many teachers untrained in these areas.

33 Campbell-Jewitt, interview, 2003.

34 Harker, *Fakesong*, 205; and Lucy Green, *How Popular Musicians Learn: A Way Ahead for Music Education* (Aldershot: Ashgate, 2001), 4.

35 Fieldwork interviews with folk and English folk-rock performers.

36 Michael Pollard, *Folk Music in School* (London: Cambridge University Press, 1978), 40.

37 Boyes, *The Imagined Village*, 3.

38 Phil Everitt, 'Exploring Folk Culture In The Classroom', *Lore and Learning – The Newsletter of the Folklore Society Education Group* 1 (1993), 17.

39 Everitt, 'Exploring Folk Culture In The Classroom', 17.

40 Everitt, 'Exploring Folk Culture In The Classroom', 18.

41 David Arthur, correspondence with author, August 2001.

42 Robb Johnson, 'Does Folk Still Exist?', *Musician: The Journal of the Musicians' Union* (June 1998), 23.

43 Stuart Hall, 'Cultural Identity and Diaspora', in *Identity: Community, Culture, Difference*, ed. J. Rutherford (London: Lawrence and Wishart, 1990), 394. (See also Stuart Hall, 'Culture, the Media and the Ideological Effect', in *Mass Communication and Society*, ed. J. Curran *et al.* (London: Arnold, 1977), 395.)

44 Martin Stokes, 'Introduction', in *Ethnicity, Identity and Music*, ed. Martin Stokes (Oxford: Berg, 1994), 7.

45 Stokes regards notions of identity and authenticity as interlinked, but he argues that authenticity is 'definitely not a property of music, musicians and their relations to an audience' (Stokes, 'Introduction', 5–7).

46 Peter Symon, 'Music and National Identity in Scotland: A Study of Jock Tamson's Bairns', *Popular Music* 16:2 (1997), 203. Scottish identity had been reduced to 'an intellectual and cultural backwater' by eighteenth- and nineteenth-century British colonialism, which Symon refers to as the period of 'cultural sub-nationalism'. Symon, *Understanding Scotland: The Sociology of a Stateless Nation* (London: Routledge, 1997), 204. (See also David McCrone, *Understanding Scotland: The Sociology of a Stateless Nation* (London and NewYork: Routledge, 1992).

47 Adam McNaughton, 'The Folksong Revival in Scotland', in *The People's Past*, ed. E. J. Cowan (Edinburgh: Polygon, 1991), 191.

48 Further points of difference emerged on a national level around variations in traditional styles in Scotland. Symon notes that 'Boundaries were drawn, and identities constructed, around oppositions and distinctions between a range of groups, some geographical, some cultural; for example, "dance band", "folk and traditional", or "Irish sound/Scottish sound"' (Symon, *Understanding Scotland*, 214).

49 Symon, *Understanding Scotland*, 214.

50 Noel McLaughlin and Martin McLoone, 'Hybridity and National Musics: The Case of Irish Rock Music', *Popular Music* 19:2 (2000), 181.

51 Tony Clayton-Lea and Richie Taylor, *Irish Rock: Where It's Coming From, Where It's Going* (Dublin: Sidgwick and Johnson, 1992), 71.

52 This new cultural presence has replaced what McLaughlin and McLoone identify as 'the stultifying and conservative Ireland of the 1930s to the 1950s' in which images of American cinema and the urban rhythms of jazz were 'positively liberating' but subject to a process of denigration from the church – unlike in England, where American popular culture was broadly accepted. (McLaughlin and McLoone, 'Hybridity and National Musics', 182–3).

53 McLaughlin and McLoone, 'Hybridity and National Musics', 185.

54 McLaughlin and McLoone, 'Hybridity and National Musics', 196–7.

55 Meic Llewellyn, 'Popular Music in the Welsh Language and the Affirmation of Youth Identities', *Popular Music* 19:3 (2000), 319.

56 Llewellyn, 'Popular Music in the Welsh Language', 319.

57 Llewellyn, 'Popular Music in the Welsh Language', 332.

58 Simon Frith, *Sound Effects* (London: Pantheon, 1983), 48–52 and Frith, '"The Magic That Can Set You Free": The Ideology of Folk and the Myth of the Rock Community', *Popular Music* 1 (1981), 162; Richard Middleton, *Studying Popular Music* (London: Taylor and Francis, 1991), 127–46. I argue, however, that dismissal of the 'existence' of folk music on socio-political grounds is, at best, a form of fluffy liberalism that in itself serves to idealise unsound social and political views of scholars who perpetuate an almost apologist (Marxist) agenda (Harker, Pickering, Lloyd *et al.*). To denigrate folk music to an invented product goes against performer and audience views that it is not a bourgeois construct drawn from an exoticised working class, but an organic musical style with its origins in an earlier working-class system. All of the performers I have interviewed, and indeed members of the folk and folk-rock audiences with whom I have discussed the subject, do not regard themselves as either purposely bourgeois or proletarian and, while most if not all hold socialist viewpoints, the imposed connections with Marxism are often anathema. For a comprehensive dismissal of views held by several Marxist scholars on issues of class in folk music, see Bearman, 'Who Were The Folk?'.

59 Llewellyn, 'Popular Music in the Welsh Language', 324.

60 Llewellyn, 'Popular Music in the Welsh Language', 329.

61 Simon Brooks, *Diwylliant Poblogaidd a' Gymraeg* (Tal-y-Bont: Y/Lolfa, 1996), 26.

62 Llewellyn, 'Popular Music in the Welsh Language', 336.

63 Hall, 'Introduction', 19–21.

64 Hall, 'Introduction', 21.

65 Bernard Crick, 'The English and the British', in *National Identities*, ed. Bernard Crick (Oxford: The Political Quarterly Publishing Co. 1991), 90.

66 Crick, 'The English and the British', 96–7.

67 Michael Gardiner, *The Cultural Roots of British Devolution* (Edinburgh: Edinburgh University Press, 2004), 106.

68 Gardiner, *The Cultural Roots of British Devolution*, 109.

69 Gardiner, *The Cultural Roots of British Devolution*, 109.

70 In Gardiner's view, one musical style that represented new notions of English youth culture was the 'rave culture', a style that circumvented political attempts to associate national politics with successful popular music artists and music industry professionals of the late 1990s, such as Alan McGee, Oasis, Blur and The Spice Girls, as well as many other artists of the time that were referred

to as 'Britpop'. The origins of the rave culture were, as Gardiner notes, in the early 1990s during a period that led to the Conservative government Criminal Justice Act of 1994, legislation that was followed by a government white paper entitled *Rural England: A Nation Committed to a Living Countryside*. This paper linked England with concepts of nationhood and the apparent renaissance of the country in which sport again became 'a close metaphor for war'. In official Anglo-British discourse, the countryside was regarded as in need of defence from incomers, such as immigrants and 'travellers', who could be arrested on suspicion. Political pressure applied by the rural electorate prompted Prime Minister John Major's statement on the followers of the rave culture (often referred to as New Age Travellers) – 'not in this age, not in any age' – a statement that aligned the rave culture with notions of political oppression at a time when 'England struggled via carnival and cultural change to occupy and rejuvenate its own locales' (Gardiner, *The Cultural Roots of British Devolution*, 113–19).

71 Campbell-Jewitt is equally critical of other depictions of folk music and Morris dancers in television programmes stating that programme-makers often contact Cecil Sharp House (the central office of the EFDSS) for advice on how English folk music can be incorporated into comedy programmes (Campbell-Jewitt, interview, 2003).

72 Pete Castle, 'Is English Music Too Awkward?', *Traditional Music Maker* no. 43 (June 2000), 11.

73 Bob Pegg, interview with author, August 1997. I interviewed Pegg following his performance at the Sidmouth Folk Festival during which he sang and gave folk-orientated narratives. He was a founder member of the folk-influenced band Mr Fox during the early 1970s.

74 Graeme Smith, 'Irish Meets Folk: The Genesis of the Bush Band', in *Music – Cultures in Contact: Convergences and Collisions*, ed. Margaret J. Kartomi and Stephen Blum (Sydney: Currency Press, 1994), 193.

75 Ian Smith, interview with author, August 2005.

76 Paul Westwell, *Folk Music Report* (London: Executive Committee of the Musicians' Union, 1997), 2.

77 Bragg, 'That England', 31–3.

78 Billy Bragg, *The Progressive Patriot* (London: Bantam Press, 2006), 2.

79 Bragg, *The Progressive Patriot*, 3.

80 Bragg, *The Progressive Patriot*, 7.

81 Bragg, *The Progressive Patriot*, 277.

82 BBC Online, 'Talking Point', BBC, http://news.bbc.co.uk/1/hi/talking_point/1292380.stm (accessed 12 July 2006).

83 BBC Online, 'Talking Point', BBC, http://news.bbc.co.uk/1/talking_point/1939821.stm (accessed 12 July 2006).

84 Paul McGarr, 'Show Red Card to Nationalism', *SocialistWorkeronline*, www.socialistworker.co.uk/article.php?article_id=5400 (accessed 22 June 2002 and 12 July 2006). McGarr was writing on issues of English nationalism prior to the football World Cup competition in 2002.

85 Bragg, 'That England', 29.

86 Paul Davenport, 'Five Men and an Idea', *English Dance and Song* 66:3 (Autumn 2004), 17.

87 Chris Smith in Bragg, 'That England', 29.

88 Smith in Bragg, 'That England', 31.

89 Ed Vulliamy, 'The Alter-Ego of Englishness', *The Guardian Arts Section* (London), Friday 11 August 1995.

90 Marriot, 'The EFDSS: A Future'.

91 Arthur, email correspondence, 16 August 2001.

92 Derek Schofield, 'Seaside Shuffles', *fROOTS* no. 133 (1994), 3.

93 Derek Schofield, email correspondence with author, 12 February, 2003.

94 Livingston, 'Music Revivals', 77.

95 Arthur, email correspondence, 16 August 2001.

96 Arthur, email correspondence, 16 August 2001.

97 The Arts Council of England did, however, fund digitisation of archival material in the Vaughan Williams Memorial Library with a grant of £13,410 in 2004 as a preservation and conservation project.

98 Malcolm Taylor, interview with author, August 2003. Taylor is Library Director at the Vaughan Williams Memorial Library at Cecil Sharp House. He was awarded the OBE in 2003.

99 Taylor, interview, 2003.

100 Marriot, 'The EFDSS: A Future'.

101 Diana Campbell-Jewitt, email correspondence with author, 9 August 2006.

102 Taylor, interview, 2003.

103 Vulliamy, 'The Alter-Ego of Englishness', 10.

104 Vulliamy, 'Cropredy', *The Guardian Guide – Festivals '97* (London: Guardian, 1997), 28.

105 According to Hardy and Laing, the Grateful Dead formed their own record company in 1972, a commercial venture that gave them recording autonomy and enabled them to record and release records by other artists. This commercial independence also pro-

vided the band with financial security and artistic freedom, which they maintained throughout the rest of their career, although they signed their own musical output to Arista Records in 1976 (P. Hardy and D. Laing, *The Faber Companion To Popular Music* (London: Faber and Faber, 1990), 323).

106 Vulliamy, 'The Alter-Ego of Englishness', 10.

107 Ashley Hutchings, interview with author, April 1997.

108 Boyes, *The Imagined Village*, 145.

109 Respectively, Malcolm Taylor, interview with author, August 2003, and Niall MacKinnon, *The British Folk Scene*, 43.

110 Rosenberg, 'Introduction', in *Transforming Tradition*, 7.

111 Rosenberg, 'Introduction', 8.

112 Bruce Jackson, 'The Folksong Revival', in *Transforming Tradition*, 75.

113 Laing and Newman, *Thirty Years of the Cambridge Folk Festival*, 88–105.

114 Robert Cantwell, 'When We Were Good: Class and Culture in the Folk Revival', in *Transforming Tradition*, 54–5.

115 Schofield, 'Seaside Shuffles', 28; Laing and Newman, *Thirty Years of the Cambridge Folk Festival*, 1–2; and Bragg, 'That England', 28–35. Also, see appendix 1 for tables illustrating stylistic diversity at British music events referred to as rock festivals.

116 Barcan, email correspondence with author, September 2001 and October 2005; Steve Heap, email correspondence with author, 17 August 2001. It is also worth noting that Fairport Convention performed at the Moseley Folk Festival in 2007 and that Jethro Tull performed at the Wickham Festival in August 2007.

117 For information on previous artist rosters at Sidmouth and Cambridge, see Schofield, *The First Week in August*, Laing and Newman, *Thirty Years of the Cambridge Folk Festival*.

118 Barcan, email correspondence.

119 Laing and Newman, *Thirty Years of the Cambridge Folk Festival*, 6 and 105.

120 Barcan, email correspondence.

121 Barcan, email correspondence.

122 Schofield, 'Seaside Shuffles', 28.

123 Schofield, 'Seaside Shuffles', 31.

124 Simon Broughton *et al.*, 'Introduction: Celtic and British Festivals', in *World Music: The Rough Guide*, ed. Simon Broughton (London: Penguin, 1994), 4.

125 Irwin, 'The New Folk Uprising', 32.

126 In 2001, the Sidmouth Folk Festival included artists from Zimbabwe, Sicily and Iraq.

127 Bohlman, *The Study of Folk Music in the Modern World*, 131.

128 MacKinnon, *The British Folk Scene*, 34 and 43.

129 Westwell, *Folk Music Report*, 1. Informal sessions are folk club meetings that do not have an established performer as an attraction. These clubs are usually small, are normally held in the back rooms of pubs and the performers for the night, and 'are drawn from whoever happens to turn up' (MacKinnon, *The British Folk Scene*, 36).

130 MacKinnon, *The British Folk Scene*, 34. Livingston's observations on revivals and commercial enterprise suggest that commercial issues remain a source of embarrassment to revivalists (Livingston, 'Music Revivals', 77). This embarrassment may explain a non-profit-making policy in many folk clubs.

131 Heap, email correspondence with author, 17 August 2001.

132 The 2001 Cambridge Folk Festival sold out by mid-June of that year (Barcan, email correspondence with author, 20 September 2001).

133 Barcan, email correspondence with author, 19 November 2002.

134 Laing and Newman, *Thirty Years of the Cambridge Folk Festival*, 1–2.

135 Barcan, email correspondence with author, and Laing and Newman, *Thirty Years of the Cambridge Folk Festival*, 1–2.

136 See appendix 1 for rosters of artists presented since 1986 at the Cambridge Folk Festival. These artists appeared with performers who are regarded as 'traditional' British folk singers.

137 Michael Eavis, 'A Brief History of the Glastonbury Festival', www.glastonburyfestivals.co.uk/about_us.aspx?id=38 (accessed 16 August 2006). Since 1979, donations from all Glastonbury festival receipts have been made to various charities.

138 Livingston, 'Music Revivals', 79.

139 Livingston, 'Music Revivals', 77.

140 Barcan and Heap, email correspondence with author.

141 Livingston, 'Music Revivals', 79.

142 Ian Smith, interview with author, August 2005.

143 Musicians' Union Biennial Conference Report, 1996, paragraph 51 – 'Folk Section', and *Grass Roots*, the newsletter of the Musicians' Union Folk Roots and Traditional Music Section (September 2002).

144 Ian Smith, interview with author, August 2005.

145 Increasing public and music industry awareness of folk music is further illustrated by the Mercury Music Prize nomination of folk singer Norma Waterson's eponymous album in 1996 (Hannibal HNCD 1393), and the inclusion of Martin Carthy in the Queen's

honours list of 1998, in which he was awarded the MBE. Maddy
Prior was also awarded the MBE in 2001.

146 Val Weedon, a member of the UK Noise Association, quoted in
'Campaign Moves Up A Gear', *Musician: The Journal of the Musicians' Union* (September 2002), 26.

147 James Purnell interviewed on *You and Yours*, BBC Radio 4, 2 July
2005.

148 Purnell, interview on *You and Yours*, 2005.

149 Martin Carthy, interview with author, August 2005.

150 Simon Nicol, interview with author, August 2005. As stated earlier,
Nicol has been a member of Fairport Convention since 1968 and
is the only remaining member from the period in which the band
made the first folk and rock amalgamations.

151 Nicol, interview, 2005.

152 Arthur, email correspondence, 16 August 2001.

153 MacKinnon, *The British Folk Scene*, 33–4.

154 Max Peter Baumann, 'Festivals, Musical Actors and Mental Constructs in the Process of Globalization', *The World of Music* 43:2
and 3 (2001), 10.

155 Baumann, 'Festivals, Musical Actors and Mental Constructs', 10.

156 Chris Goertzen, 'The Norwegian Folk Revival and the Gammeldans Controversy', *Ethnomusicology* 42:1 (Winter 1998), 99.

157 Clinton Heylin, *Dylan: Behind the Shades* (London: Penguin, 1992),
100–7.

3 Ploughshares to Stratocasters

Perspectives of English folk-rock

English folk-rock, a sub-genre of the progressive rock movement of the late 1960s and early 1970s, was reinvented as a musical style of the world music genre during the late 1980s. In the context of folk-rock in the United States, which became popular following Bob Dylan's appearance at the Newport Folk Festival in 1965, American folk-rock was a primary influence on many performers who came to English folk-rock from diverse, non-folk, rock music backgrounds in the late 1960s. Those performers coming to English folk-rock from the British folk music scene were, however, often more aware of the traditional music repertoires performed in both the US and the UK. They were also receptive to innovative folk song adaptation, although they were often unfamiliar with the technical requirements necessary for authentic rock music performance. Moreover, they all described differences concerning stylistic policies, commercial success, and the stylistic directions of later careers. It is important to discuss issues arising from change in cultural and musical contexts from the perspective of folk music adapted for performance in rock music settings. As such, it is useful to attempt to contextualise English folk-rock in terms of which bands can be categorised as pioneers of this style and which bands moved away from folk influences and towards other musical styles.

In the context of Bob Dylan's influence on UK folk and rock music performers in the mid-1960s, American folk-rock was mostly based on a contemporary folk song repertoire composed by singer/songwriters of the period. This music was often 'folk-informed' rather than drawing on traditional American folk music, which largely had its origins in the folk music of the British Isles. A distinction can be made between skills required for performance of English folk-rock – which include technical skills for rock music performance – and those skills necessary for performance of the earlier folk-rock style that emerged in the United States following Dylan's amalgamation of his own music with mid-1960s rock music.

The English folk-rock style was initially part of the progressive rock movement during the late 1960s and early 1970s and that association with rock music performance and commercial marketing systems served to distance English folk-rock from aspects of folk revivalism during its formative stages. Progressive rock was financially supported by record companies in the UK that, in contrast to earlier sales strategies, promoted sales of albums in preference to singles. The 'singles' market had been the principal source of income for pop music record companies since the invention of the seven-inch vinyl disc in 1949, and from the 1950s until the mid-1960s albums (which became known as 'long players' or LPs) mainly consisted of previously released singles and B-sides, as well as unreleased material. Record-company support enabled musical experimentation in which rock musicians drew upon diverse musical styles, initiating a new genre of rock music performance and a new subcultural style. The audience for this style purchased its music in the form of LPs rather than singles, and progressive rock – from musician and record-company perspectives – was as much a question of commercial expediency as it was a deliberate musical strategy.

While the philosophy of progressive rock centred on musical experimentation, descriptors used to define and promote the various sub-genres within it enabled only a limited description of the various progressive rock styles. These include music media terms of the period such as folk-rock, jazz-rock, Afro-rock, Latin-rock and classical rock. There were several critically acclaimed bands that were initially labelled by record companies and the populist media as 'folk-rock', due primarily to their combination of acoustic and electric instruments and the folk-influenced nature of their repertoires. These bands – The Strawbs, Mr Fox,

Lindisfarne, Pentangle and Gryphon – are discussed later in this chapter. Several of these bands frequently changed musical direction during their careers and some moved away from their early folk influences. While most of these bands remained commercially successful, they were not part of what became an English folk-rock movement that endured after the decline in popularity of the progressive rock movement.

Contrary to receptive views among folk performers, the fusion of British folk music with rock music often attracted verbose criticism similar to that levelled at Dylan during the mid-1960s. Performers I have interviewed describe disapproval from factions of the folk audience who expressed outrage that contemporisation had challenged their own perceptions of the identity of British folk music. A primary criticism often concerned the electrical, rock-styled instrumentation of English folk-rock. The combination of styles consequently attracted a negative reception from some members of the folk music audience on the grounds of perceived inauthenticity. There are several other fundamental changes that occur in the adaptation of folk songs for performance in rock music settings that are as significant as the use of electric instrumentation and drum kits. These might present musical contradictions to audience notions of both rock and folk music authenticity. To explore these issues, I apply information from performer interviews that illustrate problematic issues that arose due to the absence of a shared performance skill-base. This absence often left performers from each style unskilled in the performance techniques required to play a combination of both convincingly.

As a new phase of British folk revivalism emerges, English folk-rock performance embraces change as folk songs are adapted into contemporary settings. Contemporisation makes folk music relevant to new audiences to whom change and perceptions of authenticity are no longer pivotal issues. From a performer perspective, my interviews support a view that, while debate concerning change still occurs, English folk-rock performers, as well as those connected with the promotion of folk music, regard the music as robust enough to withstand change. Folk music performance in rock contexts is merely presenting the music in another performance medium, a re-presentation that is similar to the electrification of the blues.

This chapter is not an inclusive historical or chronological account of the various protagonists in early English folk-rock, nor does it attempt to provide a comprehensive background to the progressive rock movement. Instead, it draws upon primary data provided by performers who are regarded by their peers, the music industry and folk-rock audiences as among the most established in the genre. I have structured this chapter within a socio-cultural context, although I also address certain musicological issues related to change and perceptions of authenticity in both the folk and rock idioms.

I owe my understanding of folk and blues revivalism in the United States during the 1950s and 1960s to Jeff Todd Titon, John Covach and other scholars in Neil Rosenberg's *Transforming Tradition: Folk Music Revivals Examined*.[1] In particular, Kenneth Goldstein's argument that every major technological advancement, from the invention of moveable type to the modern sound recording, helped to produce a subsequent folk-song revival accurately reflects innovation that took place in the early English folk-rock movement.[2] Burt Feintuch's proposal that each revival achieves its own momentum – with its own standard repertoire and styles and its own selective view of the past – provides a useful key to understanding the development of a current emerging phase of British folk music revivalism that draws from folk music amalgamated with other musical styles.[3]

Genuine subcultural study enables examination of elements that music alone cannot encode.[4] My argument therefore rests between both disciplines, and I integrate social and cultural criticism within English folk-rock in terms of its meaning to its performers, as well as its reflection in semiotic symbols that are encoded as musical events, such as pulse, metre, text and visual motif. Edward Macan regards the progressive bands he discusses for the purpose of illustrating the progressive rock counterculture as beyond debate, given their professional status and commercial success.[5] Similarly, my principal discussion on the origins of the English folk-rock style centres on Fairport Convention and Steeleye Span and, while I discuss approaches to performance taken by some of their contemporaries, I regard these bands as the pioneers of the English folk-rock style. In their discussions on the origins of the progressive rock style, both Macan and Richie Unterberger provide insightful narratives describing its background as in the earlier acid-rock psychedelia of the mid- to late 1960s.[6] I have concerns that Unterberger does not acknowledge the contribution to progressive rock made by blues-rock performers during the mid- to late 1960s. These musicians performed at a level of technical virtuosity that Macan perceives as a legacy drawn from classical music, as well as from the tradition of the virtuoso as Romantic hero that was absorbed by jazz music in the 1920s.[7] Macan's comprehensive account of the progressive rock style, and its subsequent counter-culture, has made me refocus my own perception of progressive rock, which often related to bands signed to record labels such as Island, Harvest, Chrysalis, Vertigo and Charisma, as well as some of the major labels that supported musical experimentation. I take issue with his perception, and those of scholars discussed below, of the style being singularly in the domain of the amalgamation of rock music with classical referents. Macan nevertheless recognises that many of the most successful progressive rock bands – for example, Emerson, Lake and Palmer, King Crimson, Yes, Genesis and Gentle Giant – drew upon elements of the classical music that many of the bands' performers had encountered in their youth or during conservatoire training. In his discussion of the components of the progressive rock style, John R. Palmer also states that the style predominantly drew upon Western art music referents, although Macan is more expansive describing the music as constituting a Wagnerian *Gesamkunstwerk* in which 'music, visual motifs and verbal expression are inextricably intertwined to convey a coherent artistic vision'.[8] While discussing folk-rock connections to progressive rock, Macan describes what he regards as two principles of English folk-rock: the introduction of electric instruments into the framework of English traditional folk music and the production of a body of original music that reflected the heritage of folk song while drawing on contemporary instrumentation.[9]

By using the phrase 'to introduce electric instruments into the framework of English traditional music', Macan implies that the early folk-rock bands had formulated a 'plan' in the adaptation of folk music for performance in a rock setting and he thus contradicts descriptions of the assembly of a traditional folk music repertoire given by members of Fairport Convention in interviews for this study. Macan also observes that 'The most obvious connection between English folk-rock and English progressive rock is the juxtaposition of electric and acoustic instrumentation, although folk-rock groups never used electronics, especially electronic keyboards, to anything near the degree of contemporaneous progressive rock bands.'[10] I agree with Macan's view of the juxtaposition of electric and acoustic instruments, although he omits that many progressive rock bands other than those playing folk-rock used a combination of electric and acoustic instruments – for example Emerson, Lake and Palmer, King Crimson, Yes and Genesis – and he erroneously suggests that use of acoustic instruments in progressive rock performance was influenced by folk music, citing the inclusion of acoustic guitar performance in music by some of the bands above as examples. His statement concerning keyboards is also erroneous and he does not acknowledge Rick Wakeman's use of a Hammond organ while performing with The Strawbs, John Evan's use of a variety of keyboards in Jethro Tull, and Sandy Denny's use of a piano in Fairport Convention and on her solo recordings.[11] 'Electronics' may mean the use of early sound synthesis, and Macan claims that the use of keyboards in a progressive context most often featured musical virtuosity, citing Keith Emerson of The Nice and Emerson, Lake and Palmer as a progressive rock keyboard virtuoso.[12] Many progressive rock keyboard players also performed supportive roles to vocalists and guitarists, such as Tony Kaye of Yes, Mike Pinder of the Moody Blues, Hugh Banton of Van Der Graaf Generator and Tony Banks of Genesis.

At this point it is useful to discuss some key concepts relevant to formulating a defining framework for English folk-rock. Andrew Blake provides a comprehensive debate on the continuous construction and invention of cultural tradition within notions of British identity in which he proposes that Britain's musical heritage is predominantly derived from music from elsewhere. Blake puts it that Led Zeppelin, a band that can be located at the transition between the blues-rock, folk and progressive rock styles, are 'at the same time paradigmatic Romantic monsters and typical British musicians of the twentieth century, playing with diverse aspects of their world-wide and local musical heritage'.[13] In his analysis of Led Zeppelin's performance philosophy, Blake argues that the band was an example of musicians moving away from 'unitary models of musical history' towards 'less linear and less categorically differentiated cultural history', a statement equally applicable to bands in the English folk-rock style. English folk-rock performers adopted innovatory technical processes to adapt often idealised versions of folk songs that existed in Victorian and Edwardian collections – unitary models of perceived musical history – for performance in an almost categorically undifferentiated cultural location. Blake has it that progressive rock had substantial input from bands influenced by ruralism, by direct links to folk music and by neo-medievalism.[14]

Allan Moore provides an invaluable aesthetic study of rock music that successfully combines stylistic and musicological analyses of rock music performance from which I partially draw a substructure supporting my arguments concerning rock instrumentation in English folk-rock.[15] The 'classic rock' style of progressive rock has antecedents in album recordings, such as *Sgt Pepper's Lonely Hearts Club Band* (1967), and Procul Harum's single 'Whiter Shade of Pale' (1967), a song that arguably became a 'model' for British progressive rock music because of its blend of rhythm and blues and classical music. Moreover, Moore also provides a model for progressive rock in which he identifies the influence of black American music on rhythmical forms in progressive rock, the importance of improvisation that creates deification of the progressive rock performer, and 'a related use of song writing forms and traditions' in which British folk music plays a significant part, that forms a partial and deliberate break from the domination of music from the United States.[16]

In his discussion on the validation of authenticity in rock music, Moore argues that the abandonment of notions of authenticity in all popular music discourse may be premature. He discusses the use of the term 'authentic' in popular music research in various hypothetical areas, providing the example of blues-rock as ethnographic evidence.[17] Moore maintains that the UK blues-rock performers' ideology concerned the veneration of the originators of blues music that consequently enabled contemporary blues-rock performers to appropriate the originators' authenticity. While Moore's description of veneration of musical originators can be equally applied to the folk performer idealisation of Victorian and Edwardian folk song collectors, in a more recent context performer idealisation of folk 'stars', such as Martin Carthy, existed among many folk performers of the British folk club scene of the 1960s.[18]

From a perspective of authenticity in folk music performance, I support Philip Bohlman's argument against restrictions made upon the understanding of folk music by issues of authenticity. The question of whether a piece is 'authentic' does not allow consideration of outside influences that may affect its performance in terms of its performers, its audiences and its places of performance. Bohlman contends that 'this interrelation of product and process – of musical text and cultural change – generates a dialectic essential to the oral tradition of folk music', thus supporting views of several English folk-rock performers interviewed who maintain that folk music withstands change.[19] Stimuli such as culture, music and psychological factors are often principal reasons for change in orally transmitted tradition, and change also occurs through flaws in perception or memory.

While issues concerning authenticity in English folk-rock were of importance in the early performance philosophies of bands such as Fairport Convention and Steeleye Span, these concerns no longer hold precedence in the bands' current repertoires, which include a variety of approaches to folk music interpretation and performance that will be discussed later in this chapter. Secondly, English folk-rock performers interviewed for this study regard performance as the central means by which folk songs and tradition are kept 'alive'. Lastly, descriptions of audience reception provided by these performers suggest a range of views concerning the combination of the traditional and innovative performance varying between outright criticism to broad acceptance on the grounds of either acceptance of creativity or a lack of knowledge in the subject area. In the combination of the traditional performance and the innovative one, audience response to change will often be seen as either drawing attention to violation of tradition or as inspiring creativity.[20]

The absence of appropriate descriptors for musical fusions remains apparent in the progressive rock music and world music styles. As mentioned earlier, I use the term 'English folk-rock' – initially a UK record industry marketing term that has been in use since the 1970s – to distinguish between folk-rock music in the US and the UK folk-rock style, although the latter style has its origins in the British progressive rock movement and consists of adaptations British folk songs regarded as traditional by folk music performers and fans. Problems surrounding descriptions of cultural artefacts are not restricted to English folk-rock music, given that many terminologies and descriptive concepts change during cultural contact. Resulting perceptions among traditional folk fans are inauthenticity and a sense of loss of notions of tradition and heritage. Any descriptor used to describe a musical style will inevitably fail to include the peripheries of that style, and in consequence will alienate factions among its audience. The problem of accurate and comprehensive musical description exists among many styles, particularly from the perspective of the ethnomusicologist. This view is illustrated by David Arthur's comments made in email correspondence with me. In his capacity of editor for *English Dance and Song* – the house magazine of the EFDSS – Arthur is critical of British folk music amalgamated with other musical styles and suggests that post-colonialism has brought a new 'cultural melting pot' to the United Kingdom, warning that 'the ultimate potential cross-cultural "world" music soup might be considerably more bland and ultimately less satisfying than the sum of its parts'.[21]

There exists a view among musicologists that cultural fusions can initiate 'the loss of sections of a repertoire' and a reduction of 'musical energy' that ultimately lead to 'total or partial extinction of a music'. [22] The case of hybrid musics can be defended, however in the context of its analogy with animal husbandry in which 'parent stocks' are mixed to create 'hybrid strength' that works to the 'advantage of the offspring'.[23] In her description of transculturation that occurs in the adoption of new conceptual principles in music, Margaret Kartomi provides a description of musical fusion that I regard as analogous to English folk-rock. She describes a need for artistic communication among groups lacking a common culture linked to the forces of commercialism that act as components of the sustaining impulse and impetus for extramusical elements in musical transculturation.[24] As she succinctly puts it, 'where borrowing ends, creative musical change begins'.

Challenging the hegemony of folk

The second British folk revival, which took place between the 1940s and the 1960s, was similar to the one that took place in the same period in the United States in that both revivals lost impetus as folk music became combined with rock music during the late 1960s. While it is not the purpose of this chapter to examine the origins of folk-rock in the United States, it is useful to briefly discuss American influences on the fusion of British folk music with the rock music of the late 1960s. One must acknowledge the contributions to folk-rock that were made by Bob Dylan, as well as by American rock bands such as The Lovin' Spoonful and The Byrds, whose album *Sweetheart Of The Rodeo* (1968) (which consists of traditional American folk and country music performed in an acoustic context) pre-dates the English folk-rock movement. The Lovin' Spoonful and The Byrds pioneered the genre known as 'country rock' that is nowadays often referred to as 'progressive country', a mixture of styles such as folk, rock, jazz, western swing, Tex-Mex, and mainstream country music. Many US rock musicians in the mid-1960s had backgrounds in folk music and were adapting to performance on electric instruments, although Dylan's performance at the Newport Folk Festival in 1965 could be seen as the beginning of folk music performance in rock settings. After The Paul Butterfield Blues Band performed their own set, Dylan joined them on stage playing a Fender Stratocaster guitar and performed three songs from his repertoire in an electric rock band context, an event that has already been well documented. Dylan's performance with an electric band is said to have drawn criticism from folk fans as well as from folk singers Pete Seeger and Ewan MacColl, who were both in the audience. As one of the Newport board in 1965, Bruce Jackson, however, maintains that the only negative response from the audience related to the brevity of Dylan's set, which had to fit with the number of other performers appearing, and that Dylan's songs were well received.[25] Significantly, Dylan's band included keyboard player and record producer Al Kooper and guitarist Mike Bloomfield, who were both signed to CBS Records. Both were established musicians outside The Paul Butterfield Blues Band and both later performed on Dylan's album *Highway 61 Revisited* (1965), his first album to feature electric instruments and his first following the 1965 Newport Folk Festival. Dylan was also signed to CBS Records, and the inclusion of these musicians in his live performance at Newport suggests that his record company was already aware of the stylistic change he was about to make before his festival appearance. Performance of folk music on electric instruments and drum kits was anathema to purist factions within the folk audience in the US and the UK, and Dylan's artistic decision to change from his familiar live performance instrumentation (an acoustic guitar and a harmonica) consequently attracted hostility from his traditional audience. By the mid-1960s, Dylan had established himself as the leading figure in the United States folk revival and his audience, which had lauded him as the successor to Woody Guthrie and the future of modern folk music, expected his repertoire to continue in the same stylistic mould as his earlier recorded material, such as the albums *The Freewheelin' Bob Dylan* (1963) and *Another Side Of Bob Dylan* (1964). Robert Cantwell suggests that Dylan's music had become 'ratified by the commercial establishment' and he posits that Dylan's rise to fame during the 1960s was assisted by the same economic constraints that enabled the hippy movement to establish itself.[26] Cantwell claims, however, that the folk revival had also become a convergence in which one could create one's own personal style, expression and rebellion, a hypothesis that can be more broadly applied as a description of the hippy movement in general.

Pete Seeger's objections extended beyond Dylan's use of an electric guitar and an electric band. Seeger also objected to Dylan's performance on the grounds that he regarded Dylan as having joined the ranks of the pop and rock performers of the time.[27] This is arguably because Albert Grossman, who managed Peter, Paul and Mary and The Paul Butterfield Blues Band, also managed Dylan. Grossman's management of Paul Butterfield therefore suggests further music industry awareness of Dylan's change of musical direction. Peter, Paul and Mary and Paul Butterfield had achieved commercial success as recording artists, and Seeger regarded Dylan's connections to these performers, and to the commercial aspects of the music industry, as a denial of his folk integrity. By 1965, the American folk revival, and the ratification of folk performers by the commercial establishment, had become particularly evident in political issues surrounding American involvement in the Vietnam War (1962–75).[28] This involvement created divisions in class, culture and race that effectively buried the American folk revival as American folk music diversified into the popular music of the period and as protest songs became part of the mainstream.

Textual content in Dylan's pre-1965 repertoire often originated from external stimuli, such as the Vietnam War and other political and social issues of the time. While Dylan's sociopolitical commentary and criticism remain primary aspects in his songwriting, he has consistently reinvented his performance style, and the media in which it is presented, to the present day. Dylan had become increasingly frustrated by the restrictions of audience expectation that he would remain in the persona of 'the rambling singer/songwriter', and he embraced all potential influences in his search for a 'multi-faceted musical language', which he found in the rock music of the period.[29] Dylan's artistic decisions were therefore made regardless of whether or not his audience thought his music was 'authentic' folk music, although, as in the folk revival in the United Kingdom, issues concerning its authenticity remained a source of debate.[30]

Dylan's change of performance style was a personal statement that established distinction between a new direction in his music and his audience's perceptions of authenticity. His change in stylistic direction was also a performance strategy that moved him towards a view that change in folk music is often an inevitable consequence of external influence, a view expressed in interviews by many English folk-rock performers. Dylan's performance at the Newport Folk Festival was a landmark in his personal evolution and he had become a songwriter whose lyrical message could be delivered to his audience through whatever musical medium and style he chose. His music also influenced many British artists and bands in the 1960s that were not part of the second folk revival, such as The Beatles, Manfred Mann, Nick Drake, Donovan, The Jimi Hendrix Experience and Fairport Convention.

The progressive rock culture

I have already stated that the progressive rock movement facilitated the existence of several sub-genres within it. One of these was English folk-rock, and this style had a significant impact on how the progressive rock audience perceived folk music and folk performers. Moreover, English folk-rock performers interviewed suggest that progressive rock was considered to be part of the search for new boundaries to break in the new progressive rock movement. The central paradigm of performance philosophy in progressive rock in the late 1960s and early 1970s related to musical experimentation involving fusions of rock music with many other musical styles. The stylistic boundaries of rock music in the UK had broadened to the extent that the term 'rock' had become non-specific, and blues-based performers such as Cream and Jimi Hendrix further extended these boundaries through use of extended improvisation and instrumental virtuosity. Progressive rock enabled musicians to escape from the restriction of the three-minute pop song and to explore improvisation within a range of stylistic constructs as a means of legitimising musical status. In this context, rock performers in the United Kingdom did not regard the question of the performance of folk songs with contemporary instrumentation as problematic during the late 1960s.

The emergence of the progressive rock style was assisted by growth in the United Kingdom economy during the late 1960s that enabled record companies to support bands that wished to experiment musically and deviate from the standard three-minute 'single' format. A record company policy change towards marketing stylistically diverse conceptual albums instead of placing emphasis on sales of formulaic three-minute singles was a reflection of record company awareness of the growing progressive rock following in the UK university and club circuits.[31] As previously stated, the singles market had been a primary source of income for pop music record companies since the invention of the seven-inch vinyl disc in 1949 and, from the 1950s until the mid-1960s, albums consisted of previously released singles and B-sides. The recording of *Sgt Pepper's Lonely Hearts Club Band* (1967) enabled The Beatles, however, to establish the concept of album as separate and distinct entities to singles. The production techniques used in the recording of this album established the concept of the recording studio itself as a creative rather than functional tool and stimulated experimentation in recording and production techniques, an integral element in the progressive rock music era that followed.

The political and economic climate in the UK by the end of the 1960s was such that both the established major record labels and newly founded independent labels supported musical experimentation by performers that would normally have been considered too unconventional to sustain career longevity in the mainstream popular music market.[32] In his discussion of the music of Yes, John Palmer cites Yes guitarist Steve Howe's comment that, prior to the progressive rock era, there had previously never been as many opportunities for bands to 'put out records *they* wanted to make' and that the role of the record producer had been subsumed by the production role of the artist.[33] Perceived artistic ownership of recorded output was a common criterion among progressive rock performers, and Simon Nicol supports Howe's comment while describing Fairport Convention's relationship with their recording company. Fairport Convention were signed to Island Records, which had a roster of successful progressive bands, such as Free, Jethro Tull (who were later signed to Chrysalis Records), Spooky Tooth, Traffic, King Crimson, Mott The Hoople and Blodwyn Pig, all of which established Island Records' reputation as a progressive rock music label. Nicol describes the period during which Fairport Convention were recording *Unhalfbricking* (1969) and *Liege and Lief* (1969):

They [Island Records] had been very lucky picking their acts, or very skilful picking their acts, and very good at marketing them. There was a feeling that nothing could really go wrong, we were a young band and if we kept making albums every seven or eight months, or however frequent it was in those days, then you would eventually hit the jackpot, have a chart album and you'd be up and running. This hadn't happened to Fairport yet, and if we had chosen to take off in that particular route, you must remember this is '68 and '69 ... freedom was there to be exploited. They were an enabling company, they weren't a company that said 'You must do this', they weren't trying to squeeze us into a particular suit of clothes.[34]

As with other progressive rock record labels, Island Records' reputation in the early 1970s was that of a facilitator for emerging progressive rock bands, rather than for bands within the commercial mainstream. Martin Carthy shares Nicol's view in his description of the financial policies of record companies towards progressive rock music. Carthy maintains that record companies were willing to invest in experimental music in the early 1970s: 'In the late 1960s and early 1970s, you could waltz into a record company with an idea and say "give me some money" and they would say "certainly young man" and give you five grand. The Albion Country Band got eleven and a half grand out of Island and spent it all.'[35]

At this time, Carthy would have become aware of the commercial dichotomy that existed between the folk sphere and the rock music sphere, particularly during his tenure with Steeleye Span. Moreover, Nicol's and Carthy's statements suggest that the initial music industry and recording environment for English folk-rock music was the same as for progressive rock music, and that its performance attracted larger and more cosmopolitan audiences than those that attended the more intimate performance environment of folk music.

Progressive rock is often situated within the influential sphere of Western art music, although there are many other fusions of rock music with other styles that they relegate to the status of sub-style. For instance, Soft Machine, Family, Colosseum and Caravan drew upon influences from jazz; Quintessence drew influences from Asian music; Osibisa fused the music of West Africa with rock music; Jethro Tull's repertoire was influenced by blues, British folk music and jazz; Pentangle referred to themselves as a jazz-folk ensemble; and Fairport Convention and Steeleye Span both adapted folk songs of the British Isles into rock music settings.[36] Partly in order to identify what was regarded as progressive rock in the 1960s, I interviewed Ed Bicknell, the manager of Dire Straits and Mark Knopfler. I asked him about the artistic climate in live progressive rock music performance in the UK during the late 1960s. Bicknell explained that he started his career in the music industry as the social secretary at the University of Hull in the mid-1960s at which time he booked many of the bands of the progressive rock period such as Led Zeppelin, Jethro Tull, Pink Floyd and Fairport Convention. While studying at the University of Hull, Bicknell became an entertainment secretary and booked bands such as Pink Floyd, The Moody Blues, Joe Cocker and The Greaseband, and Jethro Tull between 1967 and 1970. He hired many other famous bands of the time (most of which were booked for a fee of around £100), but he recalled Fairport Convention between Led Zeppelin (a band Bicknell described as 'folksy as anybody'), Scaffold and Soft Machine. For Bicknell, Fairport Convention was a progressive rock band during a period in which record companies invested in bands that were successful at selling albums rather than singles. Bicknell regards the band's move towards the electrification of traditional folk music as one variation in the number of musical experiments that went on with the financial support of record companies.[37] Bicknell also regards Fairport Convention as a product of a rock club circuit that was frequented by progressive rock bands such as Led Zeppelin, Soft Machine, King Crimson, Pink Floyd and Jethro Tull. While this circuit was vital to a progressive rock band's existence, another major source of their financial income was the weekend bookings at universities that paid three to four times as much as clubs that booked them on weekdays.[38] Bicknell consequently supports a view that the progressive rock audience was student-based, and musically and culturally aware of the origins of the music to which they listened.

The definition of progressive rock as primarily a fusion of rock and classical music is also contrary to comments performers made when interviewed for this study. These performers maintain that the combination of folk music and rock music was carried out by musicians who often had diverse careers as professional performers; some were solo folk artists who had developed their skills on the British folk club circuit, others had been in rock bands that used amplification and electric instruments, and others still had started in bands with amplification and had purposely moved away from this performance context. Many progressive rock performers also came from rhythm and blues, and blues-rock backgrounds. Blues revivals took place in both the United States and the United Kingdom during the early 1960s and these revivals influenced many British pop bands of the period. Rhythm and blues artists in the United Kingdom such as Alexis Korner, Cyril Davies and Graham Bond led bands whose members later formed The Yardbirds, Manfred Mann, The Rolling Stones and Cream. The UK blues revival enabled American artists to perform in the UK as a result of the promotional efforts of British skiffle artist Lonnie Donegan. Rock and roll artists, such as Chuck Berry, Buddy Holly, Eddie Cochran and Jerry Lee Lewis, had performed in the UK in the late 1950s and were followed in the early 1960s by visits from American blues artists, such as Big Bill Broonzy, Muddy Waters and John Lee Hooker. These performances had a fundamental influence on UK musicians of the period.

The musical influences provided by folk music, blues, and rock and roll became apparent in the popular music of the United Kingdom in the mid-1960s, particularly among bands that later became part of the progressive rock movement. By the mid-1960s, the term 'rock music' had become a synonym for popular music that was influenced by blues revivalism while remaining detached from the more commercial styles of popular music. Unlike the United States, the blues revival in the UK was also represented in the UK popular music charts, and many British 'pop' bands of the mid-1960s achieved chart success with songs based on rhythm and blues. Many of these commercially successful British rhythm and blues bands were among those who experimented with the fusion of rock with other musical styles, and these fusions provided a basis for progressive rock. The use of electric, or rock, instrumentation was therefore common in UK performances of rhythm and blues, and blues-rock. The status of these musical styles as revivalist components in the United Kingdom during the early 1960s became less important as both styles became major influences in the UK charts from 1963 onwards. It was possible for British rhythm and blues groups to be commercially successful while retaining their musical 'credibility' – which Simon Frith and Howard Horne describe as maintaining 'one's bohemian credentials'.[39] It is also significant that rock music from the mid-1960s to the early 1970s had attracted a middle-class, student-based audience that regarded rock music as a separate entity from popular music.

Investigation into the origins of progressive rock as a subcultural style located within the boundaries of rock music indicates that British musicians who had developed their musical skills during the early and mid-1960s were familiar with performance of not only blues-rock, but a variety of rock music styles. The English folk-rock performers I interviewed are at the forefront of folk-rock performance and describe different approaches to the interpretation, adaptation and performance of folk music in an electrified rock music context. They share a range of early musical influences and experiences, the most common being a musical family environment in which they were introduced to different musical styles. They also describe listening to rhythm and blues, British pop music and American rock and roll music in their early teenage years, and several attended folk clubs in the early and mid-1960s. Despite a large number of shared musical experiences, these performers provided varied descriptions of folk and early folk-rock performance.

The emergence of the English folk-rock style

Before discussing approaches used by Fairport Convention and Steeleye Span in the adaptation of British folk music for folk-rock performance, it is worth exploring musical directions taken by their peers in order to contextualise folk influences. Consequently, this sub-section clarifies differences between those bands that are more accurately described by terms other than English folk-rock. There were other bands during the late 1960s and early 1970s that might also be considered as part of an initial English folk-rock genre from the perspectives of instrumentation, folk music influences and, to an extent, repertoire. I discuss five prominent bands of the early 1970s (The Strawbs, Mr Fox, Lindisfarne, Pentangle and Gryphon) which drew upon folk influences in the construction of popular music fusions – although the combined descriptors 'folk' and 'rock', as applied by UK record companies of the period, cannot be applied to any of them with accuracy or parity. It is significant that, whereas Fairport Convention regarded themselves as primarily a rock band, and Ashley Hutchings regarded Steeleye Span as an electric folk band, musical identities of other bands labelled by record companies as folk-rock did not always sit easily within restrictive music industry marketing descriptions.[40] For example, Pentangle drummer Gerry Conway regards the band as a jazz band, and he maintains that this was always been the audience perception of it.[41] Another example of imposed folk-rock identity is Gryphon, a progressive rock band that amalgamated English art music of the Middle Ages and music of the Renaissance with rock music in the period following band members' Richard Harvey and Brian Gulland's studies of early music at the Royal Academy of Music. This issue is further discussed later in this chapter.

The Strawbs

The pervasive impact of Bob Dylan's music and the stylistic change in his performance practice particularly influenced The Strawberry Hill Boys, a band formed by two folk club performers, Dave Cousins and Tony Hooper, in 1966. They started their performing career playing bluegrass music, as well as original songs, and were arguably the first folk-orientated band in the UK to incorporate electric instruments and a drum kit in live performance. The band was augmented in 1968 by Sandy Denny, already established as a singer/songwriter on the British folk club circuit, as a vocalist for their first album *All Our Own Work* (1968). At this point the band became known as The Strawbs. Denny left to join Fairport Convention later in 1968 and The Strawbs continued to move further towards electric instrumentation, becoming increasingly influenced by rock music before recording their second album, *Strawbs* (1969), which was made with production assistance from John Paul Jones, the bassist from Led Zeppelin. Rick Wakeman joined The Strawbs on keyboards in 1970 and the band recorded the albums *Just a Collection of Antiques and Curios* (1970) and *From The Witchwood* (1971).

Wakeman left the band to join the progressive rock band Yes in 1971 and was replaced by Blue Weaver from the pop band Amen Corner. *Grave New World* (1972) is generally regarded as The Strawbs' first album to combine rock music and rock production values with folk music, and it featured Cousin's talent for composing epic, dramatic songs, while maintaining folk elements. This stylistic change provides distinction between the music of The Strawbs and the music of Fairport Convention. While its members have always regarded Fairport Convention as a rock band, the band's style has remained close to folk influences since 1969 whereas The Strawbs gradually moved further away from them. A further distinction between The Strawbs and both Fairport Convention and Steeleye Span is illustrated by The Strawbs' early repertoire at the time when they were still considered to be a folk band, despite their gradual move towards electrification. All of the songs on the band's first album, *All Our Own Work*, were, as the title suggests, composed by Cousins, Hooper and Denny, a song-writing policy that continued throughout their recording career. Despite the band's use of song titles such as 'Sheep' and 'Cannondale', which were used to 'score idyllic points', the band's music ultimately failed to impress the aesthetes among the rock audience and it did not 'engage the grassroots sensibilities of folk connoisseurs'.[42]

From 1969, The Strawbs became the most commercially successful folk-influenced band in the United Kingdom, from which time they were signed to A and M Records with whom they had two hit singles, 'Lay Down' (1972) and 'You Won't Get Me, I'm Part Of The Union' (1973). The latter song became a recruiting anthem for the Transport and General Workers Union, resulting in leader columns in *The Times* and *The Sun* newspapers, as well as questions in the House of Commons, regarding whether the song should be banned because its lyrics might be seen as 'rabble-rousing'.[43] These events provided useful publicity for The Strawbs although, perhaps ironically, in the years 1999 and 2000, 'You Won't Get Me, I'm Part Of The Union' was used in an advertising campaign for the Norwich Union Insurance Company. By the mid-1970s, The Strawbs had achieved a reputation as a progressive rock band both in the United Kingdom and in the United States but, as with other progressive rock bands, they experienced a reduction in popularity in the late 1970s during the punk rock period and temporarily disbanded. While The Strawbs were the first folk band to incorporate electric instruments, which might arguably define them as a folk-rock band, they cannot be categorised as English folk-rock, on the grounds that their folk influences became less apparent as their rock influences and song-writing style became predominantly rock-influenced. This change was concomitant to the growth in their commercial success.

As Ian Smith suggests, there have been many successful bands in the UK whose music is 'folk-based' and uses 'the idiom of the tradition', or, as Malcolm Taylor puts it, whose music is 'informed by the tradition'.[44] I maintain that, while The Strawbs' music was folk-informed, the band's repertoire was predominantly a combination of influences that produced a consistently changing formula aimed at the progressive rock market in both the UK and the US and that the band periodically changed its overall style to suit its current song-writing direction. From a commercial perspective, The Strawbs' success in the singles market would have alienated factions of their progressive rock audience, as well as any folk following they may have retained since the late 1960s. Progressive rock had a different audience from that of the pop mainstream, and the progressive rock audience was student-based. Issues surrounding commerciality and authenticity were, however, of equal importance to the progressive rock audience, who would have viewed The Strawbs' success in the singles chart as 'selling out', an issue that also changed the progressive rock reputation of Steeleye Span in 1975.

Mr Fox

Another British folk band that drew upon rock influences was Mr Fox. Formed by folk music scholars Bob and Carole Pegg, Mr Fox performed original songs that were inspired by traditional themes and combined the sounds of English traditional singers and bands with those of rock. While advances in recording technology have made older recordings of folk music widely available, Carole Pegg observes that this availability initiated change in contemporary folk music performance practice that 'exacerbated the raging debate about sounds'.[45] Moreover, given her performance background in what she refers to as a folk-rock band, Pegg accurately maintains that issues concerning 'sound', such as the shape, speed and decorations of melodies, the uses of harmonisation rather than drones and the timbres produced, were a cause of debate among revivalists in the 1950s and 1960s. Pegg's participation in Mr Fox during the early 1970s would have provided personal experience of any debate that surrounded the amalgamation of folk music and rock music although, surprisingly, Pegg does not cite the work of Fairport Convention, while claiming that Steeleye Span and Mr Fox were the principal bands in English folk-rock movement.[46] Bob Pegg describes Mr Fox's repertoire as consisting of 'new songs' played with a variety of instruments that would normally be used in a traditional context.[47] The band did not receive the same degree of record company support as that given to The Strawbs, Fairport Convention and Steeleye Span, despite the band recording two albums, *Mr Fox* (1970) and *The Gypsy* (1971). Mr Fox disbanded in 1972. Contrary to Carole Pegg's and Laing's views, I do not regard Mr Fox as a folk-rock band on the basis of their inclusion of a bass guitar and a drum kit into a band instrumentation that consisted of organ, melodeon, tin whistle, fiddle, cello, flute, clarinet and bassoon. The band performed British folk music with diverse instrumentation during the early 1970s, a period during which there was growth in a discerning rock audience. According to the website that distributes re-issued recordings of Mr Fox's albums, the band's music is currently described as folk music and the band itself is described as a 'contemporary folk band'.

While discussing folk and rock music amalgamations, Bob Pegg told me that he regards the combination of folk and rock styles as a 'blind alley', arguing that a folk song performed in a rock setting should 'stand or fall totally on its own merits'. He maintains that folk-rock should avoid being associated with what he refers to as the 'American rock band format with rhythm guitar, lead guitar, drums, bass and synthesiser'.[48] Bob Pegg's views on the combination of folk-influenced music and rock instrumentation further supports my view that The Strawbs were not a folk-rock band, and that their later sound aesthetics might be more accurately described as a 'soft rock' band in the American sense, while still in a progressive rock context.

Lindisfarne

Another band to which I apply a similar description is Lindisfarne, whose repertoire demonstrated only minor influences taken from traditional folk music. During the early 1970s, Lindisfarne was signed to Charisma Records, a progressive rock music label that also signed Genesis, Van Der Graaf Generator, Audience and the cast of Monty Python. The title of Lindisfarne's first album, *Nicely Out of Tune* (1970), reflects the band's view of their musical style that was, as they saw it, out of step with popular musical trends of the period, a view indicative of their progressive rock origins. Both Genesis and Van Der Graaf Generator produced repertoires consisting of epic, dramatic textual narratives and music that drew upon classical referents. Lindisfarne's repertoire also consisted of original band compositions, although their songs were shorter – and often anthemic – works, several of which achieved chart success.[49] While the band is often placed in the folk-rock category, their connections to folk music centre on the band's inclusion of acoustic instruments usually associated with folk music – such as mandolin, violin and banjo – situating the band in a broad folk-influenced category. Lindisfarne's folk-influenced identity also relates to the band's origin in the north east of England. References to local identity are apparent both in the band's name and in textual themes, an association particularly apparent in the band's single 'Fog on the Tyne' (1971), which was the title track of their second album. Success in the singles charts enabled various Lindisfarne incarnations to perform until 2004, although the band often attracted criticism from earlier fans on the grounds of the commerciality of some of their later recordings. For example, Lindisfarne's *C'mon Everybody* (1987), a thirty-four-track album of 1950s rock and roll hits, was condemned by many of the band's fans on the grounds that they regarded it as a 'party album' publicised by the band's annual Christmas performances in Newcastle during the 1980s. Links to the commercial mainstream gradually eroded the band's progressive rock fan base during the mid-1970s as the band changed stylistically towards a more pop-based format, although Lindisfarne's acoustic/electric instrumentation – with its inherent notions of folk influence – enabled the band to maintain distinction in the popular music arena.

Pentangle

Pentangle, on the other hand, eschewed popular music influences. The band was founded in 1968 by two acoustic guitarists, Bert Jansch and John Renbourne, both of whom were already established as solo performers on the British folk circuit. The other members of the band were vocalist Jacqui McShee and jazz musicians Danny Thompson on double bass and Terry Cox on drums. Pentangle was part of a musical trend in which established solo artists and duos from the folk, jazz and blues idioms began to form bands, a trend that was also influential in the formation of Steeleye Span in 1970. Robin Denselow describes Pentangle as a 'British folk fusion band' that 'took folk-blues out of the folk club scene and on to the international concert circuit'.[50] While Denselow is partially correct in this statement, Pentangle also mixed folk music with extended jazz improvisation and achieved international recognition and commercial success, particularly with their song, 'Light Flight' (1969) – which was used as music for the first BBC television broadcast in colour – and their live album *Basket of Light* (1969). Pentangle was often criticised for being 'too easy on the ear' and, as a band that is often categorised in the folk-rock genre, their music demonstrates no influences from rock music. Band members take a similar stance on the band's identity. Renbourn states that, in his view, 'About the worst thing you can do to a folk song is inflict a rock beat on it', adding that 'Some of the old tunes from the British Isles will stand it, but not many'.[51] Thompson takes a similar view, commenting that 'Without question, it was a folk-jazz band. It was never a folk-rock group'.[52] Thompson bases this view on Pentangle's instrumentation, which included banjo and sitar, instrumentation that he does not associate with rock music, despite their use by The Beatles and The Rolling Stones. As with descriptions of criticism from the folk audience that were gleaned from interviews for this study, Pentangle also attracted criticism for their combination of folk music with elements taken from jazz and blues. The band received death threats from folk fans on the grounds of their use of amplification, despite its use as a public address system for acoustic instruments in large performance settings.[53] Apart from attracting folk purist criticism, association with the folk-rock category can be primarily linked to Pentangle's acoustic instrumentation and to their rock-music-orientated management in the UK. The band also appeared at rock festivals presenting bands such as Canned Heat, the Grateful Dead, Alice Cooper and the Jimi Hendrix Experience. Despite these rock music associations, Pentangle cannot be categorised as folk-rock, despite a populist view that they were among the first British folk-rock bands.

Gryphon

Richard Harvey and Brian Gulland, two multi-instrumentalists specialising in art music of the English Middle Ages and the Renaissance, formed Gryphon in 1972, and the band initially adapted early music for performance in a rock setting. Harvey describes becoming interested in rock music when he first heard *The Yes Album* (1970) – which was a 'revelation' to him – and he adds that, while Gryphon started as a serious early music band, it had, within a year, started using a large public address system and electronic effects to amplify krummhorns, mandolins and recorders, as well as an electric harpsichord, electric guitars and a drum kit.[54] The repertoire of Gryphon's first album consisted mainly of early music performed in a rock setting, although their second album included several British folk songs that were performed with a combination of medieval and rock instruments. The band's third album, *Red Queen to Gryphon 3*, demonstrated the influences of progressive rock bands such as Yes and Gentle Giant and consisted of a four-movement instrumental suite lasting thirty-five minutes. Albums that followed continued in a similar direction away from Gryphon's original early music and folk music influences and, as with many progressive rock bands, the band's recording contract was cancelled in 1977 and its members disbanded. Gryphon might be described as a folk-rock band based on the material recorded on their second album, although their subsequent change of musical direction towards a more rock-focused conceptuality on later albums suggests that they are more accurately described as a rock band that fused diverse musical instrumentation and classical referents with rock music as part of the broad progressive rock music style.

The Strawbs, Mr Fox, Lindisfarne, Pentangle, and Gryphon – five bands often regarded as part of the early folk-rock movement in the UK – all contributed to growth in audience awareness of folk music of the British Isles. While all performed folk music, or folk-influenced music, combined with other popular music styles to lesser or to greater degrees, most changed stylistic direction away from the influence of folk music towards rock music. Others disbanded due to lack of record-company support, as in the case of Mr Fox, or because of perceived musical sterility among band members, as in the case of Pentangle. What becomes apparent in an examination of progressive rock is its eclecticism in that no other popular music style in the 1970s drew upon so many diverse stylistic sources. In the case of the amalgamation of folk and rock music it is significant that while heavy rock audiences did not listen to folk music, and vice versa, there were factions from each audience that showed interest in the combination. Unlike the bands above, Fairport Convention and Steeleye Span performed British folk songs in a rock setting while retaining most of the original lyrics, melodies and metres. Fairport Convention's early repertoire included original songs, such as 'Crazy Man Michael' and 'Sloth', both of which were composed by band members Richard Thompson and Dave Swarbrick. As with all of the original songs recorded by the band, both songs assimilate the style of the 'traditional' folk music that is also on these recordings. Steeleye Span did not record original material, and most of their recorded output consists of rear-rangements of British folk songs. They also occasionally recorded cover versions of songs that had been featured in their live performances.[55] Given that the recordings and live performances of Fairport Convention and Steeleye Span have mostly consisted of folk songs of the British Isles – as well as new folk-informed songs – performed in rock settings throughout each of these band's careers, they currently define contemporary English folk-rock. They also remain influential in the emergence of new folk revivalism that has become apparent since the mid-1990s.

Pioneers of English folk-rock

Since Macan regards his examples of the principal bands in the progressive rock counterculture as irrefutable, my discussion on the origins of the English folk-rock style centres on Fairport Convention and Steeleye Span, although I do not intend the following to be a comprehensive biography of either band.[56] I regard the repertoires and performance practices of these bands as key factors in the establishment of peer and audience recognition of each as pioneers of the English folk-rock movement. I also regard the reputations, stylistic parameters and significant contents of repertoire of these bands as having become established by the 1980s. The bands are still performing many of the songs that were recorded on their earlier albums, and these have become an integral part of their identities. For example, Nicol states that 'Matty Groves' is a song that has never been out of the Fairport Convention live repertoire since it was recorded in 1969.[57]

Fairport Convention can be described as an electric rock band that plays folk music. The band was originally influenced by late-1960s American 'acid-rock' music as well as by the songs of Bob Dylan and Joni Mitchell. When Fairport Convention formed in 1967, the original members were Richard Thompson and Simon Nicol on guitars, Ashley Hutchings on bass guitar, Martin Lamble on drums, and Judy Dyble and Ian Matthews as vocalists.[58] They initially performed in their native London before they toured the United Kingdom rock club and university circuits, and their early performances at the Middle Earth and UFO clubs in London often supported the embryonic Pink Floyd. Performances of this nature indicate that Fairport Convention performed on a rock circuit that established several progressive bands of that period, despite the 'soft rock' description of the band given by Nicol during a fieldwork interview.[59] Dyble left the band after the recording of the first album, and the band continued with one lead vocalist, Matthews. Audiences were aware, however, of the lack of a female voice and so the band decided to replace Dyble in order to fulfil contractual obligations. After several auditions, Sandy Denny was invited to join the band. As there was little time to create a completely new repertoire, the band and new singer decided to meet on what Nicol refers to as 'common ground', agreeing that each party would learn some of the other's material. Nicol describes this as 'putting arrangements around the repertoire Denny had performed in folk clubs'.[60] The reason for this amalgamation of the singer's and band's sets is that most rock bands of the time relied on regular live performance as a source of income, and time spent rehearsing a new set would be an interruption of the band's live performance schedule. Album recordings usually took place twice a year and were another impediment to live performance, although new albums were a means of further promoting live engagements.

Fairport Convention's first two albums, *Fairport Convention* (1968) and *What We Did On Our Holidays* (1969), were influenced by the rock music of American West Coast bands, which often performed songs composed by Bob Dylan and Pete Seeger. Fairport Convention added 'cover' songs to original band material, as well as songs that had become standard repertoire of the 1950s and 1960s American folk music circuit, such as 'Wild Mountain Thyme' and 'John Riley'. When asked about the band's choice of cover songs, Nicol explained that Fairport Convention was influenced by bands that were broadcast by the off-shore radio station, Radio Caroline. He added that the chosen songs were purposely obscure in order to avoid the familiar 'Lennon and McCartney catalogue' performed by most 1960s cover bands.[61] Fairport Convention had not included British folk music in their repertoire prior to Denny joining the band before the recording of *What We Did On Our Holidays*. This album includes the songs 'Nottamun Town' and 'She Moves Through The Fair', both of which were, according to Nicol, arranged and recorded as they were performed in Denny's solo performances. Nicol describes the recording of 'Nottamun Town' as an early musical experiment that led Fairport Convention towards the *Liege and Lief* album (1969). 'Nottamun Town' is another song that Denny brought into the band and, unlike many of the other traditional songs that they performed, was not what Nicol describes as a 'story song':

> It had in it images which [are] dated images, they're resonant of a period of time past. They're historical but they don't tell a tale in the way a classic folk song does, to me, anyway. And those are the songs ['story songs'] which I find I enjoy singing even more and more as I get older – songs which are story driven rather than image driven.[62]

Nicol's statements suggest that members of Fairport Convention were not as familiar with the traditions inherent in British folk music performance as they were with the repertoires of folk-influenced singers such as Bob Dylan, Tom Paxton and Joni Mitchell, and that their approach to British folk music's amalgamation with rock music was primarily to adapt Denny's repertoire into a rock format as quickly as possible. Denny's experience in The Strawbs had prepared her for performance in an electrified band, and Fairport Convention's third album, *Unhalfbricking* (1969), contains a song generally regarded as the first folk-rock recording, 'A Sailor's Life'. This is a British folk song performed in the style of the American 'acid-rock' bands of the late 1960s and it features an extended improvised guitar solo by Richard Thompson. The inclusion of this extended guitar improvisation is significant because, prior to the advent of what is referred to as folk-rock from 1969 onwards, there was a difference between folk musicians, who were completely acoustic, and musicians who used electric guitars and amplification and who were considered by folk audiences and folk performers alike to be the antithesis of folk music culture. This issue further supports the argument that a perceived difference between folk and folk-rock is often a question of the relative volumes of both styles.

In an article in the *New Musical Express*, Denny describes the direction the band was planning to follow after *Unhalfbricking* as: 'digging into the archives of the [English] Folk Dance and Song Society – the British Museum of folk music', but she adds 'we're not making it pop though, in fact it will be almost straight, only electric. What does it sound like? Heavy traditional folk music.'[63]

Ashley Hutchings described to me what he regarded as major changes occurring in the band's repertoire when they recorded *Unhalfbricking*, and he describes the recording of 'A Sailor's Life' as 'a one take improvisational recording of the traditional song'. Hutchings explained how the song's arrangement was formed: 'It had fallen into place just playing, just jamming in a dressing room at a gig. Sandy started to sing and play and we fell in behind her. We went on stage that night and performed that song. One took risks like that in those days.'[64]

This statement is representative of Hutchings' earlier statement that the band's record company regarded them as 'freaks', or members of the underground movement that comprised 1960s hippies. The notion that music could 'fall into place by jamming' was common to this movement. Nicol takes a more pragmatic view to the long improvisational section in the band's version of 'A Sailor's Life' and Thompson's seven-minute guitar solo. He suggests that Thompson was not necessarily aiming to be a 'rock' or 'folk' guitarist playing electric guitar. He also describes the band policy of extending the length of songs to fulfill their performance contracts:

The band did used to stretch out to give Richard his head in those days partly because we had to play such appallingly long sets…I think 'A Sailor's Life' is another turning point. It was a live performance, what you hear on record is what was played at the time by all of us and we were hearing it ourselves for the first time. That was the first time we had assembled together to perform that song. We knew that it had six verses and that Sandy was just going to tell the story but we didn't know, for instance, that it was going to fall into a pulsing rhythm, at a certain point. We would allow Richard to play around with his musical ideas which he did with quite remarkable maturity and total unselfconsciousness. He was trying to sound like John Coltrane, I think, when he was playing electric guitar.[65]

This statement illustrates that, while Fairport Convention were initially a rock band, their musical eclecticism embraced influences not only from rock and folk music, but also from jazz. In an interview, Thompson discusses the band's reputation as a rock band in the late 1960s and describes some of the occasions when Fairport Convention performed at The Speakeasy club in London during which Jimi Hendrix would often improvise with the band: 'On occasion he'd [Hendrix] sit in with Fairport when we were playing The Speakeasy; he'd jump on stage, grab one of our guitars, which was strung the wrong way round for him – and played as well as if it had been the right way round!'[66]

Despite the band's associations with rock and folk musicians, Nicol posits that the band's change of direction from rock to folk-rock was almost accidental, despite his own awareness of the work of Dylan and Tom Paxton, as well as his and other band members' visits to folk clubs and Cecil Sharp House. Hutchings describes the period in a similar way and maintains that there was no conscious effort to become a folk-rock band because much of Denny's material 'sat very neatly' with the band's existing repertoire. Given the enabling nature of Island Records as a facilitator of musical experimentation, it is not surprising that the band would have regarded Denny's contribution as convenient rather than ground-breaking. Furthermore, Hutchings describes the band as being 'underground' in the psychedelic period of 1967–68, indicating that he regarded Fairport Convention as a psychedelic rock band at this time, rather than as a part of the progressive rock movement, and that the band themselves may not have viewed themselves as having a fixed stylistic identity.[67]

The band's fourth album, *Liege and Lief*, is generally considered to be the seminal English folk-rock album and it is at this point that Nicol places a line between Fairport Convention being initially a rock band and becoming a folk-rock band playing folk music of the British Isles.[68] He maintains that, having listened to what The Byrds had done to Dylan's songs, it was a natural and easy process that approached what might nowadays be described as 'soft-rock'. Hutchings gives much of the credit for *Liege and Lief* to Swarbrick and Denny, and adds that the criteria used by Fairport Convention to decide which songs to record was 'largely down to anything we really liked, anything that grabbed us'.[69] Nicol adds that the band was not being purposely 'scholarly' about their approach to a new repertoire and, although he states that Hutchings may have been more 'academic' than any of the other band members, the new material 'had to be something that appealed'.[70] The band policy was that the repertoire had to be 'music that touched you and illuminated your life and that you could present in an attractive and entertaining way'. These descriptions of repertoire assembly suggest, therefore, that the band's change of direction towards innovative adaptation of traditional songs was based on their enjoyment of the performance of folk music rather than a concern for authenticity as a means of furthering its preservation. All the folk and folk-rock performers I interviewed supported this aspect in the adaptation of folk songs for performance in a rock setting and, as previously stated, I do not regard the adaptations of folk and rock music by these performers as being solely for the purpose of commercial gain.

Fairport Convention continued an informal policy in the assembly of their folk-rock repertoire and Denny, and violinist Dave Swarbrick, brought their personal repertoires into the band, providing songs already familiar to their own folk audiences.[71] Nicol and Hutchings both maintain that there was no formal plan to create a fusion of folk music and rock music. The assembly of a repertoire of what were thought to be rarely performed folk songs is a common factor among many of the performers I interviewed, many of whom were concerned that the originality of their repertoire should remain as individual as possible. Nicol describes the band's early choice of material as 'purposely obscure', despite the absence of any folk-rock blue-print.[72] Despite Hutchings' view that credit is mainly due to Sandy Denny and Dave Swarbrick, Nicol maintains that Hutchings worked 'with a consuming passion' to bring traditional songs into a contemporary popular music format. Hutchings was still comparatively inexperienced in terms of folk song repertoire, and his perceptions of what could be considered obscure folk songs in that period may have been inaccurate given that Fairport Convention performed folk songs that were often already familiar to folk music audiences.[73]

In his discussion of the origins of folk-rock in the UK, Richie Unterberger describes Joe Boyd and John Woods, the production team that recorded both Fairport Convention and The Incredible String Band, as 'suited for the needs of folk-rooted musicians chafing to break out of the British folk scene's more close-minded conventions'.[74] Unterberger notes that Wood regarded folk-orientated bands such as these as 'looking to different horizons' and that they were not quite so 'precious' as the earlier generation that was 'much more purist'. In an interview, Boyd refers to 'Ashley's fanaticism' as a zealous convert to folk music.[75] He also describes Denny's amusement when Hutchings would claim to have found a 'magnificent' folk song at Cecil Sharp House only to find that it was already a part of Denny's personal repertoire. The pre-existing familiarity of Fairport Convention's folk-rock repertoire could therefore have been responsible for the popularity of the band in both folk and rock music circles, in terms of success in live performance and album sales, a familiar concept among the progressive rock audience, despite the reticence of revivalists who were critical of the fusion of the two styles.

When Fairport Convention's van was involved in a road accident in June 1969, the original drummer, Martin Lamble, was killed and other band members were injured. Hutchings was one of the most seriously injured, and Nicol describes Hutchings' work to rebuild the band during his recovery as 'very motivated, very directed, very professional and unquestionably the work of a driven man'.[76] Hutchings has achieved a reputation as a folk researcher since the time he spent at Cecil Sharp House finding material for *Liege and Lief*. Nicol described to me how

Hutchings did 'ninety per cent of the legwork' for *Liege and Lief*, and how he would arrive at rehearsals 'with tapes of the old wax cylinders' preserved at Cecil Sharp House. Hutchings' emphasis on the performance of British folk music is apparent as Fairport Convention moved from rock to folk-rock, and he continued this approach in the formation of his next band, Steeleye Span. As with many of the progressive rock bands, Fairport Convention's career foundered in the late 1970s during the punk rock period that, according to Hutchings, made folk-rock unfashionable. The band reformed for a charity performance in 1979, which became an annual event leading to the band reforming on a permanent basis.

Fairport Convention attracted recent criticism from purists among the folk audience on the grounds of inauthenticity in terms of the inclusion of original songs in their repertoire. Ed Vulliamy describes this criticism as follows: 'Fairport were (and still are) criticised by the finger-in-the-ear folk purists for adding elements of rock and country music into their brew. Some of the work was and is traditional...but most of their songs take a contemporary theme and narrate it in a traditional way...crafted in the appropriate language.'[77] Vulliamy suggests that Fairport Convention's music links the past with the present and states that:

> It is a line drawn from medieval ballads, through 17th century madrigals and sea shanties, to Vaughan Williams and Durham miners' songs, the work of the folk-song collector Cecil Sharp and the formation of the English Folk Dance and Song Society, the early days of CND and the development, via various Bob Dylan imitators, of the protest song movement, right up to the Pogues and Kirsty MacColl.[78]

Vulliamy also suggests that Fairport Convention could not continue to exist in between 'rock and roll' and 'crude political nationalism' and maintains that they were ultimately seen as too 'folky' by rock fans and too 'rocky' by folk fans.[79] Despite his broad description of the sources of Fairport Convention's material and the band's effect on later artists, Vulliamy recognises that the band's music often alienated factions in both the folk and rock audiences, and this is arguably the reason that Fairport Convention did not achieve the same level of commercial success as The Strawbs, who became successful in the broader rock mainstream performing original material.

In contrast to Fairport Convention, Steeleye Span can be described as a folk band that plays electric instruments. After the release of the *Liege and Lief* album, both Denny and Hutchings left Fairport Convention, Denny to pursue a solo career and Hutchings to take his folk music research further in the formation of Steeleye Span. Hutchings described his activities in that year as making contact with many established folk performers:

> In the year, or less than the year, leading up to *Liege and Lief*, I was mixing and mingling with a lot of people on the folk scene – Tim Hart, Maddy Prior, The Sweenies Men, who were guys from Ireland, Terry Woods, Johnny Moynihan, Andy Irvine, Bob and Carole Pegg – many others, but those in particular. I was building up a real fanatical interest in British folk song traditions. So, although we had Dave Swarbrick and Sandy Denny in the group who'd worked on the folk scene, and although I really hadn't, I would say I was the most fanatical with regard to getting traditional music into the repertory of the band. I'd spent a lot of time at Cecil Sharp House, as well as folk clubs, and I'd done a lot of delving, a lot of searching and I was enjoying that.[80]

Steeleye Span was formed after a discussion between Maddy Prior, Tim Hart and Hutchings concerning the electrification of folk music. Prior and Hart expressed frustration that innovatory developments in folk music were being made by rock musicians, and both felt that folk musicians should adapt to performance on electric instruments. The decision to form a band was also influenced by a contemporary trend in which solo and duo performers were performing – and becoming commercially successful – in larger ensembles, a factor that influenced the formation of Pentangle. Steeleye Span band members, other than Hutchings, Prior and Hart, were Gay Woods and Terry Woods. Hutchings also hired session drummers Gerry Conway and Dave Mattacks, for the recording of the first band album, *Hark! The Village Wait* (1970).[81] The first Steeleye Span line-up disbanded after the recording of this album, and Hutchings assembled a new band with the same name that retained Prior on vocals and Hart on guitar and vocals, while adding Martin Carthy on guitar, banjo and vocals, and Peter Knight on violin and mandolin.[82]

Hutchings' concept was that Steeleye Span would be the first English folk-rock band whose repertoire would consist solely of folk music from the British Isles, particularly England. The band's repertoire was to consist of British folk songs outside the popular repertoire of folk singers of the time. Much of the material recorded by Steeleye Span was also in the repertoire of folk performers who were already established and whose recorded works had existed for twenty years. This raises the question of to whom the source material was actually obscure, when Hutchings describes working with established folk performers during the formation of the band. He maintains that 'There was a lot of knowledge within the group and, very quickly, I brought my knowledge up to their standard by a lot of research, a lot of reading and a lot of burning the candle late at night.'[83] The issue of how much experience and knowledge of traditional British music Hutchings gained in a limited period of time is questionable, given that his musical background was based in the American-influenced rhythm and blues and rock music of the 1950s and 1960s. Knowledge and experience of folk music possessed by performers with whom Hutchings associated, such as Swarbrick, Prior, Hart, Bob Pegg, Carole Pegg and Terry Woods, would have been superior, however laudable and rigorous Hutchings' research may have been.

Given Hutchings' folk song sources, aspects of audience familiarity with Steeleye Span's repertoire may have contributed to the early and continued success of the band in the same way that the familiar folk repertoire of Fairport Convention made that band accessible to folk audiences. Hutchings' notions of the obscurity of folk songs therefore contributed to the success of both bands. After his departure, the band continued to perform a British folk music repertoire, as well as occasional covers, with almost unchanging personnel until 1975. The obscurity of the band's repertoire was no longer an issue, as illustrated by one song on the album, *Parcel of Rogues* (1973). 'The Spotted Cow' first appeared in the late eighteenth century and was mentioned in Thomas Hardy's *Tess of the d'Urbervilles* in 1891. It was collected by Sabine Baring Gould in Devon in 1889, Frank Kidson in Yorkshire in 1891, Cecil Sharp in Somerset in 1904, the Hammond brothers in Hampshire in 1907, Percy Grainger in Lincolnshire in 1908 and Vaughan Williams in Wiltshire in

1923. A song found in such a wide area of collection might be regarded as 'popular' in folk circles and certainly not obscure, further contradicting Hutchings' notion of a band that aimed to fuse folk and rock music and performing a repertoire outside the standard folk repertoire.

Hutchings left Steeleye Span in 1971 and formed The Albion Band. This band has performed ever since, along with several of his other folk-orientated projects. His dedication to British folk music is also reflected by the other directions he has pursued, such as the combination of rock and Morris music for the albums *Morris On* (1972) and *Son of Morris On* (1976), as well as his one-man show, *An Evening with Cecil Sharp and Ashley Hutchings*, in 1984.

Even though the first Steeleye Span album instrumentation had featured drums, following band line-ups did not. The arrangements of songs on the albums *Please To See The King* (1971), *Ten Man Mop, Or Mr Reservoir Butler Rides Again* (1971), *Below The Salt* (1972) and *Parcel of Rogues* (1973) are constructed rhythmically around the interplay between bass and guitars. There is one song on *Parcel of Rogues* on which Rick Kemp plays drums as well as bass guitar. Kemp was an established rock bass player when he joined Steeleye Span on Hutchings' departure, and he told me that he often felt that the band sound was not powerful enough without drums. He described proving this view to the other members of the band by playing both bass and drums on the song 'Wee Wee Man' in order to demonstrate how drums could provide more rhythmic impact.[84]

Steeleye Span added a permanent drummer, Nigel Pegrum, for the recording of *Now We Are Six* (1974), which was produced by Ian Anderson of Jethro Tull, and this became the band's first top twenty album. In January 1975, the band released the album *Commoners Crown* (1975), and in October of that year they released the album *All Around My Hat* with the title track released as a single. This single was produced by Mike Batt and entered the top twenty of the UK record charts, although the commercial success that the band achieved, together with their association with Batt, alienated both their folk and progressive rock audiences and placed the band in the commercial mainstream, with many television appearances and extensive touring. One cause of this alienation was Batt's associations with popular music. Batt is a song writer and producer who composed and produced the music for *The Wombles*, a children's television series in the early 1970s, that resulted in several top twenty hit albums for *The Wombles*, which became a touring band performing for children. Steeleye Span's commercial success, however, does not change their 'English folk-rock' description. Their repertoire has always consisted of folk songs from the British Isles performed in rock settings and their performances of cover versions of songs, as well as their later folk-informed, original songs, have been assimilated into the style of their familiar folk-rock repertoire. In this sense, the construction of their repertoire is similar to that of Fairport Convention, who adapted original material using a process that might be regarded as 'traditionalisation' to assimilate the material into a British folk song repertoire.

Steeleye Span recorded and toured during the 1980s with changing line-ups but the band personnel became relatively stable during the 1990s until Maddy Prior left the band in 1996 to pursue a solo career. She was replaced by Gay Woods, who had sung on the first Steeleye Span album, *Hark! The Village Wait* in 1970. The band stopped live performances in 2001 but reunited during 2005 and performed a fortieth anniversary tour in 2010.

Performer perspectives on early English folk-rock performance practice

Issues arising from change in performance practice had a significant impact on the development of English folk-rock. Describing folk musicians as rock musicians when they perform with an electric instrument is debatable.

Performance of folk music by a rock band brings about other more fundamental changes that have previously been overlooked. These changes are further discussed later in this book, but they often include the addition of a structured rhythmical pulse that alters folk music performance far more than does the use of electric instruments. The presence of a drum kit, itself a relative newcomer to twentieth-century popular music through 1920s jazz, often restricts the freer pulse of certain types of folk music. The invention of the drum machine in the late 1970s has added computerised regularity to the pulse when folk music performance is amalgamated with rock and pop, and the amalgamation of folk music with diverse popular music styles has so far continued for four decades. This amalgamation has been typified more recently by artists such as Eliza Carthy and Jim Moray – who have both used modern Afro-American rhythms and music programming technology to perform traditional British folk songs – and the combination of pop and Irish folk music performed by The Corrs, which became popular during the 1990s. It is therefore worth considering descriptions of early folk-rock adaptations from members of both Fairport Convention and Steeleye Span as they provide an insight into the acquisition of performance skills as folk and rock performers experimented with combining and maintaining authenticities inherent in both folk and rock performance.

The adaptation of folk songs for English folk-rock performance was not part of any formal musical plan. Fairport Convention's collaboration with Sandy Denny was a matter of expediency, and the gradual amalgamation of her repertoire with that of the band was a mutually convenient means by which the band could continue live performance in the progressive rock arena. Simon Nicol maintains that the band never set out to 'bang a drum for traditional music in the way that Ashley [Hutchings] was when he guided us into the *Liege and Lief* experiment and even more so when he founded Steeleye Span'.[87]

Nicol describes Fairport's *modus operandi* at the time as: 'doing things naturally without really trying to put fences up around them saying "This is folk", "This is rock", "This is some sort of grey area in between"'.[88] These statements reflect the experimental nature of progressive rock music fusions during the early 1970s. I asked Nicol about the band's rehearsal process and their policy to retain original texts and melodies as notated by Victorian and Edwardian collectors. He explained that it was a question of the source of each song, although he stated that he regards Sandy Denny's contribution to the band as introducing material that she was already performing as an experienced folk club performer. This material was unfamiliar to Richard Thompson, Ashley Hutchings and Nicol.[89] Nicol situates Denny's early career in the second folk revival that was still taking place in the 1960s and, due to the band's inexperience in this area, it was decided that the band would 'follow her lead'. When Fairport Convention prepared for the recording of *Liege and Lief* in 1969, Nicol describes the band as having 'the luxury of time' prior to the actual recording process, a factor unlike the policy of mutual convenience and expediency that existed when Denny first joined the band and that is indicative of record company support available during the progressive rock movement. The material recorded on *Liege and Lief* was 'more considered and discussed and experimented with', although Nicol regards Denny's personal repertoire recorded by the band at that time as 'a direct result of the people she had been exposed to', such as Annie Briggs, an influence Nicol regards as 'a long way from the Walter Pardons of this world'.[90] Moreover, Nicol maintains that Denny had not been exposed to singers who were 'in a direct line of the oral tradition of the way songs were told', and consequently he regards the band's English folk-rock repertoire of the time as one step removed from what he perceives as 'the genuine dying tradition'. In distancing the band from notions of revivalism at that time, Nicol describes early band policy as a combination of the people involved 'bringing their own interpretation or spirit to the collective ideal', and he adds that he regards folk music as 'available for interpretation in whatever context you choose to place it'.[91] Nicol states that 'You're never going to damage the purity of the original because, whatever you do to a song, it's not going to flaw it in any way…It may not be to your taste as a listener, it may not chime with your political standpoint, but you are not going to make it worse than unlistenable. To quote Mr Plant [Robert Plant of Led Zeppelin], "The Song Remains The Same"'.[92] Nicol summarises his view by stating that the essence of the material is inviolable and that there are only two types of music – 'the type you listen to and the rest'.[93] Martin Carthy shares Nicol's views, and he suggests that there is permanence about folk music that is manifest as 'a continuity' that remains unaffected by variation.[94] Carthy's statement, and his perception of unassailable folk songs, raises the issue of where a song 'resides'. Given the nature of oral transmission and use of printed text in both traditional folk music and English folk-rock, songs exist primarily in two locations – with the performer and with the audience. Moreover, a consequence of twentieth-century technology is that perceived song location also exists in recorded media. The recording process has enabled a canon of folk music to be permanently available to performers and audiences, and I discuss the issue of canon in folk music in a later chapter.

Carthy describes the Steeleye Span policy in the early 1970s as also retaining original elements from source songs – a process he describes as 'doing them [the songs] straight' – although he adds that the band often 'messed around' with songs as, in his view, folk music is 'a work in progress'.[95] This description of folk song reinterpretation is indicative of his view that source versions of folk songs represent only a 'snapshot' of a song's life. Carthy is critical of those who regard folk songs as 'standing still' and for study purposes only. He contends that 'you can't damage the inevitable, it's not anybody's business to put songs in aspic, you can't nail them down for ever' and that the folk song collectors 'were taking a three minute forty second snapshot…in that song's life' that 'interrupted the work in progress' as they notated the song.[96] He refuses 'to accept that this is the end of [a folk] song's life'.[97] On the subject of authenticity in English folk-rock performance, Carthy maintains that folk music has always had a progressive element and that the often indeterminable age of folk songs is a contributing factor to the difficulty many modern musicians experience in playing them, particularly guitarists, although in his view this is a particular factor that makes them interesting.[98] He also regards issues of authenticity in folk music performance practice as problematic and suggests that musical exchange is a positive aspect of stylistic fusion in which musicians learn from each other and resist 'locking themselves into a box'.[99]

As well as challenges offered by folk music to contemporary guitar performance practices, a significant aspect of stylistic exchange in the adaptation of folk songs for rock settings resides in the addition of a drum kit and the consequent use of constant pulse and regular metre. Many British folk songs, however, do not adhere to one metre in the same way that pop and rock songs do. Hutchings regards the 'Swarbrick-influenced' 'Tam Lin' from *Liege and Lief* as 'a very special track' because its irregular metre demonstrates the importance of the Fairport Convention drummer, Dave Mattacks.[100] Nicol maintains that Mattacks'

contribution to the adaptation of folk songs for rock performance is often overlooked, and he regards Mattacks as a musical
innovator who came from the 'strict world of ballroom dancing'
and who adapted skills learnt from military drumming to enable
him to perform with 'discipline' and with 'the imagination to
create a new style of drumming'.[101] While describing his experiences of playing folk songs that used irregular metre, drummer
Gerry Conway maintains that his rock recording experience had
not prepared him for the performance of folk-rock.[102] In a discussion of his experiences during the recording of Steeleye Span's
first album *Hark! The Village Wait* (1970), Conway described how
Hutchings had to verbally describe the metric arrangement for
each song:

> I suppose that if you hear a new song, a new piece of any sort, you
> would struggle to learn it. I can certainly remember struggling to
> learn them [folk songs] because of the strange shapes in the back-
> ground [the metric structure]. I certainly didn't have a lot of expe-
> rience playing in fives and sevens and things like that and
> suddenly these were appearing and I suppose, if I'm truthful
> when I look back on a lot of it, as soon as you sort of find out what
> a seven is, and you think 'It's a seven, it's fantastic', and as soon
> as you'd got it, you'd probably overplay it to death.[103]

While this statement is arguably representative of many rock
drummers of the late 1960s whose performance skills were
mostly centred in common time, it does reflect the openness to
new challenges that was common among progressive rock musicians. 'One Morning In May' from the more recent Jaqui McShee,
Gerry Conway and Spencer Cozens album, *About Thyme* (1996)
is a more contemporary example of Conway's approach to irregular metre, and his description of the arrangement process suggests a similarity to the earlier approach taken by Fairport
Convention in the modernisation of folk songs: 'We were doing
a song called *One Morning in May* and that is a kind of $\frac{6}{8}$ sort of
feel. But we drifted into $4[\frac{4}{4}]$ and a whole bar of $3[\frac{3}{4}]$ here and
there. Everyone said, "How are we doing it?" It was interesting
to play and, hopefully, to listen to as well. That's the shape of
the new stuff that's happening, but hopefully it's a little more
refined than when I was doing it in the seventies'.[104]

Conway adapted his skills to enable performance of metrical structure in source folk songs, although other folk-rock performers adopted different approaches to adaptation. Unlike the 'mutual convenience' of Fairport Convention's combination of folk and rock, the formation of Steeleye Span was based on Ashley Hutchings concept of an electrified folk band playing traditional songs from the British Isles. Folk musicians who were previously used to performing on acoustic instruments, however, did not always sound convincing playing electric instruments in a rock-oriented ensemble. When I asked Martin Carthy about his first experience of playing the electric guitar on joining Steeleye Span in 1970, he described it as 'a completely new thing' and explained the transition from acoustic to electric guitar in the following way: 'It made me play much more economically, I just played less. I was playing electric which meant that I just learned to play less. It taught me economy'.[105] There is an irony in this statement, given that Carthy's reputation as a virtuoso acoustic guitarist would have been a factor in the decision to invite him to join the band. His existing fans would have expected his virtuosity to transfer onto the electric guitar, but this was not the case and his recorded electric guitar performances in Steeleye Span are relatively subdued.

Hutchings describes the combination of folk music and rock music in Fairport Convention as 'very natural', given that the band were already used to playing electric instruments. His description of the adaptation to electric instruments in Steeleye Span suggests a more problematic experience for musicians who were previously used to acoustic instruments:

> I think with Steeleye it was a lot harder... people like Tim [Hart] and Martin [Carthy] hadn't played electric and they were learning those instruments at the same time as they were adapting material, so the material, the Steeleye performances were a bit more, how shall I say, academic, a bit more studied, a bit more arranged, still very good, very musical.[106]

Playing the electric guitar involves performance techniques that are different from those used with the acoustic guitar, and they include the use of the instrument in conjunction with its means of amplification. The mastery of these techniques is a question of experience normally gained through performance over a period of time, although Carthy describes his first rehearsals with Steeleye Span as playing 'as loud as possible' until the band's sound technicians advised them to turn the volume down.[107] He suggests that the electric guitar must be played 'at a particular level', which he describes as 'level 7 or 8' (most amplifier controls go up to 10) for the instrument to sound as it should.

English folk-rock performance is neither a question of performance on an electric instrument by a musician previously accustomed to an acoustic instrument, nor one of rock performers performing traditional British folk songs with electric instruments and drum kits. The musical uncertainties experienced by previously acoustic folk music performers using rock instrumentation and by rock musicians relocating their playing techniques from blues-based influences to English folk-rock music may have contributed to the alienation of folk-rock on the part of factions of the existing audiences for both folk and rock music.

Preservation and transformation

While there are certain commonalities in the origins of the bands I have discussed, there are also significant differences concerning stylistic policies, respective commercial success and the stylistic directions of their careers in the late twentieth century. The influence of American folk-rock, and Bob Dylan in particular, was apparent in many British rock bands' repertoires in the late 1960s. However, it would be inaccurate to suggest that this influence was significantly evident in all of the early folk-rock influenced bands in the UK. Dylan's influence in these cases primarily acted as a catalyst in the move towards stylistic amalgamations. Most of the early English folk-rock bands, as well as the folk-influenced bands, were supported by a consumer-driven marketing process aimed at a listening, rather than a dancing, youth market. Few of these bands, however, had a formal plan for a repertoire amalgamating folk and rock music. For the majority, it was a question of chance, rather than design, and their development was often instituted by stylistic and cultural trends of the period and enabled by record company support.

Fairport Convention and Steeleye Span were the first bands to amalgamate British folk songs with rock music, and consequently these bands can be described as 'English folk-rock' rather than by diverse descriptions that might be pertinent to the varied stylistic amalgamations of the other bands I have discussed. Both Fairport Convention and Steeleye Span have at the time of writing had almost continuous careers lasting over thirty years during which their repertoires have continued to maintain each bands' original musical policy of performing folk, and latterly folk-informed, music in rock settings. Neither band has deviated from this policy. Descriptions given by performers interviewed suggest that, throughout the formative years of English folk-rock to the present, tradition has co-existed with innovation. This relationship has continued as contemporary British folk music has gradually encompassed a broader, and more representational, stylistic mix of influences from other British musics. The consensus of all interviewees is that British folk music is robust and withstands change, and that it can change with its environment. They also agree that folk music in the United Kingdom at the beginning of the twenty-first century is more stylistically diverse than it was fifty years ago at the beginning of the second folk revival.

I suggest that these performers were modern successors to the early collectors through their populist approach to performance practice and by their performance of folk music to large audiences in a wide variety of venues. There are similarities between ways in which folk music has been re-presented to audiences in popular music settings and the way in which the early collectors presented folk music to the Victorian and Edwardian public in edited, published formats. Changes to the performance practice of folk songs made by modern performers have arguably increased the popularity of British folk music, without which British folk songs might once again have faced obscurity. The combination of folk music with various forms of popular music has increased folk music's accessibility. A similarity exists between the modern performance of folk music and the views of collectors such as Sharp, who regarded the dissemination of folk music in easily accessible forms as vital to its preservation. Conversely, despite positive comments made by English folk-rock performers concerning the folk and rock music amalgamations, there is also the possibility that the amalgamation of British folk music with other musics can result in a homogeneous mix in which none of the folk music elements are identifiable. The national heritage that the Victorian and Edwardian folk song collectors sought to preserve would thus be lost – a situation in which continuity of folk music performance might be regarded as ultimately destructive. Change in folk-music performance styles is, however, inevitable, and contemporary performance no longer reflects notionally authentic adherence to Victorian and Edwardian collections. Concerns for authenticity are often not apparent in audience reception of new folk-influenced recordings, many of which have been critically and commercially well-received, or among audiences at multi-style folk festivals. I have sought to demonstrate that folk-rock music performance in the late twentieth and early twenty-first centuries presents folk music in new contexts and in a new phase of revivalism, despite the potentially negative effect of homogenisation. Since the early 1970s, the transient nature of the English folk-rock movement has evolved into a new folk revival that fulfils Livingston's criteria for revivalism and that has, as Burt Feintuch puts it, transformed the subject of its efforts.[108]

Following this discussion of English folk-rock performer experiences in the use of rock instrumentation, the next chapter examines other areas of change that take place when folk songs are adapted into rock music settings, particularly from the perspectives of pulse, metre and text. In the adaptation of folk songs for rock performance contexts, performers attempted to retain many of the songs' traditional elements as a means of making folk songs relevant to contemporary audiences while retaining aspects of perceived authenticity. The next chapter discusses change that is concomitant with the maintenance of the respective authenticities inherent in both folk and rock music.

Notes

1 *Transforming Tradition: Folk Music Revivals Examined*, ed. Neil Rosenberg (Urbana and Chicago: University of Illinois Press, 1993).

2 Kenneth Goldstein, 'A Future Folklorist in the Record Business', in *Transforming Tradition*, 107–21.

3 Feintuch, 'Musical Revival as Musical Transformation', 183–93.

4 Macan, *Rocking the Classics*, 8; Robert Walser, *Running with the Devil: Power, Gender, and Madness in Heavy Metal Music* (Middletown, CT: Wesleyan University Press, 1993), xiii.

5 Macan, *Rocking the Classics*, 10.

6 Macan, *Rocking the Classics*, 15–21; Richie Unterberger, *Eight Miles High: Folk-Rock's Flight from Haight-Ashbury to Woodstock* (San Francisco, CA: Backbeat Books, 2003), 11–38.

7 Macan, *Rocking the Classics*, 46.

8 John R. Palmer, 'Yes "Awaken", and the Progressive Rock Style' *Popular Music* 20:2 (2001), 243; Macan, *Rocking the Classics*, 11.

9 Macan, *Rocking the Classics*, 134.

10 Macan, *Rocking the Classics*, 134–5.

11 Further examples of recorded piano and electric keyboard performances on Denny's work are *What We Did On Our Holidays* (1969) by Fairport Convention, on which Denny plays keyboards; *Rock On* by The Bunch (1972), on which Ian Whiteman and Tony Cox play piano; *The North Star Grassman and the Ravens* (1971), on which Denny and Ian Whiteman play piano; and *Sandy* (1972), on which John Bundrick plays keyboards.

12 Macan, *Rocking the Classics*, 22.

13 Andrew Blake, *The Land Without Music* (Manchester: Manchester University Press, 1997), 128.

14 Blake, *The Land Without Music*, 147. As examples of each of these styles within progressive rock, Blake suggests for ruralism, Jethro Tull and aspects of Led Zeppelin, for folk music, Fairport Convention and Pentangle – although he omits Steeleye Span – and for neo-medievalism, Jethro Tull and The Strawbs, the latter a dubious inclusion when he omits Gryphon.

15 Allen F. Moore, *Rock: The Primary Text: Developing a Musicology of Rock* (Aldershot: Ashgate, 1993), 83–100.

16 Moore, *Rock*, 71–5, 83–8 and 107–9.

17 Allan F. Moore, 'Authenticity as Authentication', 210–15.

18 Sweers, *Electric Folk*, 219.

19 Bohlman, 'World Music at the 'End of History', *Ethnomusicology* 46:1 (Winter 2002), 17.

20 Bohlman, *The Study of Folk Music in the Modern World*, 74.

21 Arthur, email correspondence, 16 August 2001.

22 Margaret Kartomi, 'The Processes and Results of Musical Culture Contact: A Discussion of Terminology and Concepts', *Ethnomusicology* (May 1981), 228.

23 Kartomi, 'The Processes and Results of Musical Culture Contact', 229.

24 Kartomi, 'The Processes and Results of Musical Culture Contact', 244–5.

25 Bruce Jackson, 'The Myth of Newport '65: It Wasn't Bob Dylan They Were Booing', *Buffalo Report* (2002), http://buffaloreport.com/020826dylan.html (accessed on 1 July 2006).

26 Cantwell, 'When We Were Good', 54–5.

27 Pete Seeger, *The Incompleat Folksinger* (Lincoln: University of Nebraska Press, 1972), 460. Seeger later suggested, however, that the electric guitar 'may prove to be the most typical folk instrument of the twenty first century' adding that 'average citizens can ignore the fashions of the day – which usually change for no better reason than [the fact that] rapid obsolescence is profitable'.

28 Cantwell, 'When We Were Good', 54.

29 Sweers, *Electric Folk*, 30.

30 Hardy and Laing, *The Faber Companion To Popular Music*, 230–1; Donald Clarke, *The Rise and Fall of Popular Music* (New York: St Martin's Press, 1995), 456.

31 Ed Bicknell, interview with author, September 1997.

32 Palmer, 'Yes "Awaken", and the Progressive Rock Style', 244.

33 Steve Howe, quoted in Palmer, 'Yes "Awaken", and the Progressive Rock Style', 244.

34 Simon Nicol, interview with author, December 1996.

35 Martin Carthy, interview with author, March 1997.

36 As an illustration of the musical diversity of progressive rock performance and the varied musical tastes of its audience, it was not uncommon for several progressive bands to appear at the same concert. In the early 1970s, I attended a concert at which The Groundhogs, a blues-rock band that had expanded its stylistic base and had recently released a concept album relating to schizophrenia, supported Osibisa, a group of West African and Trinidadian musicians, which combined West African music and rock music.

37 Ed Bicknell, interview with author, September 1997.

38 Bicknell, interview, September 1997.

39 Simon Frith and Howard Horne, *Art Into Pop* (London: Routledge, 1987), 94.

40 Nicol, interview, 1996, and Ashley Hutchings, interview with author, May 1997.

41 Gerry Conway, interview with author, January 1997.

42 Stump, *The Music's All that Matters*, 148–9.

43 Dave Cousins, interview by Ralph McTell, *Who Knows Where The Time Goes: The Story of English Folk-Rock*, BBC Radio 2, 16 November 1994.

44 Respectively, Ian Smith, interview with author, August 2005, and Malcolm Taylor, interview with author, August 2003. Ian Smith is

the Head of Music at the Scottish Arts Council and was a founding member of the Musicians' Union Folk, Roots and Traditional Music Section.

45 *The New Grove Dictionary of Music and Musicians*, 2nd ed., s.v. 'Folk Music'.

46 *The New Grove Dictionary of Music and Musicians*, 2nd ed., s.v. 'Folk Music'.

47 Bob Pegg, interview with author, August 1997.

48 Bob Pegg, interview, 1997.

49 Lindisfarne's hit singles included 'Meet Me On The Corner' (1972), 'Lady Eleanor' (1972), 'All Fall Down' (1972) and 'Run For Home' (1978).

50 *The New Grove Dictionary of Music and Musicians*, 2nd ed., s.v. 'The Pentangle'.

51 John Renbourn, quoted in Unterberger, *Eight Miles High*, 143.

52 Danny Thompson, quoted in Unterberger, *Eight Miles High*, 143.

53 Thompson, quoted in Unterberger, *Eight Miles High*, 146.

54 Richard Harvey, interview with Chris Welch, 'Gryphon: The 13th Century Slade', *Melody Maker*, 4 August 1973.

55 For example, the single 'Rave On' (1971), along with 'To Know Him Is To Love Him' and 'Twinkle, Twinkle Little Star' on the album *Commoners Crown* (1975), and 'The Black Freighter' on the album *Storm Force 10* (1977).

56 For a biography of Fairport Convention, see Patrick Humphries, *Fairport Convention: The Classic Years* (London: Virgin Books, 1997).

57 Nicol, interview, 1996.

58 Matthews called himself Ian MacDonald on the band's first album, *Fairport Convention* (1968).

59 Nicol, interview, 1996. Nicol's use of 'soft rock' as descriptor for Fairport Convention accurately represents the modern identity of the band, given that they have moved away from their more fundamental heavy rock music origins.

60 Nicol, interview, 1996.

61 Nicol, interview, 1996.

62 Nicol, interview, 1996.

63 Sandy Denny, interviewed by Nick Logan, 16 August 1969, and quoted in Kingsley Abbott, *Fairportfolio* (Norfolk: Abbott, 1997), 54.

64 Ashley Hutchings, interview with author, May 1997.

65 Nicol, interview, 1996. This is a concept that Roger McGuinn, the lead guitarist with The Byrds, had aimed to achieve with the song 'Eight Miles High' (1966), and both McGuinn and

Thompson admired the improvisation of bebop saxophonist John Coltrane.

66 Richard Thompson, interview with Jim Irvin, 'The Angel Of Avalon', *Mojo* 49 (January 1998), 76. Fairport Convention also improvised with musicians from Led Zeppelin, a band that became one of the most influential rock bands of the latter part of the twentieth century. Fairport Convention maintained a long connection with Led Zeppelin that originated from the friendship between the second Fairport Convention bassist, Dave Pegg, and the Led Zeppelin drummer, John Bonham. The Speakeasy was a rock club in Margaret Street in the West End of London. Established rock artists frequented it in the late 1960s and early 1970s as it was a place of leisure away from fans and audiences. It was a club for which the only entrance criterion was 'rock' status, and it was not a folk club.

67 Hutchings, interview, 1997. 'Underground music' was an early description for what became progressive rock music.

68 Fairport Convention, *Liege and Lief.* Island ILPS 9115 (1969).

69 Hutchings, interview, 1997.

70 Simon Nicol, interview with author, August 2005.

71 Dave Swarbrick had been a session violinist on *Unhalfbricking* (1969) but was, by the recording of *Liege and Lief* (1970), a band member. He had previously performed with The Ian Campbell Folk Group, with Bert (A. L.) Lloyd, and in a duo with Martin Carthy.

72 Nicol, interview, 1996.

73 For example, 'The Deserter', 'Matty Groves', 'Tam Lin' and 'Reynardine' (*Liege and Lief* (1969)), 'Sir Patrick Spens' and 'Flowers of the Forest' (*Full House* (1971)), 'Banks of the Sweet Primroses' and 'The Bonny Black Hare' (*Angel Delight* (1971)), 'The Hexamshire Lass' and 'Polly on The Shore' (*Nine* (1973)), all of which came from either Denny or Swarbrick's personal repertoires.

74 Unterberger, *Eight Miles High*, 151.

75 Joe Boyd, quoted in Humphries, *Fairport Convention*, 63.

76 Nicol, interview, 1996.

77 Vulliamy, 'The Alter-Ego of Englishness', 10.

78 Vulliamy, 'The Alter-Ego of Englishness', 10.

79 Vulliamy, 'The Alter-Ego of Englishness', 10.

80 Hutchings, interview, 1997.

81 Conway also played on the Fairport Convention album *Rosie* (1973 ILPS9313), and joined the band as a permanent member in 1998, replacing Mattacks. Hutchings, Mattacks and Conway are the

only musicians to have performed in both Fairport Convention and Steeleye Span.

82 At this time, Carthy had already established a reputation as a solo artist and as a member of a duo with Dave Swarbrick, who had recently become a full-time member of Fairport Convention.

83 Hutchings, interview, 1997.

84 Rick Kemp, interview with author, August 1997. Kemp became a professional bass player in the late 1960s and had been a member of the progressive rock band King Crimson prior to joining Steeleye Span.

85 Georgina Boyes, interview with author, August 1997.

86 Boyes, interview, 1997.

87 Nicol, interview, 1996.

88 Nicol, interview, 1996.

89 Nicol, interview, 2005.

90 Nicol, interview, 2005.

91 Nicol, interview, 2005.

92 Nicol, interview, 2005.

93 Nicol, email correspondence with author, 28 June 2007.

94 Martin Carthy, interviews with author, March 1997 and August 2005.

95 Carthy, interview, 2005.

96 Respectively, Carthy, interview, 1997 and interview, 2005.

97 Carthy, interview, 2005.

98 This is a significant statement given that Carthy's guitar playing is revered among guitarists, and that his reputation in the UK and the US has attracted the attention of C. F. Martin Guitars, who now manufacture a Martin Carthy signature model.

99 Carthy, interview, 2005.

100 Hutchings, interview, 1997. Dave Mattacks joined Fairport Convention in 1969 before the recording of *Liege and Lief* and had to adapt his personal technique on the drum kit because British folk music was usually performed with a minimum of percussion instruments or with no percussion at all. Both Hutchings and Simon Nicol agree that Mattacks fitted into the band quickly and both maintain that he was the first folk-rock drummer.

101 Nicol, interview, 2005.

102 Gerry Conway has been a professional drummer since the 1960s and his performance credits also include Cat Stevens, Jethro Tull and Sandy Denny's band, Fotheringay. In the early 1990s he joined Pentangle, whose reputation from the 1970s was built as a band performing folk music with jazz and rock influences. In my

capacity of a professional musician, I worked with Conway, once backing Elvis Presley's guitarist, James Burton, and later while performing with Jerry Donahue, an former Fairport Convention guitarist, at music festivals in the Middle East.

103 Conway, interview, 1997.
104 Conway, interview, 1997.
105 Carthy, interview, 1997.
106 Hutchings, interview, 1997.
107 Martin Carthy, interview by Ralph McTell, *Who Knows Where the Time Goes: The Story of English Folk-Rock*, BBC Radio 2, 9 November 1994.
108 Livingston, 'Music Revivals', 69; Feintuch, 'Musical Revival as Musical Transformation', 192.

Tradition and authenticity in adaptation processes for English folk-rock

4

Some issues of folk musicology

The question arises, was there a 'folk-rock formula'? In order to consider the formulation of this music, it is necessary to make comparative analyses of traditional folk and English folk-rock performance practice. I focus on musicological issues of change in folk music in the context of how adaptation of folk songs for performance in English folk-rock settings has been carried out by both folk and rock performers. I also demonstrate how English folk-rock performers aimed to retain many of the original elements in the folk songs that were used as source material in order to maintain notions of authenticity by the manipulation of pulse, metre and text.

Of Cecil Sharp's proposed three principles, continuation and variation come to the fore in discussion of the adaptation of traditional folk music for English folk-rock performance, and performance of folk music by a rock band initiates other fundamental changes beyond the use of contemporary instrumentation. These include the addition of a constant rhythmical pulse that is most often set by the presence of a drum kit, a relative newcomer to twentieth-century popular music via jazz, restricting the freer pulse of traditional folk music performance and limiting interpretive vocal expression. Restrictions that may occur in vocal interpretation may be partially countered by manipulation of metrical structures outside the familiar common time metre used in most rock music performance.

Therefore change occurs in text settings performed in English folk-rock contexts due to the constraint of constant pulse and combinations of regular and irregular metrical structures, although change to lyrics also occurs in a process of contemporisation as original textual content is re-located into modern contexts. Implied authenticity remains apparent in newly composed English folk-rock songs, and contemporary textual content – which often draws upon older folk themes in a process of folk song signification – relocates representations of folk song authenticity in a process of traditionalisation.

During my examination of differences between folk music and English folk-rock performance, I have become indebted to Niall MacKinnon, who has provided a comprehensive examination of the 'traditional' folk club scene in the United Kingdom that presents an insight into aspects of folk music performance that took place during the 1970s and 1980s.[1] I have also drawn from the works of Georgina Boyes and Tamara Livingston, who have both examined twentieth-century folk music revivalism and its links with the preservation of traditions.[2] Music journalist Colin Irwin provides a useful discussion on change that took place in folk music performance during the 1990s in relation to the growth in popularity of folk festivals.[3] His concept of a new generation of musicians delving into English and Celtic traditions 'with a wonderful disregard for notions of purity' aptly describes some of the amalgamations of folk music with other musical styles achieved by the English folk-rock performers interviewed for this study.[4] Ashley Hutchings further supported Irwin's view in an interview for this study when he commented that:

> Nowadays you can switch on the television and you can see someone with an acoustic guitar, maybe someone playing a fiddle in a rock band, doing a rap-influenced pop song. It's all mixed up. Similarly, other people who are playing folk music, who are playing it in a kind of raucous and rocky way also might be called folk, even though I wouldn't probably call it rock music. So a lot of the fences have been knocked down, and it's all there, everyone's influencing everyone else.[5]

Irwin's statement does not refer to discourse between traditionalist and modernist viewpoints concerning notions of authenticity in modern British folk music. While Dave Laing and Richard Newman are dismissive of debate of this kind, the English folk-rock performers I interviewed take a different view and maintain that there has been an anti-amalgamation faction in the folk audience since folk music was first combined with other musical styles, especially rock music, and that is critical of English folk-rock on the grounds of perceived inauthenticity.[6] This issue is further discussed in the following chapter.

Issues concerning perceived authenticity also relate to the initial assembly of an English folk-rock repertoire that had to be at once feasible from a performance perspective as well as convincing to folk and rock music audiences. As stated earlier, much of the early repertoires of Fairport Convention and Steeleye Span were adapted from existing folk song repertoires of band members, and several of these songs are still performed by both bands. Moreover, the recorded versions of these songs are now part of a canon of English folk-rock. Debate remains, however, concerning the relative values of repertoire and canon and their construction by performer or critic. Adaptation of folk songs for performance in rock settings becomes a question of certain musicological elements that govern issues of performance feasibility when aspects of perceived folk music tradition and authenticity are to be maintained in English folk-rock. Among the most important of these elements are pulse, metre and text, even though pulse and metre are most often imposed constructs set by notated source versions and by performers. While there seems to have been no pivotal English folk-rock 'blueprint' in the construction of what has arguably become a canon of English folk-rock recordings since the early 1970s, repertoire construction centred not only on subjective choice, but also on performance criteria that must be present in amalgamations of folk and rock music in order that authentic aspects of both styles remain apparent. Terms such as 'traditional' and 'authentic' are thus powerfully symbolic when used to describe an English folk-rock repertoire constructed within a process of adaptation and change, although new folks songs become imbued with notions of authenticity when they draw on specific historical themes and are crafted in the appropriate language.

The emergence of a canon of English folk-rock, in live and recorded contexts, has elevated elements of its repertoire to a level of significance similar to that which often exists in revivalist idealisation of Victorian and Edwardian collections. From this new perspective, many songs that have been in the repertoires of English folk-rock performers since the late 1960s have now become source versions for contemporary performers who regard certain folk-rock recordings as musical landmarks in the folk music canon.[7] Prior to my discussion of issues concerning change and maintenance of perceived authenticity in English folk-rock performance practice, investigation of debate concerning the nature of canon in musical perspectives provides a valuable insight into scholarly perceptions of repertoire as canon, particularly from the viewpoint of the performer and musician as critic.

In his discussion of means by which creative works are collectively categorised, Joseph Kerman puts it that, while 'repertory is a programme of action' that relates to the activities of performers or musicians, the term 'canon' is more easily applied to other artistic collections of exemplary standing.[8] Kerman maintains that 'repertories are determined by performers and canons by critics – who are by preference musicians'.[9] While discussing the Romantic ideal of the performer's spontaneity being equal to the composer's initial inspiration, Kerman points out that, to the musicologist as critic, there is a preferred theoretical perception of veiled instruction to the performer.[10] This perception has also been apparent in traditional folk music performance in which diversion from performance notes made by collectors was regarded as negative.

William Weber challenges Kerman's statement, proposing that he 'writes-off' musicians as shapers of canon and that he fails to acknowledge the role played by musicians in the creation of a tradition of musical craft.[11] Weber suggests that pedagogical canon has its origins in the discipline of writing and performing music, although a performed canon 'being more than a collection of judgements about individual works or composers', sprang from 'the bestowal of intellectual authority upon them'.[12] He notes that there was a shift in scholarly views of intellectual authority that existed in literary canon towards an emergent musical canon during the eighteenth century.[13] I support Weber's view that canonisation is more than 'a separating-out of musical wheat from chaff' in the 'intellectuals favourite sheets' – and that it is also subject to a variety of social forces – as this is a significant aspect of the selection process in the area of folk song performance.[14]

Folk music performance often consists of, as Kerman puts it in the context of Western art music, 'conscious efforts to extend the repertory back into an evanesced past'.[15] Robert Morgan forcefully maintains that Kerman fails to mention that concepts of music as 'evanescence' and a 'programme of action' are inseparably joined in an essential function of canon – a model of imitation in creative practice. English folk-rock performance practice is also often drawn from a synthesis of imitation in creative practice combined with nostalgic views of an invented – or evanesced – past, concepts that are also inherent in traditional folk music performance. In a fieldwork interview, Martin Carthy observes that the indeterminable age of folk songs makes notions of authentic performance problematic, a difficulty experienced by many performers notwithstanding the existence of a folk music canon of source versions to draw upon.[16] Morgan puts it that, while his model of imitation in creative practice remains integral to canon, there is also a concept of multi-canon that is the product of a fundamental rethinking of present-day musical and cultural pluralities.[17] Multi-canon is characterised by 'well-entrenched beliefs in tradition and continuity' and it is a realistic response to many types of music that cannot be fixed in any authoritative way and that change complexion in different musical contexts.[18] Multi-canon as a model of imitation in creative practice, and as a concept drawing upon tradition and continuity, is therefore an apt construct within which English folk-rock can be placed, particularly with regard to the canon of English folk-rock performances that have been recorded since the late 1960s.

In his discussion of folk music in the context of his proposed process of mediated canon, Philip Bohlman purposely avoids defining folk music on the grounds that change is 'ineluctably bound to folk music tradition…the dynamic nature of folk music belies the stasis of definition'. [19] On the other hand, this view could be equally applied to any musical idiom and proposes instead a process of 'mainstream' canon that, in an Andersonian sense of imagined community, would bring together diverse groups of people – constituting the 'mainstream' – from large geographical areas with a common affiliation to any musical style.[20] The compilation of lists of rock music recordings that various critics regard as 'important', or as the 'finest' examples of their kind, enables canonic analysis at two levels. Firstly, one is able to view the music as a creative, artistic endeavour and, secondly, one is able to have an overview of how the recordings enable the music to become a commercial product within the confines of a tightly controlled recording industry.[21] Despite worldwide compilations of what fans and critics regard as 'The Greatest' and 'The Best of', discussion about what constitutes popular music canon is mostly limited to populist media publications. Ralf von Appen and André Doehring maintain that, since the emergence of rock journalism, writers and readers have been the arbiters of lists of new recordings that replace older ones that have not stood the test of time. They also note that those passing the test often become labelled as 'masterworks'.[22] The deeper function of canons may be their provision of an orientation process towards the vast offerings of music that listeners are exposed to in a lifetime, and the music's use as a guide to the history of popular music.[23] Moreover, von Appen and Doehring foresee a future point at which recordings from current musicians deemed as 'authentic and suitable for distinction' and as 'innovative, original, expressive and diverse' will be canonised in about five years, a process distinct from canonisation that occurs due to, for example, the death of a famous musician.

Significantly, therefore, while Kerman maintains that there is a distinction between the act of musical performance and the tangible musical score, he also observes a contemporary paradox in that musical recordings 'have brought music in one important sense close to the condition of literature' in that they can be used and absorbed as 'freely' as books and have consequently contributed to canonisation of recorded performances.[24] He warns that as works become recorded and re-recorded, a process that often occurs in the reification of particular rock 'masterworks', there is the possibility of standardisation with a potential loss of spontaneity for the performer.[25] This view is similar to that taken by Simon Nicol who, in a fieldwork interview, stated that:

I have never personally really relished the recording process. I've never gone for that final, perfect unimprovable take, you know, because who wants to listen to it? Other than, perhaps as a reference as to where you were at a certain time, I mean [it's] like a milestone. I'm just a live musician myself, and certainly that's the way Fairport's always been.[26]

While Nicol may not relish the actual recording process on the grounds of the impossibility of the 'perfect, unimprovable take', the inclusion of band songs recorded in the late 1960s and early 1970s in the band's current performance repertoire indicates that a canon of Fairport Convention's songs has emerged during the decades of their performance history, an issue that is common to Steeleye Span. The commercial success of both Fairport Convention and Steeleye Span – firstly as pioneering progressive rock bands and latterly as leading figures in the English folk-rock movement during a new phase of revivalism – has also acted as a catalyst in the production of a canon of recordings. For example, in an interview for this project, I asked Nicol about Fairport Convention's current repertoire and which songs from earlier recordings were still performed by the band. While discussing 'Matty Groves', Nicol commented, 'It's still in the Fairport repertoire, a song that's never been off the song list, on all gigs since it first entered in about 1969 and lots of us [in other ensembles drawn from Fairport Convention members], wherever we go, are singing it'.[27] I also asked Nicol about his views on other Fairport Convention recordings, such as those on Fairport Convention's *Liege and Lief* album, becoming regarded as seminal versions of folk songs. He stated that this was never the band's intention but added:

I'm only guessing here but I would like to think [that this was] so, I would like to hope so. I would like to hope that those songs can find their way in. I mean in a way 'The Hiring Fair' [a song composed for the band by Ralph McTell] because it is so you know misty and romantic and sub-Hardyesque. As a set of images it has a timelessness to it which is already kind of there.[28]

In another interview, Ashley Hutchings also referred to the influence of a canon of English folk-rock recordings on more recent performers. He stated that 'We approached the music, not necessarily with reverence, but we had a love and a great knowledge of the music, and I think people are getting it second- and third-hand, now, as youngsters'.[29] This statement is a further reflection of the perceived inviolability of folk music among English folk-rock performers, and among new performers drawing upon earlier folk-rock recordings as source versions. Given the commercial success of contemporary folk performers such as Eliza Carthy, Jim Moray, Bellowhead, Cara Dillon and Kate Rusby, this perception is also apparent among factions of the folk audience.

Commercial success occurring in the production of a canon of English folk-rock raises further issues relating to Marxist debate concerning perceptions of manipulation by dominant capitalist forces. While Martin Carthy regards the permanence of folk music as beyond perceptions of denigration caused by variation in its adaptation for English folk-rock performance, Ian Watson is critical of Carthy's performance of the 'Blackleg Miner' during his tenure with Steeleye Span. Watson argues that the song's performance in the context of an English folk-rock band removes it from its original aesthetic setting.[30] Watson's view is similar to other late twentieth-century Marxist critique of capitalist production and consequent negation of notions of authenticity all of which, according to Marxist schol- ars, centre on issues of class.[31] As noted earlier, Chris Bearman argues that Marxist ideology condemns English folk song to becoming a subject of a class war and that Marxist notions of the expropriation of 'the folk's' cultural property by 'bour- geois' collection and publication processes, which was fed back to them as their 'cultural heritage', fits Hobsbawm's concept of 'invented tradition'.[32]

David Atkinson's characteristics of permanence, stability and authority, with which he discusses the textualisation of folk music, are now inherent in a recorded canon of English folk-rock music.[33] Moreover, recent English folk-rock performers often regard these recordings as source versions in a similar respect to the source versions from early twentieth-century anthologies that were adapted by members of Fairport Convention and Stee- leye Span. Despite Marxist notions of the denigration of folk music through perceived domination by capitalist hegemony, commercial success of modern English folk music – or, in contrast to the way some Marxist scholars might put it, folk music that has been altered to appeal to a broader audience – provides a valuable resource.

Change beyond instrumentation

All of the performers interviewed for this analysis, whose careers span more than thirty years, agree that folk music progresses through change and the use of modern technologies, and that it often draws on influences from other musical cultures. From these perspectives, the issue of a folk music repertoire being played and recorded on electric or amplified instruments becomes part of a global trend that has affected most Western popular music, similar to the electrification of the blues. The main significance of English folk-rock, however, lies outside the electrification of folk music and within the continuity of folk music change that followed the second folk revival, and in the development of a canon of recorded works from which contemporary performers are able to draw.[34] As discussed in chapter 2, commercial distribution of these recorded works provides further links to preservation, as continuity in folk and English folk-rock settings provides a connection between performance styles that preserve folk music in both modern and traditional contexts. Although revivalists often reject manifestations of mass culture and modernity, early amalgamations of rock music and folk music might be regarded as a unifying factor, linking aspects of preservation and commercialisation. This unification has gradually enabled British folk music to establish a commercial, world music identity especially since the 1990s, which, as Tamara Livingston puts it, retains belief in the music's 'timelessness, unbroken historical continuity, and purity of expression', while attracting a new audience with diverse musical tastes.[35]

The initial amalgamation of folk music and rock music can be regarded as part of a process of change in rock music that started in the late 1960s and early 1970s. This process is ongoing as English folk-rock music combines aspects of tradition and transformation that are detached from twentieth-century notions of folk music as a static construct, which remain among some factions of the folk music audience. Performer descriptions of ways in which folk songs were adapted for performance in a rock setting provide the basis for a descriptive framework for the combination of folk music with popular music styles in the United Kingdom. These combinations most often fall into one of the following categories:

1. folk songs performed by rock musicians using mainly electric and amplified instruments and drum kits;
2. folk songs performed by folk musicians using a broad combination of acoustic and electric instruments, and drawing on other musical styles in the arena of popular music;
3. folk songs performed with the use of computerised music technology and/or any form of instrumentation that might be considered representative of current popular music styles;
4. folk songs performed in a manner that assimilates the music styles of other non-Western cultural and ethnic groups present in Britain.

These categories support both Georgina Boyes' view that English folk-rock is simply folk music with a contemporary style of instrumentation, and Hutchings' view concerning the differences between the techniques of adaptation employed by Fairport Convention and Steeleye Span.[36] As I have already stated, I regard these bands as principal influences in the English folk-rock style. My categories also acknowledge some of the approaches used by the early English folk-rock bands in the adaptation of folk songs into rock settings and that folk songs continue to be adapted for performance in a variety of other popular music settings. Diverse audience tastes enable folk music to be performed in a variety of styles, while on the one hand its identity remains intact and on the other it becomes assimilated into a modern social, cultural and musical milieu. The popularity of a modern folk music style may consequently reflect no more than what its audience regards as folk music at any particular time. Thus, while the collection of folk songs by Victorian and Edwardian enthusiasts was valuable as a historical narrative and as a means of early twentieth-century folk song preservation, it gives an indication only of how folk music was performed at that point in time.

The authentic/inauthentic debate that often surrounds change in British folk music, and which often centres around the use of modern instrumentation, does not acknowledge other types of change that occur as folk music merges with other musical styles in the process of adapting to its current environment. The following discussion therefore addresses three further areas of change – pulse, metre and text – all of which have a more significant effect on folk music performance than contemporary instrumentation. As Boyes maintains, the electrification of folk music as English folk-rock in the late 1960s and early 1970s was merely a question of adding 'an extra dimension to the performance of folk music' that did 'nothing more than accompany it'.[37] When folk songs are adapted for performance in rock settings, the result establishes a particular identity for folk music at that time, and the use of new instrumentation – and, more importantly, new performance practices – becomes a further part of the folk music continuum, which includes a process of continuation that contributes to growth in the music's popularity.

Pulse

Besides the use of electric amplification, the performance of folk songs in a rock or popular music setting often introduces a regular pulse. In order to comply with any theoretical rule that would ally folk music with rock music, a structured, constant, repetitive rhythmical pattern would have to be introduced into a folk song, thus changing the freer rhythmic nature that is characteristic of many performances of folk songs. Performances by 'traditional' folk singers, which are often unaccompanied or accompanied by a single instrument, rely on the singer's lyrical and rhythmic interpretation, whereas many folk bands and English folk-rock bands performing in Western popular music styles maintain a regular pulse. Most Western popular music ensembles use a constant metric pulse to keep band members in time with each other, although there are many styles of music played by ensembles where the musicians are able to increase and decrease the tempo in unison.

Most Western popular music performed and broadcast in Europe and the United States, and described as 'rock', adheres to constant tempos. Constant tempo is particularly evident in the use of programming technology in the popular music genre that has been described as 'dance' since the 1990s. In order to make comparisons between what might be regarded as a 'traditional' folk song performance and an English folk-rock performance, I have used a computer metronome to analyse several vocal performances of folk songs recorded by solo folk performers and by English folk-rock bands.[38] The songs analysed below are 'The Spotted Cow' recorded by Bob Lewis and by Steeleye Span, and 'Polly on the Shore' recorded by George 'Pop' Maynard (1872–1962) and by Fairport Convention.[39] While both songs were selected because they have been performed by traditional folk singers and by English folk-rock bands, it is also significant that the traditional versions remain in the canon of the traditional folk scene and the versions by the folk-rock bands were high points in both bands' live performances. The English folk-rock performers interviewed in fieldwork made no connections between these particular traditional folk singers' interpretations of these songs, which are both less restricted by a regular pulse than the same songs performed by a band in a rock or pop setting. My computer analyses below provide graphic views of the first verse of each song performed by both traditional folk singer and by English folk-rock band.

Bob Lewis' version of 'The Spotted Cow', recorded on the album *When the May Is All in Bloom*, is an unaccompanied vocal performance.[40] Bob Lewis, born in 1936, lives in Saltdean in Sussex; 'The Spotted Cow', which he learned from his mother, has been part of his repertoire since his teenage years. He sang the song in folk clubs during the 1960s but abandoned it for nearly twenty years after Steeleye Span released their version.[41] He describes hearing the band and the way in which his version of the song has gradually changed:

> I heard them live in concert on a couple of occasions at hundreds of megawatts! The experience was almost like being brainwashed. After that, any attempt of mine to perform the song was assumed to be a copy of Steeleye Span, which seems to have become the definitive version. Even now I am not totally happy that my performance is exactly the way I learnt it from mother and may have become something of a hybrid.[42]

Lewis' version of 'The Spotted Cow' shows little adherence to a regular pulse, and it is unlikely that he intended to maintain one. According to the computer metronome, the average tempo of his performance is 75 beats per minute, but the last words of

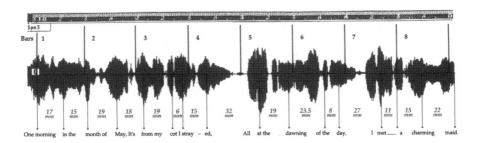

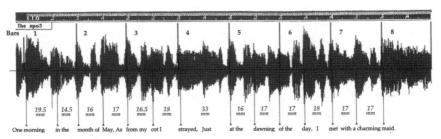

Oscillographic diagrams of sound waves in the first vocal lines of   4.1
'The Spotted Cow' by Bob Lewis and by Steeleye Span   4.2

the second and fourth lines of verse 1 ('strayed' and 'maid' respectively) are sustained. This has the effect of making the pulse slower at these points. The repetition of 'All at the dawning of the day, I met with a charming maid', at the end of the verse also slows the pulse and causes verse 2 to start at a slightly slower tempo. None of the verses is performed identically, although they are basically similar and are all subject to the implied $\frac{6}{8}$ metre. In Figures 4.1 and 4.2 the metronome bar numbers at the top of the diagram show each bar divided into two sections with an ellipse over each complete bar. The numerical divisions each have the value of a dotted crotchet, meaning that each pair of sections is equal to one bar of $\frac{6}{8}$ metre. The width of each of the two half-sections of each bar is 17 mm and a whole bar is, therefore 34 mm wide. In this way 'time' in music is represented by the width of each bar.

The words of verse 1 of Lewis' version are as follows:

One morning in the month of May,
It's from my cot I strayed,
All at the dawning of the day,

I met a charming maid.
All at the dawning of the day,
I met a charming maid.

In both versions of the song, the first word of verse 1 ('One') falls over the quaver upbeat before bar 1 and the syllable 'mor' is on the first crotchet of bar 1. The syllables shown in capitals below are emphasised, and fall alternately near the first and fourth quavers in each bar:

One MORning IN the MONTH of MAY, It's FROM my COT I STRAYED,
All AT the DAWNing OF the DAY, I MET – a CHARMing MAID.

Lewis' vocal performance is illustrated by the oscillograph pattern in the centre of the diagram and the larger 'spikes' represent the emphasised syllables in the words of the song. These spikes rarely correspond to the numerical metronome bar structure and often fall before or after the numbered bar divisions at the top of the diagram. The performance does, however, maintain an almost regular pulse throughout the first two bars. This can be illustrated in the following way, given that the distance in millimetres between each emphasised syllable remains relatively constant. The distance represents the length of time between each syllable, and so there is an almost regular pulse at this point in the song:

MORning – 17 mm – IN – 15 mm – MONTH – 19 mm – MAY – 18 mm – FROM (just after the beginning of bar 3 according to the metronome)

From bar 3 onwards, the pulse becomes more irregular:

FROM – 19 mm – COT – 6 mm – STRAY – 15 mm – ED – 32 mm – AT (almost in the middle of bar 5)

The final word of line 2, 'strayed', is sustained, but once the third line starts there is a return to a regular pulse for nearly two bars before it becomes irregular again:

AT – 19 mm – DAWNing – 23.5 mm – OF – 8 mm – DAY – 27 mm – MET – 11 mm A 15 mm – CHARMing – 22 mm – MAID

Steeleye Span recorded 'The Spotted Cow' on their album *Below the Salt* (1972) and their version maintains a tempo of 91 beats per minute in $\frac{6}{8}$ time (see Figures 4.2 and 4.2a).[43]

'The Spotted Cow', arranged by Steeleye Span (transcribed by author)   **4.2a**

As with Lewis' version of the song, the word 'One' falls onto the quaver upbeat before bar 1, with the syllable 'mor' on the first crotchet of bar 1. The Steeleye Span version uses the word 'Just' instead of 'All' at the beginning of lines 3 and 5.[44] The higher tempo means that the distance in millimetres between some of the emphasised syllables is lower than in Bob Lewis' version, but it remains more constant in the Steeleye Span version, illustrating the regularity of the pulse:

> MORning – 19.5 mm – IN – 14.5 mm – MONTH – 16 mm – MAY – 17 mm – FROM – 16.5 mm – COT – 18 mm – STRAYED – 33 mm – AT (beginning of line 3)

The last word of the second line, 'stayed', is sustained throughout most of bar 4, and the 33 mm between 'strayed' and 'at' is almost a whole bar in ⅜ time (34 mm), unlike Lewis' version, which stresses both syllables of 'strayed' for 47 mm. The third line of the Steeleye Span version starts with a regular pulse, but there is a slight vocal sustain on 'day' in the first occurrence of the double refrain:

> AT – 16 mm – DAWNing – 17 mm – OF – 17 mm – DAY – 18 mm – MET – 17 mm – CHARMing – 17 mm – MAID

The slight elongation of 'day' could be related to what might be regarded as the 'pitch climax' of the song, given that there is a varying degree of sustain in the vocal performance in both the Lewis and Steeleye Span versions at this point. Tempo fluctuations such as this are common in both folk music and English folk-rock performance, although less apparent in English folk-rock due to the regular pulse.

Lewis' solo performance of 'The Spotted Cow' is not restricted by the pulse employed by a band performing in a rock music setting, and so an element of interpretative freedom is available, allowing him to stress words in order to emphasise their meaning. He is also able to sustain notes at various points in each line and at the end of verses, a technique often employed by folk singers to encourage audience participation.[45] The regularity of pulse in Steeleye Span's version of the same song does not permit these interpretative effects, and the only slight deviation from a regular pulse in Maddy Prior's vocal performance is the sustained 'day' at the end of line 3. Given that the space between each computerised bar line is 34 mm, it could be argued that Prior's interpretation relies on her placement of emphasised syllables within each bar. For example, in bar 1 the second emphasised syllable, 'in', is 19.5 mm after 'mor', which is on the first beat of bar 1; and the third emphasised syllable, 'month', is 14.5 mm after 'in'. The total space between these three syllables is therefore 34 mm, the exact number in one bar; and the spaces between the syllables in each of the following bars add up to between 33.5 and 35 mm. This further illustrates the limitations placed on interpretative freedom by the presence of a regular pulse.

George 'Pop' Maynard was another folk singer from Sussex, and his version of 'Polly on the Shore', originally recorded in 1956, can be heard on the compilation album *Hidden English*.[46] There are similarities between Lewis' singing of 'The Spotted Cow' and Maynard's performance of 'Polly on the Shore', although Maynard sings in approximately $\frac{4}{4}$ time, with the first bar maintaining a relatively constant pulse. As with Lewis' performance of 'The Spotted Cow', Maynard stresses certain syllables and elongates others in order to emphasise certain words and impose his own interpretation of the song. The words of Maynard's version are as follows, with the second line of the verse being repeated, arguably to encourage audience participation:

O come all you wild young men,
A warning take by me,
And never to lead your single life astray,
Into no bad company.
And never to lead your single life astray,
Into no bad company.

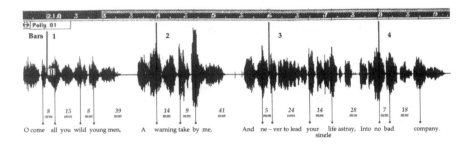

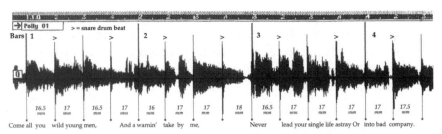

Oscillographic diagrams of sound waves in the first vocal lines of   **4.3**
'Polly on the Shore' by George 'Pop' Maynard and by Fairport   **4.4**
Convention

The large oscillograph spikes on the computer metronome (Figures 4.3 and 4.4) again represent the emphasised syllables (in capitals below). The unequal spaces between these spikes demonstrate the irregularity of the pulse.

The words 'O come' are sung as two semiquavers preceding bar 1, and the first emphasised syllable is 'all', which, according to the metronome, falls on beat 1 of bar 2. The alignment of this syllable to beat 1 enabled the computer to calculate an approximate tempo of 68 beats per minute for the rest of Maynard's performance. From bar 2 he sings without a regular pulse, lengthening and emphasising syllables and words – the longest being words at the ends of lines ending with the vowel sound 'ee' (that is, 'me' and 'company', neither of which is stressed). The lengthening of these vowels also has the effect of slowing the tempo slightly at the end of each line:

COME – 8 mm – ALL – 15 mm – WILD – 8 mm – YOUNG – 39 mm – WARNing – 14 mm – TAKE – 9 mm – BY – 41 mm – NE – 5 mm – VER – 24 mm – YOUR – 14 mm – LIFE – 28 mm – NO – 7 mm – BAD – 18 mm – COMPany

Come all you wild young men And a warn – in' take by me,

Ne –ver lead your sin – gle life a – stray Or in -to bad com – pa – ny.

4.4a 'Polly on the Shore', arranged by Fairport Convention (transcribed by author)

The emphasis placed on certain words may reflect George Maynard's personal interpretation of the text. In stressing the following words the song takes the form of a warning to those who intend to follow the life of a privateer, with themes of war, lost love, and despair.

> O COME ALL you WILD YOUNG men,
> A WARNing TAKE BY me,
> And NE-VER to lead YOUR single LIFE astray,
> Into NO BAD COMPany.

The computer analysis of Fairport Convention's recording of 'Polly On the Shore' (see Figures 4.4 and 4.4a), recorded on their album *Nine*, indicates a regular pulse throughout the performance, which is also in $\frac{4}{4}$ time.[47] The lyrics of the first verse are as follows:

> Come all you wild young men,
> And a warnin' take by me,
> Never lead your single life astray
> Or into bad company.

The regularity of the pulse is illustrated by the similar lengths of the spaces between each of the spikes, all of which correspond with the crotchet beats in each of the bars of the computer metronome. There is also a large spike on the snare drum beats occurring in each bar on crotchets 2 and 4, which coincide with syllables falling on beat 2 of each bar of the vocal performance. A comparison can be made between the performance of 'The Spotted Cow' by Steeleye Span and of 'Polly on the Shore' by Fairport Convention in terms of the limitations imposed on the vocal performance by the regular pulse. In the latter case, this restriction has made it necessary to make slight alterations to the words in order to make them scan within a regular pulse. This is indicated by the regular spaces between each emphasised syllable:

ALL – 16.5 mm – WILD + snare beat – 17 mm – MEN – 16.5 mm – snare beat – 17 mm – WARNin' – 16 mm – TAKE + snare beat – 17 mm – ME – 17 mm – snare beat – 18 mm – NEVER – 16.5 mm – LEAD + snare beat – 17 mm – SINGLE – 17 mm – ASTRAY + snare beat – 17 mm – INTO – 17 mm – COMPA + snare beat – 17.5 mm – NY – 16 mm – snare beat

Scope for interpretation by the Fairport Convention vocalist, Trevor Lucas, is limited by the snare drum on the second crotchet beat of each bar throughout the song. His interpretation of the words is more subdued than that of Maynard, and he imparts a sombre and perhaps more despairing undertone to the sailor's description of his wasted life. The emphasis placed on various beats of the bar by the use of the drum kit means that Lucas does not have to emphasise syllables in order to maintain a regular pulse. This is illustrated by the size of the spikes on syllables that do not coincide with a snare beat, which are 10–15 mm smaller than those on the emphasised syllables in Steeleye Span's performance of 'The Spotted Cow', where emphasis was necessary to maintain the regular pulse in the absence of a drummer. This lack of emphasis further adds to the sombre nature of Lucas' vocal delivery. Further comparative computerised analyses of folk songs performed by both traditional folk singers and by English folk-rock bands are included in appendix 2.

Metre

As further examples of continuity and variation in modern British folk music performance, I will demonstrate how the manipulation of metrical structures in the performance of a folk song adapted to a rock context permits elements of vocal interpretation that are usually only present in a traditional unaccompanied performance. The performance of a folk song in a rock context most often involves the use of electric and amplified instruments and of a drum kit, which supports the band's maintenance of a constant pulse while also often employing Afro-American polyrhythms. Bass drum beats usually emphasise beats 1 and 3 in $\frac{4}{4}$ bars, although the bass drum also employs rhythmical variations that are dependent on the popular music style within which it is played. The hi-hat and ride cymbals usually play constant quavers or crotchets, acting as a form of metronome, although they too are subject to stylistic rhythmic variation. Snare drum beats in $\frac{4}{4}$ bars of most popular music styles have, traditionally, fallen on beats 2 and 4, and are often referred to as the 'backbeat'. Of all the percussive components of the drum kit, it is the snare drum pattern that provides the most commonality between different styles within the rock music genre.[48] My distinction here between metre and rhythm is that metre accents are taken from the first beat of a bar whereas rhythm accents can occur anywhere within a rhythmic group. British folk songs sometimes use irregular metres, and are performed by singers quite able to sing without difficulty in complex bar structures. It should be noted that the occurrence of regular or irregular metre in notated folk songs is most often a consequence of the imposition of Western art music notation, and therefore represents the interpretation of the transcriber.

In traditional practice, the performance of a folk song renders the metre familiar, which is vital if the song is to be sung by inexperienced singers. This point can be illustrated by reference to the Bulgarian and Romanian folk songs collected and transcribed by Béla Bartók (1881–1945), which have multiple bars of irregular metre rapidly following one another. Most of these songs were in common, simple duple, simple triple, or compound time, and many were children's songs, such as 'Raina Katsarova' (Figure 4.5), a song collected in 1906, which is transcribed in $\frac{5}{16}$.

Other Eastern European folk songs collected by Bartók change metre several times within the space of just a few bars; for example, Figure 4.6, a folk song collected in Balatonberény in the Somogy district of Bulgaria in 1906, starts in $\frac{5}{8}$ for two bars,

4.5   'Raina Katsarova' from *Bulgarian Children's Folksongs* (quoted in Halsey Stevens, *The Life and Music of Béla Bartók* (New York: University of New York, 1981), 272)

Folk song collected in Balatonberény in the Somogy district of   4.6
Bulgaria (Halsey Stevens, *The Life and Music of Béla Bartók* (New York:
University of New York, 1981), 272)

before it changes to $\frac{3}{4}$ for three bars, $\frac{2}{4}$ for one bar, and then
returns to $\frac{3}{4}$ for the final two bars.[49]

In English folk-rock performance, the drum kit provides the
most fundamental link between the component styles, combining the metrical structure of folk songs with the maintenance of
aspects of the rock idiom, which is most often in $\frac{4}{4}$ metre. To
further my research into drum kit performance and use of metre
in the English folk-rock genre, I interviewed veteran English
folk-rock drummer Gerry Conway. While describing his experiences of playing folk songs using irregular metre, Conway maintained that his previous rock performances had not prepared
him for the performance of English folk-rock and its use of metrical structures outside those used in mainstream rock music. It
was band policy in Steeleye Span to perform folk songs in the
metrical structures in which the Victorian and Edwardian collectors had notated them. Rick Kemp provided a further example
of Steeleye Span's policy of preserving original elements of
notated source folk songs, such as metre, melody and lyrics,
in their adaptation for English folk-rock performance.[50] He
described how the band followed a structured approach to retention of notated metres in the recording of 'The Weaver and the
Factory Maid' on the album *Parcel of Rogues*.[51] This performance
is Maddy Prior's arrangement of two folk songs concerning the
rural weaving trade and social change imposed by the introduction of mechanisation during the Industrial Revolution. Prior
sings the first section of the song with accompaniment from
Peter Knight on the violin. The arrangement for voice and violin
– reflective of traditional folk song performance – arguably
creates a mood of nostalgia for the loss of perceived rural simplicity, as described in the text, which is supported by the use of
$\frac{3}{4}$ metre (Figure 4.7).

The second section of the song is in $\frac{5}{4}$ and is based on a version
of the song collected by A. L. Lloyd in Widnes in 1951.[52] Lloyd's

4.7   'The Weaver and the Factory Maid', first section, as arranged by Maddy Prior (transcribed by author)

4.8   'The Weaver and the Factory Maid', second section, as arranged by Maddy Prior (transcribed by author)

transcription had only the melody line, text and the imposed metre, all of which were retained in the Steeleye Span version of the song. Steeleye Span's electric bass and guitar arrangement retains the source version's $\frac{5}{4}$ metre, and it is in the form of a louder, repetitive, almost mechanistic figure that provides a stark contrast to the earlier lilting $\frac{3}{4}$ metre.

The third section of the song returns to the earlier $\frac{3}{4}$ metre in an unaccompanied, multi-tracked vocal arrangement of the first theme. The two metres provide contrasting moods within the arrangement, although they do not deviate from the source versions of the song used by the band. The main contrast exists within an interpretative dynamic arrangement that juxtaposes a traditional approach to performance in one section of the song with a contemporary rock approach to performance in another.

Fairport Convention followed a policy similar to that of Steeleye Span and retained the metrical elements notated by collectors in their recording of 'Lord Marlborough' on the album *Angel Delight*, although this recording features a drum kit, in contrast to the Steeleye Span line-up of the same period, which had no drummer.[53] As stated above, the inclusion of a drummer in an English folk-rock context provides a fundamental rhythmical link between both component styles. In this case, the drum arrangement situates itself between a conventional rock pattern, with two snare drum beats in each bar, and the retention of the metrical structures notated in source versions, in keeping with Fairport Convention's musical policy. The text of 'Lord Marlborough' relates to a battle in the War of the Spanish Succession (fought between Britain and France and ending in 1706).[54] Fairport Convention used lyrics from a version of the song collected by the Hammond brothers in Dorset in 1906, which was transcribed in $\frac{5}{4}$ metre. The metrical arrangement of bars in Fairport Convention's recording of the song is, however, closer to a version collected and notated by Cecil Sharp in Somerset in 1906, which has two repeated four-bar phrases, each with three $\frac{5}{4}$ bars followed by one in $\frac{3}{4}$. These are followed by a four-bar phrase of three $\frac{5}{4}$ bars followed by one in $\frac{4}{4}$, and then another four-bar phrase of three $\frac{5}{4}$ bars and a $\frac{3}{4}$ bar (Figure 4.9).

Fairport Convention's arrangement has similar phrases of three $\frac{5}{8}$ bars followed by one $\frac{6}{8}$ bar. The $\frac{5}{8}$ bars use additive rhythm with each bar split into three quaver values followed by two quaver values (Figure 4.10).

'Marlborough', sung by John Culley (74) at Farrington Gurney, Somerset, 22 August 1906, melody as collected by Cecil Sharp (from *Cecil Sharp's Collection of English Folk Songs* (London: Oxford University Press, 1974), ed. Maud Karpeles)

4.9

4.10   'Lord Marlborough', arranged by Fairport Convention (transcribed by author)

ⓥ = snare drum beat

4.11   'Lord Marlborough', arranged by Fairport Convention, verses 3 and 4 showing snare drum arrangement (transcribed by author)

In verses 3 and 4, the first, second and fourth of these four-bar cycles have a snare drum beat on the first quaver of the second $\frac{5}{8}$ bar, as well as another on the fourth quaver of the $\frac{6}{8}$ bar, in phrases one, two and three (Figure 4.11).

This snare drum pattern performs a similar role to that in most rock music drum arrangements and serves as a link between the rock and folk music styles present in Fairport Convention's arrangement. The fact that the drum kit is played in a half-time pulse in relation to the rest of the band further emphasises the snare drum beats. The instrumental verses of the song, verses 2 and 5, have military-style side drum patterns played on the snare drum, and verse 6 combines these patterns with accented single snare drum beats at the beginning of, and during, each bar of the verse (Figure 4.12).

⊽ = snare drum beat

'Lord Marlborough', arranged by Fairport Convention, verse 6   4.12
showing snare drum arrangement (transcribed by author)

The snare drum arrangement maintains the military style of
the song before it finally plays the same full-time pulse as the
rest of the band, supporting the final lines of the text: 'Come on
you boys, for old England's sake / We'll conquer or we'll die!'

The metre and bar structures of Sharp's notated version remain
largely unchanged in Fairport Convention's recording of the
song, and the drum kit arrangement supports the melody and
follows the notated metrical structure while providing a constant pulse and maintaining an authentic rock music context.
Thus the drum kit part in this performance is integral to the
combination of folk and rock music performance. The only
other performance aspects placing this version of the song in a
rock setting, and which are central to the process of transformation, are the regularity of pulse and the use of modern instrumentation, given that the metrical structures, as well as the
lyrics of the song, are almost identical to those of the notated
source versions.[55]

A further example of irregular metre bars occurring in English
folk-rock performance is Eliza Carthy's recording of 'Billy Boy',
although the metrical arrangement in this song fulfils a different purpose from that in 'Lord Marlborough'. Recorded on the
album *Red Rice* (1998), 'Billy Boy' is in a reggae style, using a
drum pattern referred to as 'one drop'.[56] This means that, unlike
the standard beat 1 and beat 3 rock bass drum pattern described
above, the bass drum on the first crotchet of a $\frac{4}{4}$ bar is often
omitted, or 'dropped'. The bass drum beat on the third crotchet

remains and the snare drum often coincides with the bass drum at this point in a $\frac{4}{4}$ bar. Martin Carthy recorded an earlier version of 'Billy Boy' on the album *Sweet Wivelsfield* (1975), although this is unlikely to be the only source version employed by Eliza Carthy, given that the song was also collected and notated by both the Hammond brothers and Sharp in the early twentieth century and the words appear, for example, in James Reeves' collection, *The Idiom of the People*.[57] On the earlier recording, Martin Carthy accompanies his vocal performance on acoustic guitar, whereas the instrumentation on Eliza Carthy's version includes electric and acoustic guitars, accordion, electric bass, drums and percussion. The difference in metre between the two versions is more significant than the difference in instrumentation, even though both are melodically the same. Both versions have bars of irregular metre, but they differ in that each performer has arranged these bars in a different order. Both performances start with three bars of $\frac{4}{4}$ metre, followed by a fourth bar in $\frac{5}{4}$. Martin Carthy's version has a tied crotchet from bar 4 sustaining into bar 5, a $\frac{2}{4}$ bar, for one crotchet, and this interpretation allows him to sustain the vowel sound 'oh', a common feature in folk song performance (Figure 4.13).

In Eliza Carthy's version of the song, the fourth bar is followed by one in $\frac{3}{4}$, where the lyrics also have an elongated 'oh' tied for three crotchets: the last crotchet of bar 4 and the first two of bar 5 (Figure 4.14).

The snare drum arrangement in Eliza Carthy's version maintains a half-time pulse in relation to that played by the rest of the band, similar to that of Fairport Convention's drum arrange-

4.13 'Billy Boy', arranged by Martin Carthy (transcribed by author)

'Billy Boy', arranged by Eliza Carthy (transcribed by author)   4.14

ⓣ = snare drum beat

'Billy Boy', arranged by Eliza Carthy, showing snare drum   4.15
arrangement (transcribed by author)

ment for 'Lord Marlborough'. The first three bars have a snare drum beat on beat 3, a drum technique common to the reggae style of the arrangement. Bars 4 and 5, in $\frac{5}{4}$ and $\frac{3}{4}$ respectively, have a snare drum beat on beat 3 of the $\frac{5}{4}$ bar and on beat 2 of the $\frac{3}{4}$ bar, giving the feel of two $\frac{4}{4}$ bars (Figure 4.15).

This drum arrangement enables the drummer to play a $\frac{4}{4}$ part for five bars while the rest of the band are playing in different metres. After bar 6, the drum part continues into another three bars of $\frac{4}{4}$, and the final $\frac{2}{4}$ bar has a drum fill linking verse 1 to verse 2. This performance thus combines a reggae drum arrangement (given that reggae music is most often in $\frac{4}{4}$) with the implied non-metrical structure familiar in traditional British folk music vocal performance.

Martin Carthy's version differs in that, after the $\frac{2}{4}$ bar at bar 5, there are three $\frac{4}{4}$ bars and a final $\frac{5}{4}$ bar. This difference most likely relates to his personal vocal phrasing and choice of source material. Self-accompaniment on acoustic guitar enables more interpretive freedom in vocal performance than does accompaniment by a rock band with a drum kit that usually plays a repetitive figure in a constant pulse. The lyrics of the two versions are almost identical, and so the use of irregular metre becomes a question of individual vocal interpretation, source and performance medium. Furthermore, the use of irregular metre enables extended vocal expression and interpretation within the parameters of constant pulse and metre in Eliza Carthy's version of the song, since bars have been elongated which in some cases enables the extension of note lengths in the vocal part. By rearranging bar structures in the drum arrangement, the drummer is able to play in $\frac{4}{4}$ for the majority of the verse, despite the irregular metrical structure played by the rest of the band, thus maintaining an authentic reggae feel (Figure 4.16).

This argument is further supported by the fact that the instrumental section in this version, where there is no requirement to consider vocal interpretation, remains in $\frac{4}{4}$ metre.

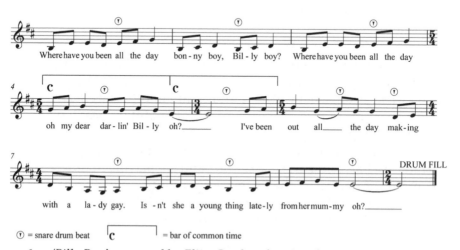

4.16   'Billy Boy', arranged by Eliza Carthy, showing drum arrangement (transcribed by author)

If songs such as these were, and are, easily sung, then the 'question' of irregular metre in English folk-rock adaptations is simply, to whom does the metre appear irregular? Vocal performances of folk songs that are unaccompanied, or are accompanied by an instrument played by the singer, often use a form of rubato. This enables the performer to give an individual interpretation of a folk song without any restriction from constant pulse or metrical structure. The use of irregular metre in a rock context enables bars to be shortened or lengthened within an arranged bar structure, permitting a degree of interpretive freedom in the vocal performance because bar lengths can be arranged according to the vocalist's interpretation of the song. It is perhaps ironic that use of irregular metre, in order to provide interpretative freedom in English folk-rock, actually restricts change from performance to performance, which is a familiar concept to many traditional folk song performances.

Text

I approach my investigation into textual change from two perspectives – continuation and variation – although selection remains part of an overall question of choice for the performer, particularly if a folk song's original message remains pertinent in modern contexts. Change in text is often relatively minor when an English folk-rock performance retains existing textual content from an earlier source version as part of a policy of maintaining perceived authenticity. The following discussion therefore centres on a process of continuation that occurs in different versions of the same song published and performed in traditional and in English folk-rock contexts. For example, while performance of many folk song texts by English folk-rock performers is subject to certain interpretative restrictions imposed by regular pulse inherent in rock performance, the text of Fairport Convention's recording of 'The Banks of the Sweet Primroses' is almost the same as those in versions published and recorded during the 1950s and 1960s. The song was recorded Fairport Convention on the album *Angel Delight* (1971), although it was also recorded by Ron and Bob Copper in the early 1950s, by Louis Killen on the album *Ballads and Broadsides* (1964) and published as notated music and text in *The Penguin Book of English Folk Songs* (1959), an anthology that was, according to Martin Carthy, a source of material for many folk singers during the late 1950s and early 1960s.[58] The text of 'The Banks of the Sweet Primroses' has a 'rejected suitor' theme with a strong hint of sexual innuendo.[59] While there are relatively small differences in the lyrics of each that arguably relate to personal interpretation, there are variations in the order of verses and the inclusion of some verses, and the Fairport Convention version has been adapted in places to scan with a constant metric pulse.

The Penguin, Copper and Killen versions of the song start with the familiar 'As I walked out one mid-summer's morning'. The Fairport Convention version starts with the same line but has a slight variation with 'As I walked out *on a* mid-summer's morning'. The second line of the Penguin version says to 'To view the fields and take the air', although each of the recorded versions starts with 'For to view', possible as a means of scanning text with music, given that the Penguin version is in $\frac{3}{4}$ metre and the versions by Ron and Bob Copper, Louis Killen and Fairport Convention all maintain $\frac{4}{4}$ metre.[60] The Copper and Killen versions also add an extra syllable in the word 'prim-er-oses', which elongates and emphasises the title of the song.

Verse 1 of the Penguin version:

As I walked out on a mid-summer's morning,
To view the fields and take the air,
Down by the banks of the sweet primroses,
There I beheld a most lovely fair.

Verse 1 of the Copper and Killen versions:

As I walked out one mid-summer's morning,
For to view the fields and to take the air,
Down by the banks of the sweet prim-er-oses,
There I beheld a most lovely fair.

Verse 1 of the Fairport Convention version is almost identical to the Copper and Killen versions, although it omits the extra syllable, 'er', in 'primroses' and has more in common with the Penguin version. The Copper and Fairport Convention versions also have a second verse that is omitted in the Killen and Penguin versions. The texts of these verses are almost identical, apart from the discrepancy concerning length of step in the first lines and the Copper version's further use of inserted extra syllables in 'stepp-ed'.

Copper second verse:

> Three long steps I stepp-ed up to her,
> Not knowing her as she passed me by,
> I stepp-ed up to her thinking for to view her,
> She appeared to be like some virtuous bride.

Fairport Convention second verse:

> Three short steps I stepped up to her,
> Not knowing her as she passed me by,
> I stepped up to her thinking for to view her,
> She appeared to be like some virtuous bride.

In interviews for this project, Simon Nicol made no references to the Coppers' 1950s recording of the song, and he maintains that its inclusion in Fairport Convention's repertoire came from that of Dave Swarbrick, the band's violinist, who had worked extensively with A. L. Lloyd.[61] Fairport Convention adapted many songs from Swarbrick's folk song repertoire into rock settings throughout Swarbrick's tenure with the band.[62] Martin Carthy explained to me that Lloyd was often 'inventive' with his use of lyrics from various folk songs – 'putting traditional ideas together in the belief that it was his "duty" to create his own interpretation of a song'.[63] The addition of the second verse in the Fairport Convention version of the song may therefore be a result of Lloyd's influence on Swarbrick, given that Lloyd was an active performer during the 1950s and 1960s in the period after the Copper version had been recorded.

While the third Copper and Fairport Convention verses, and second Penguin and Killen verses are also almost identical, albeit with slight variations, each contains the line 'If you will grant to me one small relief'.[64] This hint of innuendo is used very subtly and is in common with many traditional songs that deal with what would have been a very delicate subject at the time with a slightly humorous approach. In the following verse, the Penguin version uses 'thou' whereas the Copper, Fairport and Killen versions use a more contemporary 'you', and the Copper, Killen and Penguin verses' fourth line has slight variations of 'And to give me comfort is all in vain', while Fairport

Convention finish the verse with 'And in your comfort lies no refrain'. The Copper, Killen and Fairport Convention versions have a final verse that is omitted in the Penguin anthology and that provides a warning to young men who 'go a' courtin'' (Copper and Killen) or 'go a' wassailing' (Fairport Convention), and yet offers hope to the lovelorn singer who has, in the penultimate verse, vowed to hide away 'where no man on earth shall there me find'. All the recorded final verses have it that 'There is many a dark and cloudy morning turns out to be a sunshiney day'. A positive ending to a song about unrequited love is not uncommon in folk music and this may be one of the reasons for this song's unchanging text and continued popularity.

There is little difference between the texts of each of these versions of 'The Banks of The Sweet Primroses', except for the addition of the second verse of the Copper and the Fairport Convention versions of the song and the omission of the final verse in the Penguin version. The lyrics of all three recorded versions are almost identical, despite the differences in their performance media, and the only major difference between the English folk-rock setting of the song and the Penguin version is in what Vaughan Williams and Lloyd describe as its 'presentation', which they suggest should be solely the unaccompanied voice.[65]

Fundamental change to text may occur as a result of a process of contemporisation – or variation – in which folk songs are adapted for the purpose of relocating an earlier narrative to a contemporary social setting, while the song's message remains the same. I demonstrate variation in modern folk song performance practice by analysing the texts of two versions of the same song – 'To the Beggin', a song that was recorded during the second half of the twentieth century and adapted for different contemporary audiences. While both of these versions are relatively recent recordings, one is sung using the Scottish text with which the song was published in 1899, while the other is a modern reworking pertinent to the Thatcher era of Britain in the late 1980s. The versions are titled 'Tae the Beggin'', recorded by The Battlefield Band, and 'The Begging Song', recorded by Martin Carthy and Dave Swarbrick.[66]

The Battlefield Band's recording of the Scottish version of the song contains satirical elements in the lyrics, which suggest that the life of a beggar is more rewarding than that of a king. The first verse argues that begging means the absence of a master, and the next verses describe the clothing needed to follow the trade successfully:

Of a' the trades that I do ken [know], the beggin' is the best,
For when a beggar's weary he can, aye, sit down and rest.
Say I'll gang [walk] tae the cobbler and get him tae sort ma shoon [shoes]
An inch thick around the bottom and clouted weel aboon [well patched above].
Then I'll gang tae the tailor wae a dod [piece] a [of] hod [abbreviation of 'hoddin', a hoarse homespun cloth] in grey
An' I'll gat 'im make a cloak fir me to help me night an' day.

Subsequent verses describe the beggar's freedom from care about personal hygiene and outline a plan to ensure a supply of food and money:

An' after I begin ma trade I'll let ma beard grow strang [strong]
Nor pare my nails this year an' a day for beggars wear them lang [long].
An' I'll put nae [no] water on ma hands, as little on ma face
An' I'll gang about just like I am an' there ma trade I'll grace.
I'll gang tae the farm towns, I'll stand wi' hat in hand
Can a beggin' man get quarters here, alas, I canna stand.
An' if there's a weddin' in the town, I'll let mae tae [lit. 'more toe'] be there
An' I'll pour my kindest blessin's upon the happy pair.

An' some will gie [give] me beef an' bread, an' some will giecheese
An' out among the weddin' folk, I git all the bawbees [halfpennies].

If beggin' be as good as a trade, as well I hope it may
It's time that I was out o' here an' haudin' down the brae [heading down the hill].[67]

Satirically, the lyrics then pose the philosophical view that the beggar's intended trade will grant him a personal freedom that is not apparent in any other lifestyle, including that of a monarch:

An' if beggin' be as good a trade, it's true for I can tell
Then who would be a monarch, when a beggar lives sae [so] well.

The subject matter in Carthy's version of the song remains unchanged, but it has several new verses that refer to the conditions of the homeless in the UK during the 1980s. While placing the song in an English setting, Carthy's new lyrics maintain elements of despair and resignation as well as the satire and black humour present in the Scottish version. The opening verse is very similar to that of the Scottish version, maintaining that begging grants a form of personal freedom, but following verses describe the harrowing life of a beggar in London at the end of the twentieth century:

Of all the trades in England, the beggin' is the best,
For when a beggar's tired, he can lay him down and rest.
And a-beggin' I will go
And a-beggin' I will go.
I got on the train at Carlisle, they kicked me out at Crewe,
I slept on every paving stone from there to Waterloo.
And a-beggin' I will go
And a-beggin' I will go.
I got breakfast off the Embankment, I got my lunch and tea
And only the finest cardboard made a home that was fit for me.
And a-beggin' I will go
And a-beggin' I will go.
We sit on the stair at Leicester Square from seven o'clock till ten,
Then round the back of the Connaught Towers for dinner from
    out of the bin.
And a-beggin' I will go
And a-beggin' I will go.
I can rest when I am tired and I heed no master's bell,
You men'd be daft to be a king when beggars live so well.
And a-beggin' I will go
And a-beggin' I will go.
The law came down to see us, they came down three together,
They put out the fire, they left us there, oh, Lord, how we did
    shiver.
And a-beggin' we will go
And a-beggin' we will go.
I am a Victorian value, I'm enterprise poverty,
Completely invisible to the state and a joy to Mrs T.
And a-beggin' I will go.[68]

(The next four verses are from a 1996 recording of the song)

There were three young fellas jumped out of the rubbish, their
    clipboards all a-flutter,
They said, 'Poverty has its pluses, y'know, and you could present
    it better.'
And a-beggin' I will go
And a-beggin' I will go.
'For we've got funds and we've got plans and we've got time in
    hand,
So we're launching a plan for the market place to take begging to
    all the land.'
And a-beggin' I will go
And a-beggin' I will go.
'We're Poverty PLC, we are, we want you all to know,
And everyone says that our share of the market will grow and
    grow.'
And a-beggin' I will grow
And a-beggin' I will grow.
Then they dressed us in all of their merchandise, I had a logo all
    over me hat,
It said 'Poverty Rising Above the Time' but the others all thought
    it said 'PRAT'.
And a-beggin' I will go
And a-beggin' I will go.[69]

The earlier, Scottish version of the song takes a philosophical
and humorous view of a future career as a beggar, whereas
Carthy's version is couched in the past tense and is less satirical
because its elements of realism relate to events in recent history.
In an interview for this study, Carthy justified changing the text
by maintaining that the song's original message made it 'topical'
and that, as such, the song belongs to a throwaway tradition
that can be updated.[70] Moreover, the retention of the original
subject matter within the modern context of the additional new
verses makes the song pertinent to modern audiences, who are
likely to be more aware of contemporary events than of those
that may have occurred centuries earlier. Michael Pickering supports this view, observing that folk songs are the products of
cultural processes and that they are subject to social variables
brought about by changing historical settings, which continue
to change as songs are performed to new audiences over a period
of time.[71] Carthy's performance of 'The Begging Song', while

maintaining the original elements of the earlier 'Tae the Beggin', is in the style of a modern 'protest song', and this form of con-temporisation enhances its relevance for a modern audience.

New folk songs and the re-adaptation of historical balladry

The composition of historical songs and the adaptation of exist-ing folk songs is a further area of change that often occurs in modern British folk music, and particularly in English folk-rock. This area would include use of a historically factual text in a ballad context that is performed in a newly composed, rock-style setting. An example occurs in 'I'm Already There', a song recorded on Fairport Convention's album *Over The Next Hill*.[72] The lyrics and music of 'I'm Already There' were composed by Chris Leslie, a member of Fairport Convention since 1997. The song's text refers to the voyages of arctic exploration carried out by Sir John Franklin (1786–1847) between 1819 and 1829. The assimilation of traditional language and images in the text is apparent in the first verse:

> Across the ocean we set sail,
> It was a rough and mighty sea,
> Our strength and courage beat the gale
> Till our ship, she landed free

In the third, fourth and sixth verses, references to exact histori-cal events locate the song into the context of a new historical ballad in a rock music setting:

> *Verse 3*
> At Hudson Bay we made our camp
> To heal our wounds and take on stores
> With Native Indians as our guides
> We found the Coppermine shore.
>
> *Verse 4*
> We headed down for Canada
> Our bough was breaking through the ice
> And it got thicker when we stopped
> Held in a frozen vice.
>
> *Verse 6 (first two lines)*
> Franklin said we had to leave
> And take our chance with dog and sleigh

A further example of the use of historical fact in a new historical ballad in a rock setting appears in 'Over the Falls', recorded on the same album.[73] Opening verses of the song are about The Great Blondin's preparation for the first crossing of Niagara Falls on a tightrope in 1859, although the later verses of the song mainly concern his personal thoughts while he is crossing:

> He's standing on the edge
> Looking out across the flow
> He puts his feet up on the rope
> To feel the tension with his toe
> Now he knows the time is right
> A final dust of chalk on hand
> A certain dryness in his mouth
> Everything is how he planned

While 'Over the Falls' does not provide the same level of historical detail as 'I'm Already There', it does centre on a specific event. Nicol states that band member Chris Leslie has a talent for writing biographical songs, particularly in respect to 'The Fossil Hunter', a song about Mary Anning, an amateur palaeontologist who lived in Lyme Regis in the mid-nineteenth century and who eventually became a celebrated member of the palaeontology community.[74] Nicol particularly admires Leslie's combination of historical fact in the song with the 'nursery rhyme' quality of its chorus – 'She sells sea shells on the sea shore' – and states that Leslie 'has found this clever way of looking at the people he admires as strong individuals, like herself [Anning] and Blondin'.[75] He puts it that Leslie's curiosity is the basis for his songwriting:

> Intellectual curiosity, local interest, holiday trips to Lyme Regis where he became aware of Mary Anning. It's brilliant, I mean those songs are keepers, they are definitely keepers and I look forward every time he comes up with a new song with that kind of direct theme, I think it's like a little slice of history which has been neatly parcelled up and can be passed on to the next generation, disguised as a song.[76]

While Nicol acknowledges Leslie's songwriting skills and his use of historical narrative, Fairport Convention have often adapted songs outside the traditional folk idiom using a process that might be regarded as 'traditionalisation', which may have implied notions of authenticity to audiences used to hearing English folk-rock adaptations of folk songs. Simon Frith regards this reshaping of a genre as 'transgressive performance' in which old genres fail 'when their rules and rituals come to seem silly and restrictive'.[77]

Steeleye Span also followed a policy of 'transgressive performance' in the creation of new folk songs by adapting traditional formats on the band's 2004 recording, *They Called Her Babylon*.[78] This album includes a version of 'Van Diemen's Land', a folk song well documented by collectors in the early twentieth century.[79] Unlike many of their previous albums, Steeleye Span's sleeve notes on this album do not provide details of source versions they may have used, although they refer to the song as an adaptation of 'The Gallant Poachers'. Their text, however, closely resembles versions of the song published in both Peter Kennedy's and Ewan MacColl's anthologies. Steeleye Span's version starts with the introduction of the narrator, Susan Summers, who also appears in a variation of the song, 'Poor Tom Brown of Nottingham Town'. Following verses describe the other poachers being transported, living conditions during transportation and on arrival in Van Diemen's Land, the sale of the prisoners, the marriage of the female character, and a desperate longing for home, although the verses are not in the same order as other published versions. Moreover, Steeleye Span have changed the melody of a verse warning of the penalties for poaching for use as a chorus, giving the song an arrangement structure common in the popular music idiom.

The use of source texts in a popular or rock music setting such as this is simply an extended variation of the methods used in the contemporisation of a folk song that may be regarded by its performers and audience as becoming old fashioned and restrictive.[80] The inclusion of existing folk song texts within newly composed rock settings is a further means by which notions of authenticity are retained in English folk-rock performance. Moreover, the presentation of historical topics both in original texts and in newly composed rock contexts implies authenticity while providing alternative repertoire possibilities to those previously utilised in the adaptation of folk songs for English folk-rock performance. English folk-rock performers are able to extend their traditional folk song repertoires by the addition of new historical ballads that are imbued with notions of authenticity. Similarly, the use of song texts 'crafted in the appropriate language' is apparent in the composition of new, folk-influenced material in older musical forms.[81]

While discussing the composition of new folk music in an interview for this study, Ashley Hutchings commented: 'As to what is folk, what is not folk in the future, . . . I personally don't care. I just think the important thing is the music has integrity, and that . . . we have knowledge of what's gone before, so that we can build on that'.[82] This statement may appear somewhat *laissez-faire* but it is reflective of the changes in folk music performance style that have occurred since the late 1960s and that are still apparent in contemporary folk performance among a new generation of folk performers.

A continuum of change

A key characteristic of English folk-rock from the late 1960s to the present is its location within a continuum of folk music change that followed the second folk revival. This continuum has been driven by contemporisation – both textual and musicological – within a combined framework of notionally maintained authenticity and a process of traditionalisation, and it has led to a canon of recorded works that provides a regenerative approach to the field of folk music performance and preservation. English folk-rock, initially a broad description of the amalgamation of folk and rock music that took place during the progressive rock movement, can be regarded as part of a contemporary trend in the development of both rock and folk musics that are culturally and historically separate from twentieth-century folk revivalism. This trend has enabled British folk music performed in the context of English folk-rock to become a popular music style for new audiences with diverse musical tastes, despite criticism from factions within the traditional folk music scene.

Musicological analyses of English folk-rock described above indicate not only that British folk music can be performed in a variety of musical styles, but also that its identity remains intact as it becomes absorbed and adapted into a contemporary social, cultural and musical milieu. Folk music remains no more than what its audience regards as 'folk music' at any particular time and, while the collection and preservation of folk music by Victorian and Edwardian folk song collectors remains an invaluable historical social and cultural narrative, it only reflected what folk music meant at that point in time and only what it meant to the collectors personally. Folk music has been adapted into rock settings since the late 1960s, and the result has been to establish a particular identity for folk music during that time, despite the absence of a formal plan for this endeavour. Contemporary performance practice in British folk music, within frameworks of notionally maintained authenticity and traditionlisation, thus remains part of an ongoing process of change that can be regarded as a positive phenomenon contributing to growth in the music's popularity, as well as to its continued preservation in live performance contexts, and in an expanding canon of folk and English folk-rock recordings.

Notes

1 MacKinnon, *The British Folk Scene*.
2 Boyes , *The Imagined Village*; Livingston, 'Music Revivals'.
3 Irwin, 'The New English Roots', 32.
4 Irwin, 'The New English Roots', 32.
5 Hutchings, interview with author, May 1997.
6 Laing and Newman, *Thirty Years of the Cambridge Folk Festival*; Simon Nicol, interviews with author, December 1996 and August 2005; Gerry Conway, interview with author, January 1997; Martin Carthy, interviews with author, March 1997 and August 2005; Ashley Hutchings, correspondence with author, May 1997; Rick Kemp, interviews and correspondence with author, between August 1997 and July 2007.
7 Seminal English folk-rock recordings such as *Liege and Lief* (1969) mark the introduction of this particular perception of canon. Songs recorded in the late 1960s and 1970s that are still in Fairport Convention's repertoire include 'Walk Awhile', 'Matty Groves', 'Journeyman's Grace', 'Rosie', 'Genesis Hall', 'End of a Holiday', 'Dirty Linen' and 'Meet on the Ledge'. In their live performance repertoire, Steeleye Span still include 'King Henry', 'Four Nights Drunk', 'All Around My Hat', 'Blackleg Miner', 'Cam Ye O'er Frae

France' and 'Gaudete'. These songs can be regarded as significant in the emergence of the folk-rock canon.

8 Joseph Kerman, 'A Few Canonic Variations', *Critical Enquiry* 10:1 (September 1983), 107.

9 Kerman, 'A Few Canonic Variations', 112.

10 Kerman, 'A Few Canonic Variations', 113.

11 William Weber, 'The History of Musical Canon', in *Rethinking Music*, ed. Nicholas Cook and Mark Everist (Oxford: Oxford University Press, 1999), 349.

12 Weber, 'The Intellectual Origins of Musical Canon in Eighteenth Century England', *Journal of the American Musicological Society* 47:3 (1994), 490.

13 Weber, 'The Intellectual Origins of Musical Canon in Eighteenth Century England', 491.

14 Weber, 'The History of Musical Canon', 349.

15 Kerman, 'A Few Canonic Variations', 111.

16 Martin Carthy, interviews with author, March 1997 and August 2005.

17 Robert P. Morgan, 'Rethinking Musical Culture: Canonic Reformulations in a Post-Tonal Age', in *Disciplining Music: Musicology and Its Canons*, ed. Katherine Bergeron and Philip V. Bohlman (Chicago: University of Chicago Press, 1992), 44 and 62.

18 Morgan, 'Rethinking Musical Culture', 44 and 62.

19 Bohlman, *The Study of Folk Music in the Modern World*, xviii.

20 Antti-Ville Kärjä, 'A Prescribed Alternative Mainstream: Popular Music and Canon Formation', *Popular Music* 25:1 (2006), 11.

21 Kärjä, 'A Prescribed Alternative Mainstream', 3.

22 Ralf Von Appen and André Doehring, 'Nevermind The Beatles, Here's Exile 61 and Nico: "The Top 100 Records of All Time" – A Canon of Pop and Rock Albums from a Sociological and an Aesthetic Perspective', *Popular Music* 25:1 (2006): 21–39, 22.

23 Von Appen and Doehring, 'Nevermind The Beatles, Here's Exile 61 and Nico', 34.

24 Kerman, 'A Few Canonic Variations', 118–19.

25 Kerman, 'A Few Canonic Variations', 119.

26 Nicol, interview, December 1996.

27 Nicol, interview, December 1996.

28 Nicol, interview, August 2005.

29 Hutchings, correspondence, May 1997.

30 Ian Watson, *Song and Democratic Culture in Britain: An Approach to Popular Culture in Social Movements* (New York: St Martin's Press, 1983), 145.

31 For example, Boyes, *The Imagined Village*; Harker, *Fakesong*; Lloyd, *Folk Song in England*; and Pickering, 'Song and Social Context'.

32 Bearman, 'Who Were The Folk?', 773 and 775; Hobsbawm, 'Introduction: Inventing Traditions', 7.

33 Atkinson, 'Folk Songs in Print', 457–8.

34 For example, since the 1990s Topic Records have released recordings of folk songs collected between the 1940s and 1960s, and the early recordings of both Fairport Convention and Steeleye Span contain many songs that have in turn become source versions to more recent performers. The Steeleye Span version of the 'Gower Wassail', which was recorded on the album *Ten Man Mop, Or Mr Reservoir Butler Rides Again* (1971), is sometimes known as 'The Steeleye Span Wassail'.

35 Livingston, 'Music Revivals', 69.

36 Boyes, interview with author, August 1997; and Hutchings, correspondence, May 1997.

37 Boyes, interview, August 1997.

38 It is worth noting that most commercial recordings use compression tools as a means of levelling peaks in sound waves. While analogue compression would have been used in professional recording studios during the 1970s and 1980s, I do not regard its use as having a significant effect on my findings, particularly from my own experience as a studio musician at that time. Modern digital compression used in contemporary popular music has a more noticeable effect on overall production values.

39 See appendix 2 for further oscillographic comparisons of folk songs performed in both traditional and English folk-rock contexts.

40 *When the May Is All in Bloom: Traditional Singing from the South East of England* (Haughley, Suffolk: Veteran VT131CD, 1995).

41 Bob Lewis, email correspondence with author, 28 January 2002.

42 Lewis, correspondence, 2002.

43 Steeleye Span, *Below the Salt* (London: Chrysalis CHR1008, 1972). Although Steeleye Span at this time had no drummer, they adhere to a constant pulse in 'The Spotted Cow' in the same way as other bands in the rock music genre.

44 This may be because the Steeleye Span version is stated to be 'From the singing of Harry Cox' in the sleeve notes to the album.

45 MacKinnon maintains that audience participation is a distinctive aspect of the folk club scene (MacKinnon, *The British Folk Scene*, 30, 36 and 48).

46 *Hidden English: A Celebration of English Traditional Music* (London: Topic TSC600, 1964).

47 Fairport Convention, *Nine* (London: Island ILPS 9246, 1973). Dave Pegg, the band's bass guitarist, arranged 'Polly on the Shore'; he plays part of the bass line in the form of an eight-bar melodic ostinato constructed from an A Mixolydian scale.

48 In the late 1960s, before the metrical inflexibility of the 1970s 'disco' era, A. L. Lloyd (*Folk Song in England*, 35) was critical of the ways in which the use of $\frac{4}{4}$ metre in popular and art music affected Western perceptions of music. There were, however, three success-ful 'irregular' metre recordings that achieved chart success in the 1960s and 1970s. 'Take Five', in $\frac{5}{4}$, was a hit single in 1960 for the Dave Brubeck Quartet; 'Living in the Past', also in $\frac{5}{4}$, was recorded by Jethro Tull in 1969; 'Money', in $\frac{7}{4}$, recorded in 1973 by Pink Floyd, was a single taken from the album *Dark Side of the Moon*. This album remained in the UK and US charts for over ten years, demonstrating that constant $\frac{4}{4}$ metre was not a necessary criterion for commercial success.

49 Halsey Stevens, *The Life and Music of Béla Bartók* (New York: University of New York, 1981), 272.

50 Kemp, interviews with author, August 2001 and June 2005.

51 Steeleye Span, *Parcel of Rogues* (1973).

52 'The Weaver and the Factory Maid' (as collected by A. L. Lloyd in Widnes in 1951) from Roy Palmer, *A Touch on the Time: Songs of Social Change 1770–1914* (Harmondsworth: Penguin, 1974), 134.

53 Fairport Convention, *Angel Delight* (1971). The drummer on 'Lord Marlborough' was Dave Mattacks, who had joined Fairport Convention in 1969 before the recording of *Liege and Lief*. Both Ashley Hutchings and Simon Nicol maintain that Mattacks was the first drummer to amalgamate folk and rock music while retaining aspects of authenticity from both styles.

54 John Churchill, First Duke of Marlborough, led the British forces to victory in this campaign and his reward, an estate in Oxford-shire, was named after the battle at Blenheim (Blindheim), in Bavaria, in 1704. He was created Duke of Marlborough by William III (William of Orange), although the text of Fairport Convention's version of the song refers to his earlier support for King Charles II.

55 See Robert Burns, 'British Folk Music in Popular Music Settings', in *Folk Song: Tradition, Revival, and Re-Creation*, ed. Ian Russell and David Atkinson (Aberdeen: Elphinstone Institute, University of Aberdeen, 2004), 115–29.

56 Eliza Carthy, *Red Rice*, Topic TSD2001 (1998).

57 Martin Carthy, *Sweet Wivelsfield*, Deram SML 1111 (1975); James Reeves, *The Idiom of the People: English Traditional Verse* (London: Heinemann, 1958), 75.

58 Martin Carthy, interview with author, March 1997.

59 A. L. Lloyd's notes in *The Penguin Book of English Folk Songs* (Harmondsworth: Penguin, 1961), state that the song probably originated as a seventeenth-century broadside and has remained constant in text and tune in all of the places in which it has been sung, which include Sussex, the Gower peninsula in Wales, and the north of England (110).

60 According to Vaughan Williams and Lloyd, changes were made to versions of folk songs in the *Penguin Book of English Folk Songs* in order 'to make the text fit the tune' (*The Penguin Book of English Folk Songs*, 8).

61 Nicol, interview, December 1996.

62 Nicol, interview, December 1996.

63 Carthy, interview, March 1997.

64 'To' is omitted in Killen's version.

65 Vaughan Williams and Lloyd, *The Penguin Book of English Folk Songs*, 9.

66 The Battlefield Band, *At The Front*, Topic 12TS381 (1978); Martin Carthy and Dave Swarbrick, *Life and Limb*, Special Delivery SD 1030 (1990). Peter Kennedy provides an account of the sources of 'A-Beggin' I Will Go' in *Folksongs of Britain and Ireland: A Guidebook to the Living Tradition of Folk Singing in the British Isles and Ireland* (London: Cassell, 1975), 527. The song and its variants can be found in printed versions dating back to 1641, although the lyrics as sung by The Battlefield Band were published by Robert Ford, *Vagabond Songs and Ballads of Scotland*, vol. 2 (Paisley: Alexander Gardner, 1899), 118–22.

67 Scottish vocabulary taken from 'Glossary', in *The Poems and Songs of Robert Burns*, vol. 3 (Oxford: Clarendon Press, 1968), 1549–1613. Lyrics transcribed by author.

68 In 1996, Carthy sang 'and there for all to see' instead of 'and a joy to Mrs T'. At this time, Thatcher was no longer prime minister, nor leader of the Conservative party.

69 Dave Swarbrick, *Folk On 2*, with Martin Carthy, Cooking Vinyl, MASH CD 001 (1996). Lyrics transcribed by author.

70 Carthy, interview, March 1997.

71 Pickering, 'Song and Social Context', 75.

72 Fairport Convention, *Over the Next Hill*, Matty Grooves Records MGCD041 (2004).

73 The lyrics and music of 'Over the Falls' were also composed by Chris Leslie.

74 'The Fossil Hunter', Fairport Convention, *Over the Next Hill* (2004).

75 Nicol, interview, August 2005.

76 Nicol, interview, August 2005.

77 Frith, 'Music and Identity', 94.

78 Steeleye Span, *They Called Her Babylon*, Park Records B0001KJ038 (2004). Steeleye Span occasionally recorded cover versions of songs that had been featured in their live performances, for example, the single 'Rave On'. Also, 'To Know Him Is To Love Him' and 'Twinkle, Twinkle Little Star' on the album *Commoners Crown*, Chrysalis CHR1071 (1975), and 'The Black Freighter' on the album, *Storm Force 10*, Chrysalis 1151 (1977).

79 See collection details in Kennedy's *Folksongs of Britain and Ireland* (London: Oak Publications, 1984), 585, and Ewan MacColl's *Traveller's Songs From England and Scotland* (London: Routledge and Kegan Paul, 1977), 286.

80 Frith, 'Music and Identity', 94.

81 Vulliamy, 'The Alter-Ego of Englishness', 10.

82 Hutchings, correspondence, May 1997.

5 Performer perspectives of audience reception of English folk-rock

Overview

We now return to my earlier question – who makes up the audience for English folk-rock? And why, as Simon Nicol suggests, are there up to four generations attending festivals such as that held annually at Cropredy? I now discuss these topics from performer perspectives with a view that, in the amalgamation of folk music and rock music, there are specific audience expectations from both styles. I draw on interviews with English folk-rock performers, as well as my own experiences as a professional musician in rock and folk-rock contexts, and my experiences as an audience member at folk-orientated music events. While English folk-rock performers interviewed in fieldwork do not regard the involvement of aspects of the popular music industry in modern folk music as denigrating to the nature and meaning of folk music, a convergence of folk music and rock music often reinforces perceptions held by some factions of the folk audience concerning the devaluation of folk music through commoditisation. I described my earliest experience of negative audience reception at one of my own early folk-rock performances in chapter 1, and I include another more recent experience later in this chapter.

Discussion of contemporary audience reception of English folk-rock music relates not only to perceived authenticities located within aspects of performance practice that are related to its component styles, but also to the expectations from live performance that match criteria set by production values in recorded media. Change in music performance technologies during the latter part of the twentieth century – the availability of CD recordings in the early 1980s onwards to the era of music downloads – has altered audience expectation and reception criteria to the extent that live performance must often reflect an accurate representation of a recorded work. Audience reception of English folk-rock performance relates both to adaptations of folk songs for performance that demonstrate signifiers inherent in both the folk and rock genres, and to the accurate live re-creation of recorded works that have become situated within newer audience perceptions of authenticity and that relate to more recent recorded 'source versions'. My ethnographic observations of audience reception of high levels of performance and technical prowess, as well as the sophisticated sound reproduction values associated with progressive rock, are further key factors in the combination of folk and rock music as English folk-rock.

Adoption of aspects of music-industry-related commerciality and promotion processes in rock music often facilitates enhancement of performance reputation and status that reinforces notions of separateness between performer and audience. Despite the rock-music-orientated locations in which English folk-rock is most often performed, this aspect of audience perception has never been apparent at English folk-rock performances I have attended or played at since 1971, and performers interviewed espouse familiarity with their audiences. The location of an English folk-rock performance must therefore provide both a forum for aspects of rock performance as well as a sense of community between audience and performer. This is an issue familiar in the folk club scene, in which the closeness that occurs between audience and performer often negates perceptions of performer 'status' normally associated with rock music performance.

Simon Frith maintains that the most developed folk 'rituals' are the folk club and the folk festival phenomenon, noting that folk clubs often attempt to minimise distance between audience and performer.[1] The folk club perception of audience/performer contact was often transferred to early folk festivals, at which an established performer would be required to socialise and drink

with the audience after a performance, and to take part in workshops. This requirement was part of a combined audience perception that anyone in the audience community should be able
to perform before or after the main performer in an attempt to
deny the commercial separation between folk 'stars' and folk
fans. For the purpose of situating the audience of English folk-
rock, I propose a four-tiered concept in which the combination
of folk music and rock music – as English folk-rock – is at once
unifying in terms of performer/audience rapport. This amalgamation simultaneously presents and maintains aspects of rock
music 'status' from which English folk-rock performers enhance
musical reputations in a more formal forum than that of the
rock scene, but in a less formal forum that of the folk club scene.
This forum also presents English folk rock as a musical style that
embraces sound reproduction values, in both live and recorded
contexts, that are familiar to, and expected by, contemporary
rock, jazz and art music audiences. Finally English folk-rock
retains notions of its audience as community, an aspect of audience reception that has always been apparent in folk audiences,
but which, in my own experience, was also evident in the student-based, progressive rock audience.

Commenting on social values in popular music, Frith suggests
that certain styles of popular music also articulate communal
values, and he adds that English folk-rock, in particular, has
individualised the folk concept of authenticity by offering 'an
experience of community' in a similar way to traditional folk
music.[2] Communal and social values are attributes regarded by
folk revivalists as intrinsic to any description of the folk music
audience. My interviews with folk and English folk-rock performers indicate that notions of community also extend to
members of the English folk-rock audience, who are predominantly middle class. As with folk fans, perceptions of community in the English folk-rock audience often arouse deep
emotional connections, an aspect of perceived community that
often occurs, as Benedict Anderson puts it, among the 'bour-
geoisie'.[3] This aspect of perceived community is applicable to
both the traditional and rock elements in English folk-rock audiences. For example, as stated earlier in his preview of the 1997
Cropredy Festival, Ed Vulliamy describes 'hundreds of fans'
arriving at the festival 'by narrowboat and converted Telecom

vans', as well as many fans who 'purr in by BMW'.[4] Vulliamy's description of the forms of transport used by audience members attending previous festivals at Cropredy suggests that a broad spectrum of classes would, as in previous years, be present at the 1997 festival, given the differences between narrowboats, BMW motor cars, and converted Telecom vans. There is also an indication of a dichotomy in the upper and middle classes' use of an expensive mode of transport, such as a narrowboat or a BMW car, to attend an event that enables them to 'buy into' a revivalist nostalgia. Simon Nicol describes the Cropredy Festival as 'community-orientated', albeit while describing the English folk-rock audience rather than the traditional folk music audience: 'There is no such thing as a typical folk-rock fan because you've got families there with three, maybe four generations who come for the weekend. It's a reunion in a sense because people come not just from this country or Europe but from all over the planet to meet in a field because they know they're going to see so-and-so for the first time since last year.'[5]

Nicol does not mention issues of class but it is significant that the audiences at the Cropredy festivals, and those at other festivals at which I participated as an English folk-rock performer, regard these festivals as communal gatherings in a similar way to revivalists, who often regard the issue of community as a component of revivalism.[6] The life span of a revival is often governed by the revivalists' perceptions of authenticity and by questions of cost and affordability as the middle classes buy into nostalgia.[7] Cost and affordability are issues that are often of no concern to middle-class consumers, and consequently revivalist nostalgia becomes an affordable and accessible commodity. Once authenticity has become less of a concern to revivalists, limitations caused by restrictive definitions are removed, and different musical styles can be promoted within the revival. Interviews with performers and music industry operatives carried out for this study indicate that a reduction of reference points became apparent in the period following the second folk revival, and it remains apparent during a new phase of revivalism, within which exist diverse amalgamations of folk music and popular music, including English folk-rock. New revivalist traditions frequently emerge with their own new communities, and often within a few years. New traditions rapidly become established while supporting the divergence of folk music styles as they become amalgamated with popular music styles.[8] These transformations often weaken social patterns for which 'old' traditions were intended while, in the case of English folk-rock, the formalisation of 'new' traditions has promoted growth in the popularity of folk music combined with other musical styles, particularly in the world music arena. Notions of older traditions in modern folk music create a perception of antiquity, as well as new notions of community, in order to preserve imaginary historical links.

Audience reception of a musical hybrid

In order to evaluate audience reception in English folk-rock, I will briefly compare scholarly debate surrounding audience reception of art music (from which I draw comparisons to the folk music and world music scenes) as well as that surrounding the reception of rock music. Commercial distinctions between what art music and folk music audiences regard as authentic and inauthentic – and what folk music audiences often regard as 'selling out' – are similar to what Frith describes as the dichotomy between what is considered to be 'serious' and 'respectable' or 'fun'.[9] This distinction exists in the consideration of art music and rock music reception. Frith maintains that 'a good classical performance is measured by the stillness it commands, by the intensity of the audience's mental concentration, by the lack of any physical distraction'.[10] British folk clubs have often been part of a similar 'serious' versus 'fun' dichotomy in that folk audiences often have a 'structured informality' that is 'tightly bound by a series of mores and expectations as to how to behave', including 'attention to explanations of songs, glaring at interruptions [and] a general expectation of silence between songs'.[11] This view, however, concerns folk audiences prior to what Martin Carthy observes as the emergence of a 'new folk circuit', and it can be regarded as debatable in the contemporary folk club scene, particularly from the perspective of my own experiences at newly established folk venues during the 1990s.[12]

In contrast, Frith claims that rock music performance can be measured by its audience's physical response, audience relocation from seating to dance floor and by how loudly its audience shouts or screams, although he does not acknowledge the structured formality of reception that has always existed in the progressive rock music concert at which the audience is also bound by a series of mores.[13] Progressive rock audience conventions surround expectation of technological aspects of sound reproduction, shared musical knowledge between audience members as well as between audience and performers of the repertoire performed, and the musical virtuosity of its performers. These are key aspects of progressive rock. Enthusiastic rock music reception is also evident in progressive rock, although it is reserved for the end of a musical performance in a similar way to art and folk music performances. English folk-rock, as a former progressive music style, therefore provides a link between the formality of the folk music concert and the 'informal' formality of the progressive rock concert that concomitantly unifies its audience and performer, while enabling performers to establish and maintain status through performance virtuosity.

There also exists the issue of professional status among folk and rock musicians. While folk and rock performances may differ in terms of audience behaviour, more fundamental differences exist in audience perceptions of performers in both styles and the professionalism inherent in performances. Professional status provides a distinction between, on the one hand, audience perceptions of United Kingdom art music and rock music performers, who must be members of the Musicians' Union in order to broadcast and to tour internationally, and, on the other, professional folk performers, who performed in the folk club scene during the second folk song revival. The performance of traditional music during the second revival had gained a form of professionalism and publicity that detracted from audience notions of tradition or revivalism.[14] Folk music in the UK during the 1950s and 1960s also became regarded as a type of popular music providing a moral dilemma for successful British folk singers as they sought to preserve their non-professional image while folk music became 'professionalised within an ethos of non-professionalism'.[15] Professional status provides a commonality between folk and rock performers whose professionalism is demonstrated by career longevity in the same way as their art music counterparts, despite revivalist preferred notions of amateurism. As a former professional performer in both the rock and English folk-rock music styles between the 1970s and the 1990s, I was also required to perform in other musical settings, including art music. Performer professionalism extends to an audience's perception of value in art, folk and rock music performance, and it is this aspect that links not only audience reception of art and folk music, but also perceptions of folk and rock music, particularly reception of bands that emerged from the progressive rock movement.

In his description of the pub rock scene in the UK, Andrew Bennett provides a discussion that serves as an analogy between folk music and rock music reception, while providing a link that extends beyond audience perceptions of performer professionalism. Bennett maintains that the reception of pub rock centres on a perceived sense of audience community and on its performance in a network of pubs – aspects similar to the reception of folk music, which occurs in a network of folk clubs that are 'inextricably linked to the localised patterns of consumption that inform its reception'.[16] For Bennett, pub rock originated as part of what he refers to as the 'back to basics' movement in the 1970s, which was in opposition to what audiences regarded as the increasingly elitist emphasis on technical expertise and stadium-orientated performance among progressive rock performers.[17] While Bennett describes audience hostility towards progressive rock, his references to 'accessibility and intimacy', 'rapport with the audience' and 'performance and consumption of popular music in the informal atmosphere of the pub venue' can be equally applied to English folk-rock performance, which often took place in similar venues. This is an aspect of folk-rock that I experienced while performing in folk-rock bands and while attending folk-rock concerts. A recorded example of audience/performer intimacy exists on Fairport Convention's *35th Anniversary Concert* DVD (2002).[18] While the band was performing in a concert venue, introductions of songs and humorous asides between the band members and to the audience were similar to those that occur in the intimate environment of the folk club.

A further link to English folk-rock exists in Bennett's description of 'issues of musical taste [in pub rock] being inextricably bound up with forms of vernacular knowledge', an aspect of audience reception in progressive rock that had a different audience from the mainstream pop market, and which was often student-based and musically informed. In terms of musical taste and vernacular knowledge, the audience at the Fairport Convention concert are familiar with the material being performed and the manner of its presentation, given that they often applaud introductions to songs. This may be reflective of their age demographic and the length of Fairport Convention's career. Nevertheless, as Nicol observes, there exists a notional community among the band's fans.[19] Fairport Convention's intimate and informal style of stage presentation has not changed significantly since I first saw them in 1970, when they performed in established rock venues of the period. Steeleye Span's stage presentation in the early 1970s was also different from the familiar transatlantic presentation of many rock bands, and they also presented themselves to knowledgeable rock audiences with an informality and intimacy usually associated with the folk club scene. Steeleye Span often included a mummer's play in their live performances.

Progressive rock performance often occurred in small, intimate venues that were part of a rock club circuit, which included universities. In a fieldwork interview, Ed Bicknell, the manager of Dire Straits, described his experiences as a booking agent for bands during the late 1960s and throughout the 1970s.[20] Bicknell stated that the club and university circuits provided a primary source of income for progressive bands at this time, as well as a performance forum for several bands and performers that became part of the stadium circuit as their careers became commercially successful, such as Pink Floyd, David Bowie, Roxy Music and King Crimson. I attended many clubs of this kind between 1969 and 1972, particularly Friars Club in Aylesbury, Buckinghamshire, which was regarded among progressive rock musicians as the most influential club on the circuit.[21] This was because the BBC radio presenter John Peel often played records there between each band's performance, and he would later play recordings of new progressive bands on his radio programme, 'Top Gear'. Another reason for the club's popularity among performers was its location close to London, placing it within reach of record company artist and repertoire personnel. The venue was a small hall with a maximum standing capacity of about three hundred, and audiences were able not only to see and hear progressive rock performances, but also to experience intimate closeness to performers. This aspect of performance was often problematic once performers became commercially established. This intimacy between performer and audience, as in the folk club and pub rock scenes, is a key component of the English folk-rock audience reception concept, in which performer/audience rapport is aligned with aspects of rock music 'status' and audience notions of community.

In an investigation of audience reception of English folk-rock, reception theory in art music performance provides a framework with which to view the amalgamation of folk music and rock music within a progressive rock context. Reception theory has its origins in English literature in relation to the reading and understanding of texts. For Alan Lessem, the process of reading recreates meanings and realisation within texts, a process he aligns to reception and understanding of music, particularly in terms of audience perceptions of ways in which music was heard and understood in the past and how it has been understood and remade at subsequent times.[22] Lessem's observation can be recontextualised for discussion on comparative audience reception of folk music in folk club settings, as well as its reception in rock music or world music festival settings. Lessem puts it that, in a positivist study of audience reception of Western art music, music only has meaning when it is performed and heard within the 'horizons' of 'actual' recipients, who he suggests are, at best, 'hypothetically ideal' rather than 'real'.[23] He states that it is impossible to extract a 'timelessly true meaning' from the past, and he argues in favour of the abandonment of confines imposed by concerns for authenticity, a convincing view that may also be applied to folk music, which is often only authentic in terms of editorial and transcription skills of folk collectors.[24] Recorded media become a comparatively accurate platform for contemporary perceptions of authenticity in folk music, arguably in a similar way to the early recordings of folk song performances made by early twentieth-century collectors such as Percy Grainger (1882–1961) and Béla Bartók (1881–1945).

As contemporary folk music and English folk-rock become identified as a product of not only live but also recorded performance, change occurs in audience expectation and reception, or what Lessem refers to as the 'horizons' of listeners.[25] Frith, however, describes a recurring discursive clash in twentieth-century popular music in which 'nature is pitted against artifice' with live music representing 'true' music and recorded music representing 'false' music.[26] Lessem nevertheless maintains that audience horizons are often grounded in socio-cultural conditions and, while he takes a similar view to Adorno that audience aesthetic criteria become 'shaped' by the circumstances of music production, distribution and reception, he suggests that there exists a positive audience response to challenges presented by change in all art.[27] In the context of folk music, change has occurred in the re-contextualisation of folk music as popular music, and in its dissemination through the use of recorded media. From my own experiences of attending and performing at festivals since the early 1980s, Lessem's observation may be equally applied to enthusiastic audience reception and audience growth at festivals presenting folk music performed in world music contexts in an arena of folk music diversity.

Lessem also puts it that, in order to understand past developments in art music, any evaluation must include all subsequent developments that followed them.[28] From this perspective, he persuasively suggests that, in order to seek a 'common horizon' in audience reception – a concept he regards as utopian at best – there needs to be a perception of the 'musical present' from a shared perspective that will enable consensus of what this 'present' may mean.[29] Perceptions of a musical 'present' in folk music performance most often relate to performances that preceded it, and contemporary and, possibly, future evaluation and reception of folk music may therefore relate less to edited texts and more to recorded media that acquire, as David Atkinson puts it, the appearance of 'permanence', 'stability' and 'authority'.[30]

Helmut Rösing regards recorded music as a 'technological transmission train' that occurs between musical sound and listener, that is always available, that can be replayed at will and that is independent of the 'here-and-now of live performance'.[31] From the perspective of Western art music, Rösing maintains that, during the last three hundred years, audience reception of music has moved from 'social interaction' and 'performance' to what he regards as 'transmitted music' that is independent of the live performer and that has a significant impact on listening behaviour, expectations, preferences and musical understanding of audience members.[32] The independence of musical sound from its place and initial occasion of performance is part of what Rösing regards as the absence of the 'performance ritual' that previously occurred in the concert hall, as well as the absence of manifestations of audience pleasure or displeasure, an aspect of recorded folk music that is distinct from the live music ritual of folk club and festival attendance.[33]

As contemporary audience reception is altered by new patterns of listening behaviour, Rösing suggests that 'technically perfect' music production generates expectation norms that must be met in live performance.[34] This aspect of live performance presented in sound recording is apparent in English folk-rock performance, particularly among those performers whose careers have been established since the early 1970s and whose recorded catalogues have been re-released in CD formats. Many styles of music that were 'special and non-everyday' have now become 'a medium of the everyday and taken-for-granted'.[35] There are, however, styles of music that remain resistant to functional change into background music – such as 'free jazz, punk and progressive music' – due to their unambiguous potential for 'social criticism, hostility to cliché and questioning of the system'.[36] These examples could equally include traditional British folk music performed as English folk-rock, which is also regulated by art music perceptions of conformist notions of approval and confirmation and by critical awareness of possible misuse and manipulation. The English folk-rock audience is able to relate to and draw upon a broad range of musical perspectives located within the style, given its musical diversity and the aspects of perceived authenticity drawn from its component styles that its audience often expects from it.

The brief survey of scholarly views above supports a theoretical concept that reception of live performance, and of recorded media, in English folk-rock draws from a balance of performer/audience rapport and audience notions of community that are aligned with performer/audience notions of rock music 'status' demonstrated through professional levels of performance and technical prowess, and sound reproduction. In order to further investigate audience reception of the style, comparative descrip-

tions from English folk-rock performers and folk music critics
are worthy of investigation.

Perspectives of critical reception

While English folk-rock adaptations have attracted new audiences outside the existing folk club scene, many folk fans were,
and are, critical of the amalgamation on the grounds of perceived inauthenticity, and the links to aspects of commercialism, inherent in popular music. MacKinnon observes that the
folk club scene was in decline by the mid-1990s in contrast to an
increase in audience attendance at folk festivals promoted since
the mid-1990s, which became part of a globalised presentation
of folk music as world music.[37] MacKinnon's research suggests
that the largest group attending folk clubs in 1988 was between
30 and 45 years of age, and he argues that this is probably because
this age group became interested in folk music during the
'heyday' of the second folk revival.[38] In a later survey conducted
in 1993, MacKinnon observes that the largest group attending
folk clubs was between 40 and 49 years of age and he puts it
that the folk club scene 'appears to be an ageing movement'
with 'an almost complete absence' of teenagers joining folk
clubs.[39] In contrast, a further indication of increasing popularity
of folk music is an increase in younger age groups, particularly
among the festival audience and what Martin Carthy refers to
as 'the new folk circuit'.[40] These aspects of audience behavioural
trends further illustrate MacKinnon's observations of a decline
in the popularity of folk clubs, and the increase in folk festival
attendance.

Although no statistically rigorous survey was conducted, my
own performance experiences indicate that United Kingdom
folk festival audiences between 1991 and 1997 were predominantly aged between late teenage and approximately 40 years of
age. This was arguably because of the rock-influenced style of
the band with which I was performing and the reputation of its
leader, as well as the mixed folk, folk-rock and world music styles
of the artists and bands that were also appearing at these events.

MacKinnon's views on decline in folk club attendance are
countered by Helen Bell's observation that, while British folk

music in the early twenty-first century has become part of a cultural milieu that attracts media broadcasts and government-sponsored award ceremonies, there is also a resurgence of the informal pub 'session' performances, particularly among young people.[41] Bell states that these sessions provide a symbiosis among performing, listening, participation, music and song in which dance and music and song and tune evolve 'naturally'.[42] Basing her discussion on sessions visited in Dumfries, York, Sheffield, County Kerry and Oxford, Bell situates the 'session culture' at a primarily social level.[43] Bell regards them as occasions at which musicianship takes second place to the sessions' main identity as informal, social occasions and to their significance as a learning process that often acts as a 'stepladder' to professional performance.[44] Bell predicts that, as current interest in media coverage wanes, there will be a return to what she regards as 'ordinary people who do folk music type things' and performing in pubs. Bell's descriptions of the folk sessions are not reflective of the newly emerging folk club scene that Martin Carthy and music industry journalist Kate Wildblood describe as a platform for musical virtuosity in which notions of 'star' status are apparent.[45] Moreover, despite Bell's prediction, there is little evidence that the informal sessions she describes have a significant impact on the emergence of a commercially driven folk music industry that is also supported at government level.

David Arthur, a former editor of *English Dance and Song*, regards commercial aspects of promotion in modern British folk music as 'the worst hype and hyperbole that was once associated with the pop world' and contrary to the open performance platform policy available to floor singers in many folk clubs, where new performers are encouraged to participate as part of a community. Arthur is critical of what he regards as aspects of performer status in folk music and contends that an antidote would be a return to 'the grass roots level' of folk music.[46] He states that: 'At the grass roots level there are still a lot of people who are into 'folk music' for the sake of the music and not to have their egos massaged, and I suspect they'll still be around, as will the music, when a lot of today's folk 'super-stars' and wannabe 'super-stars', who believe their own publicity, will have gone on to other things'.[47]

English folk-rock audiences regard many of the performers I have interviewed as pioneers of the English folk-rock movement. All of these performers have enjoyed career longevity and their performances still attract large audiences, which suggests they retain what could be arguably referred to as 'star' status within the genre. In what might be regarded as a contradiction to his statement above, Arthur also suggests that, from a commercial perspective, the EFDSS missed the opportunity to become a festival promoter in the United Kingdom and that 'a lack of vision' on the part of the Society lost control of the Sidmouth Festival.[48]

This suggests a dichotomy for the EFDSS. If the Society adopts commercial aspects of marketing and promotion, it may be criticised by existing members who regard commercialism as anathema to the folk ethos and who may consequently leave. On the other hand, a restructuring of the Society's financial and marketing mechanisms might enable enhancement of its reputation and encourage new membership – and a consequent increase in the folk music audience – as is it becomes re-branded and located within the expanding world music arena.

The solution to this problem is not within the scope of this project, although it illustrates one of the areas of debate that have surrounded audience reception of English folk-rock among factions of the folk audience since the late 1960s. Folk music journalist Colin Irwin describes what he regards as negative aspects of the folk scene, which are also among the causes of this debate. He maintains that:

> The folk world has a long and ignoble history of shrouding itself in elitism and exclusivity, and rarefying itself to a degree deemed madly impenetrable by all but a diminishing inner sanctum. With the decline of folk clubs, the newly accessible folk music from various remote corners of the world, and the arrival of a new generation of artists with different ideas and fresh ways of being heard, we might have thought those damaging old attitudes had been well and truly kicked into touch.[49]

Irwin's statements on elitism and exclusivity among factions of the folk audience are supported in interviews for this study in which performers from the English folk-rock movement described their performance experiences during the early 1970s.

During this period, they received criticism from members of both the folk and rock audiences on the grounds of perceived inauthenticity.

One aspect of perceived inauthenticity criticised by folk fans was the performance location of English folk-rock on the grounds that the rock environment separated performer and audience and elevated the performer to 'star' status. Performance in large venues raises a further divisive issue among the folk audience concerning the identity of English folk-rock performed as rock-influenced folk music or as folk-influenced rock music. In the folk scene during the 1960s, amplification was seen either as a vital tool for performance in larger venues or as a means of distancing performers from audiences. MacKinnon describes reactions to the early use of public address (PA) systems in folk clubs and maintains that there were two conflicting viewpoints.[50] Firstly, the use of PA systems encouraged more background talking in the bar area, which prevented intense listening to performers and discouraged a 'general atmosphere' and performances by floor singers. The alternative view was that, by discouraging the use of amplification technology, folk clubs would be seen as failing to keep up with the times and would discourage younger audiences from becoming involved. Many folk clubs had a PA system set up for those who wanted to use it and those who did not were at liberty to perform acoustically. MacKinnon describes how performances in this climate often differed: 'The 'anti-camp' claimed that if one person used the PA, the volume level was set for that night and disposed towards background chatter. Then, when someone followed playing acoustically, the lowering of dynamics made that person sound flat'.[51]

Solo unaccompanied performance is a familiar part the folk club scene but many modern folk clubs have installed public address systems that enable audiences to hear every nuance of a performance without acoustic interference from background noise. While intimacy of performer/audience rapport occurs in the folk club, despite the presence of sound reinforcement, it is debatable whether the use of amplification prevents audience perceptions of close contact with the performer at a rock concert. I further discuss this issue later in this chapter. The central issue is one of the expectations of the audiences of each style, an issue that might also be indicative of the different age groups that make up the membership of the folk music audience.[52]

If folk music is performed in a rock setting, the use of highly amplified instruments and drum kits is essential to audience expectations of rock authenticity and it is one of the defining aspects of rock music. Gerry Conway stated in an interview that folk music audiences often regarded the inclusion of any electric instrument or a drum kit in the performance of a folk song as sacrilegious. Conway described audience reaction at one of his performances:

> Putting bass and drums to folk music is sacrilege in a lot of quarters. I can remember going to do a gig with the McGarrigle Sisters somewhere in Europe and they were doing their own songs, but at the end of it they didn't go down that well. We thought we'd do all right because there was a sort of 'Euro-folk' ensemble going on before us. We thought that if they liked them, they would like us but they didn't. When we enquired, we were told that they just didn't like bass and drums... not 'the' bass and drums, but just bass and drums. They were taboo and a lot of people thought that way.[53]

There are differences in accounts of audience reception given by other English folk-rock performers interviewed in fieldwork that vary between vociferous criticism to total acceptance. For example, Ashley Hutchings describes 'a great anti-feeling from a lot of folkies' towards folk-rock that was outweighed by the general audiences who came along to see both Fairport Convention and Steeleye Span, as well as his later ensemble, The Albion Band.[54] He describes a particularly negative reaction during an Albion Band concert at the Royal Albert Hall during which:

> someone stood up and shouted very loudly, he thought he didn't want to hear this, he came here to hear folk music, not rock. And there were other people who barracked, but they were in the minority. But, you know, you could draw a parallel with what they were doing in the States, and no one objected quite as vociferously as they did to Dylan.[55]

This statement suggests that the folk audience did not always attend English folk-rock performances at established rock venues and that they instead attended performances at venues that were not traditionally associated with rock music, such as the Royal Albert Hall and the Royal Festival Hall.[56]

Simon Nicol maintains that the reaction to *Liege and Lief* (1969) and, more significantly, the thinking behind it, caused heated debate among the revivalist and traditionalist factions of the folk mainstream.[57] He regards the folk mainstream of the period as 'people who considered themselves in some way guardians of a precious, almost fragile heritage. Some of those who were getting on in years would have personal memories of those whose collecting and scholarship did actually snatch the source material from the jaws of neglect and ultimately oblivion'.[58] Nicol's comments suggest that criticism of English folk-rock was a generational issue; they also suggest that there was broad acceptance from younger age groups. Nicol added that, although opinions differ concerning the adaptation of folk songs for contemporary performance, he remembers 'no angry upbraiding by those who might have felt we were being disrespectful at best and vandalous at worst'.[59]

Martin Carthy describes a generally mixed reaction to early English folk-rock and states that outright hostility was rare, although he maintains that there were sometimes positive reactions to early English folk-rock from people from whom he expected dislike. For example, Carthy stated that 'Bert [A. L.] Lloyd thought it was great' and that Dave Swarbrick (the Fairport Convention violinist) suggested to Fairport Convention that Lloyd should join the band.[60] Carthy also described to me the confused reaction of a folk music fan who had reservations about folk-rock:

> There were people who came up to me and said 'Gosh, this is immoral, I like it, I don't understand, it's immoral and I like it, cos it's electric music and that represents everything that's bad, but it's great.' The guy that said it to me actually realised that it was his problem and he went away and worked it out. He then went to our gigs, enjoyed them and then talked to us afterwards.[61]

Negative reactions to folk-rock music were not confined to folk music fans. Carthy maintains that 'rock purists' were often critical on the grounds that Steeleye Span 'was sullying their [the rock fans'] favourite form'.[62] Carthy described the negative reaction of a rock music fan:

One guy decided that what we were doing had nothing to do with rock and roll and actually stepped on the stage and tried to pull Peter Knight's fiddle out of his hand. And people at rock and roll gigs threw pennies at us cos folkies were plugging in and they didn't like that.[63]

This statement supports my view that issues of authenticity in each stylistic component within English folk-rock are paramount to audience expectations among respective fans of each style, although this particular event also demonstrates a preconception of folk performance on the part of the rock fans involved.

Carthy also described audience reception of *Bright Phoebus* by The Watersons (1972) – an album containing original songs composed by Lal and Mike Waterson – as 'hostility and bewilderment', and the recording did not become commercially successful for several years.[64] Carthy compares this example to more recent reception problems that Eliza Carthy experienced when she signed to Warner Brothers Records and began to release self-composed material. For Martin Carthy, criticism from factions in both folk and rock audiences is nowadays evenly spread and not as evident as it once was. He convincingly argues that this may reflect fragmentation in musical tastes of contemporary audiences whose tastes are more diverse and who are used to 'weirdness' in music that often promotes open-mindedness.[65]

I discussed the initial years of English folk-rock with Karl Dallas, who collaborated as a songwriter with Ewan MacColl in the 1950s and who had attended many performances at MacColl's 'Ballad and Blues Club'. During the 1970s, Dallas had been a *Melody Maker* music journalist, and, when I asked him about the negative audience reception described by performers I had interviewed, he claimed that the overwhelming reaction to folk-rock was very positive:

It was absolutely super-enthusiastic. Tim Hart [a member of Steeleye Span] goes on about how they got put down in folk clubs and on the folk scene for Steeleye's electric stuff but that wasn't my experience. Everybody thought they were great...everybody thought it was wonderful, lots of people thought it was funny, I mean it was a thing which had been growing. I have to confess though, I didn't give a bugger what the audience thought, I just thought it was wonderful.[66]

Between the 1950s and the 1970s, the weekly *Melody Maker* music newspaper was published for a readership consisting mainly of professional and semi-professional musicians, as well as musically informed popular music fans. The paper contained interviews with prominent musicians and performance previews and reviews and, significantly for musicians such as me, a classified advertisement section that acted as a musical 'situations vacant' notice board attracting the attention of musicians aspiring to professional musical employment. As a newspaper primarily for musicians, *Melody Maker* was supportive of the emergence of progressive rock in the late 1960s. Dallas, in his role as a member of the paper's review staff at that time, attended and enthusiastically reviewed diverse concerts throughout his tenure with the publication, although his favourable reviews of punk bands in the late 1970s were written with enthusiastic zeal similar to that in his reviews of the emergence of progressive rock music. In the punk period, however, Dallas' earlier complimentary reviews of progressive rock were at odds with most other rock journalists, who viewed punk as the antidote to what they perceived as the technical excesses of progressive rock. In 1981, Dallas wrote a review of a concert at which I performed with rhythm and blues pianist Zoot Money at Ronnie Scott's, the leading jazz club in London.[67] This concert took place during a week of Money's performances at the venue and band members found each performance particularly difficult, given the contradiction between our musical style – which encompassed blues, rock and funk music – and the reputation of the club as a prestigious jazz performance centre, and the musical expectations of its audience. Audience reception was sometimes enthusiastic among those who had come to see Money – whose performances were often exuberantly humorous and provocative – but it was often negative among those who had expected to listen to jazz excluding any amalgamation with other popular music styles. Dallas' review of the concert was, in keeping with the majority of his reviews, very enthusiastic and he mentioned most band members by name.[68] As in the 1970s, Dallas' broad musical views were unlike most rock journalists in the 1980s, many of whom were biased in favour of a particular musical style, and it could be argued that his positive reception of diverse styles, however commendable, might lack critical integrity. I therefore regard his views on enthusiastic audience reception of English folk-rock stated above as debatable given experiential accounts from performers. I applaud, however, the passionate nature of his musical eclecticism and open-mindedness to the musical changes in popular music that occurred between the 1950s and 1980s.

While the above descriptions of audience reception mainly relate to bands widely regarded as the founders of the English folk-rock style, they provide a valuable insight into continuing debate among folk fans and rock fans that surrounds reception of this style and reception of traditional folk music performance. Previous chapters have investigated contentious issues in English folk-rock, such as electrification and change to existing musical structures and texts of folk songs, although application of the audience reception concept suggests that debate among the traditional folk music audience often results from negative perceptions of 'star' status linked to notions of commercialism that run counter to the perceived sense of community in the folk music audience. Application of this concept to English folk-rock audiences indicates that these issues have always been able to exist concurrently within an audience framework that supports status among performers, while providing audience access to the performer within a perceived communal forum.

The following accounts present my own descriptions of audience reception of folk and rock amalgamations from both performer and audience member perspectives. These accounts are drawn from a broad range of performance locations that were often outside the rock venues in which English folk-rock was originally performed, and they provide insights into folk-rock performance, and rock performance that drew upon folk influences, from the 1970s to the 1990s.

Personal accounts of audience reception in rock music and English folk-rock

In the capacity of my own performances in bands from both the rock and folk-rock genres, as well as my attendance at folk clubs and folk festivals from the 1970s to the 1990s, I often experienced and witnessed negativity from folk audiences who were critical of the use of electric instrumentation and the performance of a folk repertoire that many perceived as inauthentic. As a performer, and as an audience member, I attended folk festivals of various sizes that took place in various parts of the United Kingdom. The demands of consistent stylistic diversity in professional performance settings equipped me with musical skills necessary to perform in a variety of musical contexts, as well as in a variety of musical environments ranging from small clubs to large open-air festivals. I was thus able to perform in all of the stylistic contexts that Frith describes in his descriptions of audience reception, including art music, folk music, pop, rock and jazz.[69] Frith notes that art music performance is often measured by the stillness it commands and by the intensity of the audience's mental concentration, although this can also be applied to performance of folk music and jazz, and in particular to my own experiences as a performer in English folk-rock bands.[70]

These experiences illustrate that an audience whose perception of community is bound by a notional series of knowledge-based mores is also able to isolate itself through aspects of disapproval to other musical styles as perceptions of purity become reinforced through elitism and exclusivity. While I apply this critical description to factions of the folk and jazz audiences in the 1970s and the 1980s, my audience reception concept for English folk-rock – performer/audience rapport, perceptions of rock status in an informal setting, professional levels of sound reproduction and notions of audience as community – does not include aspects of isolation that might be exclusionary to new audience members.

My later performance experience at diverse clubs and festivals extended to Europe, Scandinavia, Canada, Yugoslavia, Hungary, the Middle East and Australia. By this time, I had been a professional musician for over ten years and had become used to the demands of international touring. I had also become aware of a change in my attitude towards touring itself. Being asked to perform on extended trips around the world was initially similar to being on a paid musical vacation – a probable factor in my choice of career – but, by the 1980s, I found that the touring process outside of actual performance was becoming less stimulating, and I started to note differences between approaches to performance among those artists who employed me, the reaction of their audiences, and differences in reception from one geographical region to another. In analysis of this experience, I maintain that reception was particularly enthusiastic in countries whose audiences had limited opportunities to see popular music performers from the UK and the United States, and that issues concerning musical authenticity were less of a concern than the musical style of the performance and the reputation of the performer. For example, while performing with rock singer Eric Burdon during the 1980s, I often played at folk festivals in the Basque region of northern Spain.[71] These festivals had a Marxist ethos and the folk element inherent in them was closely linked to regional politics. While Burdon cannot be described as a folk singer in the traditional sense, the messages in his lyrics – which were often influenced by those of Bob Dylan and Bruce Springsteen – could be reinterpreted for a variety of ambiguous political purposes, particularly in terms of political and social protest. Burdon emphasised notions of protest during performances as a means of relocating himself from established performer to communal member of the audience, an aspect in his performances that drew upon audience notions of performer/ audience rapport, and that particularly suited Marxist-orientated folk festivals. Burdon had similar enthusiastic receptions at folk-orientated festivals in Yugoslavia and Hungary in the mid-1980s, immediately prior to political upheaval in both countries. Conversely, Burdon performed in Israel as part of a concert tour in that country during which audiences aspiring to American culture interpreted the protest-orientated content of his lyrics as pro-American. One of Burdon's performances in Israel took place at the Ben Gurion University of the Negev and it was particularly memorable because of the nationalist demonstration that followed it during which students of the university sang protest songs in Hebrew stating their claim to the state of Israel. The band was later informed by the concert promoter that the students interpreted Burdon's performance as supportive of this cause.

The descriptions above fit the audience reception concept in terms of performer/audience rapport and rock performer status, both of which are linked to audience notions of community. Given the rock music orientation of Burdon's reputation as a singer, it is mainly the audience as community aspect of his

performances that links to my hypothesis on audience reception to folk music. Performer/audience rapport and performer
status have often co-existed within the arena of rock music. For
the purpose of describing my own accounts of folk audience
reception in the UK, however, I draw from specific festival and
club experiences that I regard as significant to my hypotheses
on audience expectation and reception. Issues concerning rock
instrumentation, volume or age groups were never apparent at
any of the folk-orientated festivals and clubs at which I performed when overseas, although audience reception in the UK
was often fixed in advance of a performance.

Between 1991 and 1997, I performed with Jerry Donahue, a
guitarist who had been a member of Fairport Convention in the
1970s, and who regularly performs at Fairport Convention
reunions at the annual Cropredy Festivals. I was nearing the end
of my touring career and had become a lecturer in music at
Thames Valley University. Nevertheless, Donahue's invitation
to join his band, which came at a time when I was also working
sporadically with David Gilmour of Pink Floyd, was a welcome
alternative given that Donahue's tours were often quite short
and lasted only two to three weeks. Donahue's band, The Back-
room Boys, were all session musicians drawn from bands such
as 10cc, Jethro Tull and The Albion Band, and it was one of
several that have been formed by Fairport alumni. As such, we
toured regularly and performed in the United Kingdom, Europe
and Scandinavia. Working with Donahue, an American, provided a valuable insight into his personal approach to the performance of English folk-rock, as well as anecdotal information
on the approaches to it that were adopted by Fairport Convention. The session musician nature of the band line-up attracted
audiences mostly made up of musicians, and the performance
emphasis was based more on musical virtuosity than on the
kind of stage shows that I had performed in the 1980s. Consequently, audience reception was at its most enthusiastic when
band members, and in particular Donahue, performed intricate
musical passages and improvised solos. This provided me with
the opportunity to focus on audience reception as I did not have
to consider stage choreography.

Donahue's club and festival audiences consisted of a broad
age range, were of mixed gender and tended to be drawn by

awareness of his tenure with Fairport Convention. Due to the nature of festivals such as these, Donahue's performances were always enthusiastically received within a variety of folk-influenced music performers presented on stylistically diverse artist rosters. Donahue's performances at folk clubs in the UK, however, were sometimes greeted by an initial unenthusiastic reception that related to our use of amplification and drums, despite audience awareness of Donahue's English folk-rock reputation and the content of his recordings. Audiences often remained unenthusiastic and seemed uninterested during the early part of our performances, regardless of our repertoire consisting of familiar folk-rock songs and material from Donahue's solo albums. This disapproval gradually dissipated once we commenced performing, particularly if we were in a public-house setting.

At a performance at The Rockingham Arms folk club in Rotherham during 1993, the band was asked to lower its volume several times during the sound check, and during the first hour of performance. The folk club meeting took place in a hall adjoining the Rockingham Arms public house, which was part of a brewery chain selling organic beer. The folk club served two types of beer, one at a similar alcohol level to most other bitter beers and the other with a higher alcohol level at 6 per cent. During a break in our performance, the promoter asked the band if anyone would like refreshments and several band members asked for the lower alcohol beer. When it was served, the members realised that they had been given the stronger beer. Audience reception in the second half of the performance improved noticeably and we were asked to perform several encores. As we packed our equipment at the end of the evening, the promoter informed us that the bar staff had mistakenly sold the high alcohol beer throughout the evening believing it to be the lower option. Many members of the audience attending this performance had come to see Donahue because of his earlier reputation with Fairport Convention and most were part of an older age group whose expectation related to an arguably nostalgic view of English folk-rock. Although the audience became more receptive as the evening progressed, there is a correlation that can be made between the amount of alcohol consumed – albeit unwittingly – and the marked difference in audience reception in the latter part of the evening. Audience inhibitions, set by protocols inherent in folk club attendance, had thus become less of a concern and less apparent to audience members to the extent that the band received encores, and sold several CD recordings. Audience reception at this performance also indicated that preconceptions of what English folk-rock once was and what it had become in the 1990s were no longer compatible to factions of the folk audience who may have been receptive to the style at its inception.

In 1997, I attended an open-air performance by Maddy Prior at the Sidmouth Folk Festival, during which I witnessed audience criticism of the combination of amplification and perceived folk music performance that was similar to criticism described above. Prior was the main artist at this festival and her open-air concert provided an insight into how a founder member of Steeleye Span had been able to develop and expand a new musical identity, which included the use of electric instrumentation and Musical Instrument Digital Interface (MIDI) technology, enabling several instruments to be pre-programmed for simultaneous performance. The concert also provided a dichotomy in terms of what differing sections of the audience at this concert expected from Prior. Prior's support act was Coope, Boyes and Simpson, an *a cappella* trio whose vocal abilities featured sophisticated harmonies that would be well received at a jazz concert and whose repertoire was drawn from several musical styles. Their pre-performance sound check involved the balance of on-stage personal monitoring and was less problematic than that of Prior and her musicians, which had preceded it.[72] Prior's musicians, Nick Holland, who played a variety of MIDI-enabled keyboards, and Troy Donockley, who played electric and acoustic stringed instruments and pipes, had to check the balance of every instrument they would later use. The balance between the vocal performance and the variety of sound textures created by her musicians was crucial to the success of Prior's performance.

The generally middle-class audience ranged from young children accompanied by parents to a broad cross-section of both sexes between the approximate ages of late teenage to middle age and older people. Before the concert, the audience unpacked picnic hampers and deckchairs from parked cars, put children into sleeping bags and remonstrated with any member of the audience who was regarded as being too noisy or over-enthusiastic. The behaviour of sections of the audience was similar to audiences that MacKinnon has observed in folk clubs that have protocols for behaviour at folk music performances during which any interruption, or expression of enjoyment is regarded as detrimental to the performance.[73]

Despite their stylistic diversity, Coope, Boyes and Simpson's performance was well received, suggesting either eclecticism among the festival audience that reflected the festival's location within the world music genre, or willing acceptance of a supporting performance in anticipation of the perceived traditional folk performance that was to follow it. When Prior and her musicians performed their opening song, the sound engineer had to deal with a complex sound balance involving amplification of several electric instruments supporting a vocal performance that the audience expected to hear clearly. This was quickly achieved but, at the end of the first song, many members of the audience vociferously expressed their dissatisfaction with the sound balance and were outraged that the instrumental musicians were almost as loud as the singer. The audience members' shouting lasted several minutes and it left the sound staff in no doubt of audience members' opinions. Prior dealt with audience complaints quite calmly, although the audience reaction was unlike her descriptions of audience reception of Steeleye Span given in a radio interview in which she maintained that the band was as loud as other electric bands in the 1970s, even without a drummer.[74]

Rick Kemp, the Steeleye Span bassist following Ashley Hutchings' departure, supported Prior's description. He told me that the band was the loudest he had ever been in and that it was well received by an audience consisting of a mixture of folk music and rock music fans.[75] Kemp, however, recalls a negative reaction from folk performers at a Steeleye Span concert in London in 1971 when folk musicians Robin and Barry Dransfield left the band's performance by walking out 'noisily' to express their feelings towards English folk-rock, despite Barry Dransfield's performances on later English folk-rock projects.[76] Dransfield's more recent views concerning notions of folk music 'purity' are, however, different from his earlier criticism of folk music amalgamations. While discussing perceived differences between art music and folk music, he now states that his current recording project is intended as a means of negating 'the recent myths about art and folk music being so separate' and that 'all this music [folk music] is art music, and I wanted to put folk and classical music side by side to show that they were both as valuable to each other'.[77] It is significant that Steeleye Span did not play in folk clubs, unlike the performance forum familiar to the Dransfields, and this is a probable contributory factor to their protest in that the performance location for folk music was a rock concert.[78]

Prior describes Steeleye Span as 'loud and beefy', although she adds that long-term fans have often asked why they could not be 'like they once were, acoustic and quiet'.[79] I suggest that the audience reaction at the 1997 Sidmouth festival may therefore relate to generational issues, and, in particular, to personal expectations and nostalgia concerning what folk music – and English folk-rock music – represents to audiences who attended folk, rock and folk-rock concerts in their youth. Perceptions of English folk-rock as 'acoustic and quiet' are arguably due to nostalgic blurring of fans' first memories of English folk-rock, although these audience perceptions support my contention that folk music audience reception of aspects of rock music – such as instrumentation and volume – in English folk-rock performance relates to differences in the tastes of various age groups. It also often elicits a negative reception among members of the folk club scene.[80]

The modern folk audience and the maintenance of community

While folk audience perceptions of authenticity and identity in folk music often remain linked to notions of heritage and preservation, contemporary reception of English folk-rock relates to its relocation within the arena of world music, an aspect of re-branding that has also been experienced by many folk performers. Following Coope, Boyes and Simpson's performance at the 1997 Sidmouth festival, I asked Jim Boyes and Georgina Boyes (author of *The Imagined Village*) about their views on audience perceptions of stylistic identity of the trio, given the ensemble's live performance at what had become widely regarded as a world music festival and the trio's recent inclusion on a world music compilation of vocal music.[81] Georgina Boyes maintained that world music classification of the trio had been 'a huge step' that attracted a larger audience.[82] Jim Boyes commented that the trio enjoys playing on what he refers to as a 'mixed stage' and this aspect of performance does not change the trio's perception of itself, although he added that audience perceptions often change on hearing the ensemble and 'the barriers of 'the folk' seem to disappear, which for us is a great thing'.[83] Boyes also described performing in Europe where audiences 'don't have this narrow focus of what folk is about' and he maintains that European audiences demonstrate 'more openness to a lot of other kinds of music than there is in this country [the UK]'.[84] Jim Boyes puts it that UK reception of Coope, Boyes and Simpson is often centred on an audience perception of the trio as 'traditional', which is based upon them being a trio and the *a cappella* nature of their performance, although the word 'traditional' never appears in their publicity material. Audience expectations of tradition and authenticity therefore 'pre-brand' Coope, Boyes and Simpson before any performance takes place by a similar means to the folk audience expectations described above. Relocation to the world music genre has enabled Coope, Boyes and Simpson to attract new and larger audiences, although audience preconceptions of unaccompanied vocal music still situate them as traditional folk performers.

It would be erroneous to assume that musical diversity does not exist among members of the folk audience and that negative preconceptions govern reactions to change. I asked Derek Schofield, the editor of *English Dance and Song*, how he would compare audiences at world music festivals and those who prefer the traditional folk club scene.[85] Schofield maintains that folk audiences would have become eclectic sooner, but diversity was never made available to them. He posits that the Sidmouth festivals have always aimed for diversity, presenting 'everything from singers and performers in pub sessions and traditional performers in small scale things right the way through to dance groups and big bands'.[86] In his capacity as a folk music journalist and author, Schofield has received letters from folk fans that describe personal musical discoveries at Sidmouth that have encouraged 'new interests and new enthusiasms within the music' and he further adds that, given Sidmouth's longevity and the availability of the diverse presentations that are included within the single price of entry, 'the pop festivallers probably copied [single price-inclusive folk festival diversity] because folk festivals were there before rock festivals'.[87]

Issues of folk music authenticity remain apparent in the perception of English folk-rock among some factions of the folk audience. Georgina Boyes described meeting folk audience members who refuse to listen to folk music they regard as contemporary, maintaining that the general view is 'if it wasn't produced in the twenties or the thirties, I'm not interested in it'.[88] These issues therefore extend beyond those concerning performance practice, retention of original texts and the inclusion of protocols of behaviour that are often more in keeping with the art music concert hall, and towards issues surrounding isolationism within an exclusivist framework.

As Moore notes while discussing issues of authenticity in rock music, perceptions of authenticity are a matter of interpretation made, and 'fought for', from within an isolated, cultural and historicised position, which is an equally applicable statement among some factions of the folk audience.[89] Folk fans and revivalists often reject change to established 'customs' and 'traditions'. Change to established 'tradition' includes any amalgamation of British folk music with popular music that is often regarded by folk fans as a threat to the perceived 'purity' of British folk music. In this way, they regard past traditions as providing 'roots' – or links to the past – that are the opposite of their perceptions of the novelty of the modern world and mass culture. Factions within the folk audience often seek to preserve what they regard as vestiges of history that they perceive as links to an imagined past, or the 'roots' of the tradition being revived. These roots must be preserved from change inherent in modern society, including new popular music styles that revivalists regard as 'root-less'.

Folk audience perceptions of 'roots' as links to an invented past also imply continuity existing in notions of a folk community – albeit often exclusivist. While discussing the aspects of continuity in community – or roots – within the English folk-rock audience, however, Simon Nicol observes that the contemporary Fairport Convention audience is 'vertically stretched' with up to four generations of families attending. He describes the age groups within this audience as 'of an age with us – now in their late 50s who attended early band performances at clubs or at universities'.[90] These members also bring family members whose first experience of the band occurred when they were 'exposed to early LPs as a form of automatic baby sitting and then given a life-changing opportunity to run about in a safe festival field for a happy, muddy and liberating weekend with other five year olds from all over the world'.[91]

Nicol also maintains that there now exists a younger Fairport Convention audience, which has been attracted to the band through the acoustic folk scene in the UK, and that this audience also listens to performers he regards as the 'high profile young Turks' of the contemporary folk scene, such as Eliza Carthy, Kate Rusby and Seth Lakeman.[92] Nicol has it that members of these performers' audiences judge Fairport Convention in the context of contemporary music and that, if they wish to gain more from folk music, 'the history is there IF they choose to go back and explore it'.[93]

This statement suggests that English folk-rock – as well as more recent folk and popular music amalgamations – is listened to on various levels and that its musical identity is able to remain separate from notions of heritage and preservation. Significantly, as Martin Carthy has noted, there is 'a new folk circuit' that is independent and 'has its own rules' for 'a very young and vibrant audience'.[94] It is the same audience that Nicol has observed following Eliza Carthy, Rusby and Lakeman, as well as, arguably, Jim Moray and Bellowhead, among others. This audience is also part of the fragmentation described by Carthy and it has initiated many sub-genres of folk music, such as 'nu-folk', 'twisted folk', 'alt-folk' and 'folktronica'.[95] As music industry journalist Kate Wildblood observes, 'Folk music is a vital British tradition but without new blood, traditions die out. Today's folk scene seems to be embracing the new folk, embracing the many family ties and enjoying the genre twisting we're currently witnessing'.[96]

Within a new phase of revivalism, audience reception differs among factions of the folk audience. Performer descriptions, as well as my own, indicate that there is a faction of this audience that prefers to retain a nostalgic view of authenticity, tradition and preservation, while attending informal folk performance in the intimate environment of the folk club. This particular environment for folk performance may be in decline as folk-orientated festivals presented as world music festivals demonstrate audience growth and re-definition. Audience preferences often relate to generational issues – as demonstrated by Prior's 'like it used to be' statement – although there is also a new folk circuit aligned with festival performance. Moreover, folk performers appear at folk clubs as well as at world music festivals in the United Kingdom. This new performance phenomenon demonstrates that the new folk audience does not share a critical view of commercial issues and embraces a globalised view of folk music. Globalisation in modern folk music can be regarded as positive, given that market expansion has occurred as British folk music has become amalgamated with other musical styles while retaining its identity and creating new audiences. Global concepts of cultural diversity and relativism support preservation of individual traditions in folk music as well as the uniqueness and self-reference of musical ethnicities within it.

In the context of world music, English folk-rock has been relocated within the musical diversity of new folk sub-genres that elevate its reception above negative folk audience perceptions of authenticity and protocols of behaviour. The new folk scene, as described by Carthy, embraces both electrically and acoustically performed folk music, creating its own new 'stars' within an emerging folk industry that has been acknowledged by government-sponsored media and by the UK recording industry, while providing foundations for a new audience as community.

Notes

1 Frith, 'Music and Identity', 41.
2 Simon Frith, "'The Magic That Can Set You Free': The Ideology of Folk and the Myth of the Rock Community' *Popular Music* 1 (1981), 159 and 164.
3 Anderson, 'A Weekend of Britfolk', 4.
4 Vulliamy, 'Cropredy', 28.
5 Nicol, December 1996.

6 Livingston, 'Music Revivals', 69.

7 Livingston, 'Music Revivals', 66.

8 Livingston, 'Music Revivals', 68–9.

9 Frith, *Performing Rites*, 123.

10 Frith, *Performing Rites*, 123.

11 MacKinnon, *The British Folk Scene*, 77–9.

12 Martin Carthy, email correspondence with author, 2 July 2007. My own memorable examples of enthusiastic audience/performer interaction at live folk concerts are performances given by Carthy and by Robin Williamson at the Kings Head Folk Club in Crouch End, London during the late 1990s. Both concerts were unforgettable because audience reception included both intense listening as well as members of the audience cheering during demonstrations of technical virtuosity.

13 Frith, *Performing Rites*, 124.

14 James Porter, 'Convergence, Divergence, and Dialectic in Folksong Paradigms: Critical Directions for Transatlantic Scholarship', *Journal of American Folklore* 106:419 (1993), 78.

15 Rosenberg, 'Introduction', in *Transforming Tradition*, 7–8.

16 Andrew Bennett, 'Going Down the Pub!: The Pub Rock Scene as a Resource for the Consumption of Popular Music', *Popular Music* 16:1 (1997), 97.

17 Bennett, 'Going Down the Pub!', 97.

18 This concert took place at the Anvil Theatre in Basingstoke in 2002.

19 Nicol, interview, December 1996.

20 Ed Bicknell, interview with author, September 1997.

21 Friars Club was arguably the most influential progressive rock club during the late 1960s and early 1970s. Artists performing at the club included the Pretty Things, Free, Blodwyn Pig, King Crimson, Pink Floyd, John Peel, Principal Edward's Magic Theatre, Mott the Hoople, Genesis and Van Der Graaf Generator.

22 Alan Lessem, 'Bridging the Gap: Contexts for Reception of Haydn and Bach', *International Review of the Aesthetics and Sociology of Music* 19:2 (December 1988), 137.

23 Lessem, 'Bridging the Gap', 138.

24 Lessem, 'Bridging the Gap', 138.

25 Lessem, 'Bridging the Gap', 139.

26 Frith, *Performing Rites*, 25.

27 Lessem, 'Bridging the Gap', 139.

28 Lessem, 'Bridging the Gap', 139.

29 Lessem, 'Bridging the Gap', 148.

30 Atkinson, 'Folk Songs in Print', 457–8.

31 Helmut Rösing, 'Listening Behaviour and Musical Preference in the Age of 'Transmitted Music', *Popular Music* 4 (1984), 119.

32 Rösing, 'Listening Behaviour and Musical Preference', 119.

33 Frith, *Performing Rites*, 41; Rösing, 'Listening Behaviour and Musical Preference', 120.

34 Rösing, 'Listening Behaviour and Musical Preference', 121.

35 Rösing, 'Listening Behaviour and Musical Preference', 122.

36 Rösing, 'Listening Behaviour and Musical Preference', 123.

37 MacKinnon, *The British Folk Scene*, 43, and Heap and Barcan, email correspondence with author, 2001–05.

38 MacKinnon, *The British Folk Scene*, 43.

39 MacKinnon, *The British Folk Scene*, 38 and 43.

40 Carthy, email correspondence with author, 2 July 2007.

41 Helen Bell, 'Session Culture', *fROOTS* 27:10 (April 2006), 52. Bell is arguably referring to events such as the annual BBC Radio 2 Folk Music Awards, and to government-sponsored folk music education initiatives, such as the annual Folkworks Summer Schools in Durham.

42 Bell, 'Session Culture', 53.

43 Bell, 'Session Culture', 53.

44 Bell, 'Session Culture', 53.

45 Carthy, email correspondence, 2007, and Kate Wildblood, 'The New Folk', *M – The MCPS/PRS Members Music Magazine* 24 (2007), 27.

46 David Arthur, 'Editorial', *English Dance and Song* 63:3 (2001), 1.

47 Arthur, 'Editorial', 1.

48 Arthur, email correspondence, 16 August 2001.

49 Colin Irwin, 'The Face of Folk,' *fROOTS* 27:6 (December 2005), 21.

50 MacKinnon, *The British Folk Scene*, 121.

51 MacKinnon, *The British Folk Scene*, 121.

52 This is based on observations made by the author during attendances at folk club meetings, folk music concerts and folk festivals between 1992 and 2000 and MacKinnon's statistics of folk club attendance (*The British Folk Scene*, 38 and 43).

53 Conway, interview with author, January 1997 (italics added).

54 Hutchings, interview with author, May 1997.

55 Hutchings, interview, May 1997.

56 See Humphries, *Fairport Convention*, 43 for details of Fairport Convention's appearances at these venues.

57 Nicol, email correspondence with author, 28 June 2007.

58 Nicol, correspondence, 28 June 2007.

59 Nicol, correspondence, 28 June 2007.

60 Carthy, interview with author, March 1997.

61 Carthy, interview, March 1997.
62 Carthy, interview, March 1997.
63 Carthy, interview, March 1997.
64 Carthy, email correspondence, 2007.
65 Carthy, email correspondence, 2007.
66 Karl Dallas, interview with author, May 1997. Dallas is also a co-author of *The Electric Muse*, and co-authored the sleeve notes to the CD recording *The New Electric Muse: The Story of Folk into Rock* (1996).
67 Karl Dallas, 'Zoot Money: Caught in the Act', *Melody Maker*, 13 June 1981.
68 Despite my criticism of what I regard as Dallas' over-enthusiasm in most of his reviews, I am grateful for his description of my performance that night during which he says that I 'played a fine funky bass'.
69 Frith, *Performing Rites*, 36–9.
70 Frith, *Performing Rites*, 125.
71 Burdon was the former vocalist in The Animals. Following commercial success with this band in the 1960s, he sang with the American band War prior to becoming a solo artist. My tenure as bassist with Burdon lasted between 1982 and 1986.
72 A difficulty encountered by bands during sound checks is that the band due to perform last always has the first sound check. This obviously means that the first band to perform at a concert has had the final sound check and, therefore, has the advantage of being most recent to the ears of the person controlling the overall sound balance. The consequence on this occasion was that Coope, Boyes and Simpson's set started well and was successful, not just because of their excellent performance, but also because of the relative simplicity of their mixing requirements and the relatively short time since they had carried out their sound check.
73 MacKinnon, *The British Folk Scene*, 79.
74 Maddy Prior, interview by Ralph McTell, *Who Knows Where The Time Goes: The Story of English Folk-Rock*, BBC Radio 2, 9 November 1994.
75 Rick Kemp, interview with author, August 1997.
76 Kemp, correspondence with author, 11 July 2007. In 1972, Barry Dransfield performed on the recording *Morris On* with Richard Thompson, Ashley Hutchings and Dave Mattacks. In 1994, he toured the United Kingdom with Steeleye Span.
77 Barry Dransfield, interview with Elle Osborne, 'The Art Class', *fROOTS* 27:6 (December 2005), 35. Dransfield's project was the CD recording *Unruly* (2005).

78 The venue for the Steeleye Span performance was Hornsey Town Hall, a municipal building in north London.

79 Maddy Prior, interview by Ralph McTell, *Who Knows Where the Time Goes*, BBC Radio 2, 9 November 1994.

80 MacKinnon, *The British Folk Scene*, 38 and 43.

81 Coope, Boyes and Simpson recorded 'Jerusalem Revisited' on *One Voice: Vocal Music From Around The World* (1997).

82 Georgina Boyes, interview with author, August 1997.

83 Jim Boyes, interview with author, August 1997.

84 Jim Boyes, interview, 1997.

85 Derek Schofield is also the author of *The First Week in August: Fifty Years of the Sidmouth Festival*, which was published in 2004 to celebrate the festival's Golden Jubilee.

86 Schofield, correspondence, 2003.

87 Schofield, correspondence, 2003.

88 Georgina Boyes, interview, 1997.

89 Moore, 'Authenticity as Authentication', 210.

90 Nicol, correspondence, 28 June 2007.

91 Nicol, correspondence, 28 June 2007.

92 Nicol, correspondence, 28 June 2007.

93 Nicol, correspondence, 28 June 2007.

94 Carthy, email correspondence, 2007.

95 Carthy, email correspondence, 2007, and Ben Lane interviewed by Wildblood, 'The New Folk', 27.

96 Wildblood, 'The New Folk', 29.

The third folk revival 6

Issues of transformation surrounding contemporary folk music have been the subject of debate among scholars and folk music fans since the late 1960s. While Sharp's definitions of folk music have been justifiably criticised for being non-specific, his three principles, redefined, can provide useful descriptors that are appropriate to various aspects of English folk-rock music. As descriptors, continuity, variation and selection are relevant to folk music as it is amalgamated with rock music since various fusions of both styles continue to reflect their current environment, and since songs continue to be selected and transformed according to their performers' criteria. I have used the term 'British folk music' to distinguish between indigenous traditional folk music of the British Isles, with 'traditional' applied as a means of distinguishing between earlier styles of folk music performance and more recent electrified folk music performance that is distinct from rock influences. 'English folk-rock' is an established commercial term, although I have used it as a means of distinguishing between this music and the folk-rock styles originally popularised in the United States of America, as well as between folk-influenced rock music of Wales and the predominantly Celtic-influenced folk-rock music of Scotland and Ireland.

Fairport Convention and Steeleye Span were the first bands to amalgamate traditional British folk songs and rock music. I describe these bands in particular as 'English folk-rock' rather than by diverse descriptions that might be pertinent to other bands in the folk-rock and folk-influenced arenas, and despite the Fairport Convention and Steeleye Span repertoires having drawn on folk music from all of the British Isles. I have also used these bands as distinctive examples of English folk-rock on the grounds that both have had almost continuous careers lasting over thirty years. During this period their repertoires have continued to maintain each band's original musical policy of retaining perceived authentic aspects of the source versions they adapted, a practice that remains apparent in their more recent folk-informed songs. Neither band has deviated from this policy.

Performers' descriptions from interviews suggest that throughout the formative years of English folk-rock to the present, tradition has co-existed with innovation. This relationship has continued as contemporary British folk music has gradually encompassed a broader, and more representational, stylistic mix of influence from other British musics, thus embracing the dimensions of continuity, variation and selection. The consensus of all interviewees is that British folk music is robust and withstands change and that it can change with its environment. They also agree that folk music in the United Kingdom at the beginning of the twenty-first century is more stylistically diverse than it was fifty years ago at the beginning of the second folk revival. English folk-rock music has been subject to change since the late 1960s. The style has demonstrated the effects of culture industry commercialisation on performer and audience perceptions of folk music, as well as change in terms of performance practice and the alteration of song texts. Growth in audience attendance at folk festivals in the United Kingdom, particularly since the mid-1990s, demonstrates that commercial processes have enabled elements of continuity in folk music. These elements remain apparent through the promotion and marketing of folk music amalgamated with rock music, and attract new audiences outside the established folk club scene.

Continuity, variation and selection exist in the context of English folk music as it has become relocated from a progressive rock style to the mainstream styles of world, roots and rock music. English folk-rock consequently attracts larger audiences, while retaining notions of national identity. Within a heritage distribution model, in which culture industry hegemony supplies performer interpretation and production for audience reception and consumption, the presentation of traditional British folk music as English folk-rock becomes a nationalising, communal artefact. This artefact is produced within the hegemony of a socio-political culture industry as a means of promoting re-branding of national identity within the British Isles, particularly in the post-devolution period. While devolution of the United Kingdom since the late 1990s has enabled individual national assemblies for Scotland, Wales and Northern Ireland, the absence of an English national assembly remains antithetical to the consolidation of a modern English identity. The emergence of a post-progressive-rock English folk-rock style has, however, enabled new folk music fusions to establish themselves in a populist performance forum that is both club and festival orientated. In this way, English folk-rock has promoted the emergence of a new English cultural identity that is distinct from negative social and political connotations that are often linked to nationalism, colonialism and xenophobia. A significant contemporary national identity for British folk music consequently exists in English folk-rock as it is presented as part of a homogenous mix of world music styles.

Contemporary perceptions of Englishness – and, in particular, its location within notions of Britishness – have been influenced by the promotion of English folk-rock in the context of commercial and political relationships from the late 1960s to the present day. Connections between English folk-rock promotion and popular music-industry business techniques have also enabled a new phase of folk music revivalism that preserves notions of English and British tradition and heritage. The newly emerging folk music revival also embraces the commercial character of popular music that was often viewed as anathema by twentieth-century folk revivalists. English folk-rock performers have enjoyed a commercial advantage given that the style has its origins in a popular music industry that has both avoided negative associations with nationalism and used standard business practice as a means of marketing, promotion and distribution. English folk-rock adoption of music industry business practices has also provided the style for over three decades with a more eclectic audience base than that of the traditional folk music scene. Contemporary dissemination of British folk music

– in various stylistic formats – occurs within its own newly created culture industry and is often facilitated by a symbiotic relationship between folk and popular music styles.

Despite increases in audience attendance at UK world music festivals presenting folk music of the British Isles, there remains debate concerning English folk culture linked to earlier perceptions of English cultural identity. Negative associations in the twenty-first century still prevent relocation and re-branding of English folk music as a notional national heritage that could be endorsed in similar ways to Scottish, Welsh and Irish folk music, and thus re-contextualise English identity. An appropriate definition of modern British folk music could therefore be 'music in which the performance practice and lyric content demonstrably represent its ethnic origins and cultural identity'. An alternative view is that, if 'British' folk music were to be marketed in terms of its regional origins, then it follows that audience perceptions of English, Irish and Scottish folk music would be reinforced as separate entities, instead of being acknowledged as diverse variations of a singular folk music of the British Isles. This issue becomes compounded by the inclusion of new cultures and ethnicities present in each geographical area whose members often regard themselves as multicultural within a broad perception of Britishness.

Terms such as world, roots and international, which are often used to advertise stylistically diverse music festivals, demonstrate a blurring of boundaries that previously separated folk music performance from other performance styles. Stylistic differences between artists performing at world music festivals indicate that concerns about the globalisation of British folk music are unfounded among many folk fans. Growth in folk festival attendance is therefore an example of the interrelation of regionality with musical multi-lingualism and inter-culturalism. Audience growth further reflects diversity in musical tastes and cultural backgrounds of modern folk and folk-rock performers, modern folk audiences and, in particular, English folk-rock audiences. Potential for further expansion of the new folk music audience may, however, be compromised by a political establishment whose positive stance on values inherent in the folk music of the British Isles seems at odds with its recent legislation concerning live music performance.

Perception of English folk music as difficult to sell or sounding quaint in comparison with Irish and Scottish folk music is a subjective issue. There is some scepticism within the UK concerning a cultural mix that might amalgamate folk music from its different cultures. Commercial promotion of any folk music style may be perceived by some folk fans as commodification, leading to further globalisation and leading some critics to warn that folk music of the British Isles will ultimately become devoid of individual identity. Global concepts of cultural diversity and relativism, however, support preservation of individual traditions in folk music, as well as the uniqueness and self-reference to musical ethnicities within it. This aspect of commercialism provides the most discernible link between audience and performer perceptions of tradition and heritage in English folk-rock, and it indicates that there is a new phase of folk revivalism emerging, particularly from the world music arena. Notions of authenticity in folk music and opposition to what was regarded as commerciality were, nevertheless, central to twentieth-century British folk revivalism, and the 'Ghost of Electricity' remains a source of debate between factions of the folk music audience in the UK.[1]

Performer accounts of the amalgamation of folk music and popular music demonstrate that variation and selection become apparent in the reinterpretation of folk songs adapted to contemporary audience taste and that songs maintain continuity through the retention of original textual messages. From a perspective of debate among folk fans concerning perceived authenticity, there are many modern folk performers whose performances are regarded by traditional folk fans as inauthentic, but whose performance philosophies combine new practice with the maintenance and preservation of musical and textual aspects present in the source material adapted. A continuum is therefore apparent between the extreme views of 'purism' and 'modernism' concerning authenticity and the preservation of what audiences at both extremes regard as tradition. English folk-rock is situated at the centre of this continuum and it remains contested by folk music 'purists' and 'modernists' through the dialectics of perceived authenticity and heritage on the one hand and the influence of commercialisation on the other. At the purist extreme of the continuum, traditional British folk music is validated by invented tradition, and at the other extreme is an English folk-rock performer view that this music is transitory and constantly undergoing change. While revivalists in the second British folk revival regarded folk music amalgamated with popular music as inauthentic, notions of authenticity validated by perceptions of tradition have been present in English folk-rock since the late 1960s. Ironically perhaps, the space between the two extremes contains several commonalities that provide British folk music and English folk-rock with a unified identity.

Each extreme of this continuum defines a contested space that provides folk music with a symbolic, yet debated presence separating it from many popular music styles. A contemporary interpretation of continuity, variation and selection can therefore be regarded as enabling dissemination of folk music through its adaptation into English folk-rock settings, aided by music-industry-related aspects of commercialism. English folk-rock performers have become 'producers' of folk music and have established a recorded canon of folk music that is promoted on concert tours outside the established folk club scene. English folk-rock has, however, moved closer to aspects of tradition and historical status and has embraced a revivalist stance similar to that of the folk revivals that occurred in the UK during the twentieth century. Whereas revivalism often rejects manifestations of mass culture and modernity, the early combinations of folk music and rock music illustrate that aspects of preservation and commercialisation co-exist within English folk-rock. Rock music remains a stimulus for further change in folk music and has enabled English folk-rock to become regarded as popular music by a new audience with diverse musical tastes. When folk music is adapted into rock and popular music settings, the result represents a new and contemporary identity for folk music that attracts new audiences. From this perspective, growth in the popularity of British folk music can be also linked to its performance in a commercially driven popular music arena and to its consequent connections with culture industry marketing and promotion techniques. Recent growth in popularity can also be linked to British folk music's inclusion as a festival component presented to audiences as part of what is promoted as world music.

While there are certain commonalities in the origins of the principal English folk-rock bands, differences remain concerning stylistic policies, respective commercial success and the stylistic directions of later careers. As was the case in American folk-rock, a consumer-driven marketing process supported most of the early English folk-rock bands, although few of these bands had a formal plan for a repertoire amalgamating British folk and rock music. The first amalgamations of folk and rock music were more a question of expediency, rather than of design. Moreover, the development of English folk-rock was primarily instituted by stylistic and cultural trends of the late 1960s and early 1970s, and it was enabled by record company support. Continuity, variation and selection come to the fore in discussion of the adaptation of traditional folk music for English folk-rock performance and the construction of a canon of English folk-rock. In the transformation of folk songs for rock performance settings, performers attempted to retain many of the songs' traditional elements as a means of making folk songs relevant to contemporary audiences, while retaining aspects of perceived authenticity. Performance of folk music by a rock band initiates fundamental changes beyond the use of contemporary instrumentation, such as change to pulse, metre and text. Constant pulse restricts the freer pulse of traditional folk music performance and limits interpretive vocal expression, as demonstrated by my oscillographic representations of vocal performances in traditional folk and English folk-rock music. These limitations can be partially countered by manipulation of metrical structures that are often present in source versions, and that are outside the familiar common-time metre used in most rock music performance. Change in text settings performed in English folk-rock is often due to the constraint of an imposed constant pulse, although more significant textual changes occur as original textual content is re-located into modern contexts. Textual content in recently composed English folk-rock songs relocates representations of folk song authenticity in a process of traditionalisation (albeit invented). This becomes a further illustration of the central location of English folk-rock in a continuum between audience notions of the contemporary and the traditional. This continuum has therefore been driven by contemporisation – both textual and musicological – within a combined framework of notional maintained authenticity emerging through a process of traditionalisation. The continuum has led to a canon of recorded works that provides a regenerative approach to the field of folk music performance, research and preservation.

Musicological analyses of English folk-rock indicate not only that British folk music can withstand change, but also that its identity remains intact as it becomes absorbed into a contemporary milieu. Folk music adapted into rock settings since the late 1960s has led to a contemporary identity for folk music, despite absence of a formal plan for this endeavour. My analyses of pulse, metre and text also demonstrate that debate around the use of modern instrumentation remains a superficial concern. Equally, change in textual content of traditional British folk music often relates to relatively recent source versions and occurs in a process of contemporisation in which textual messages are adapted for modern settings. Contemporary performance practice in British folk music, within frameworks of notional authenticity and traditionalisation, thus remains part of an ongoing process of transformation that can be regarded as a positive phenomenon contributing to its canonisation through live performance and recordings.

English folk-rock has been relocated within the musical diversity of new folk sub-genres that elevate its reception above audience perceptions of authenticity. A perception of folk music denigration caused by its amalgamation with rock music still exists, however, among some factions of the folk audience. Conversely, adoption of music industry promotion processes facilitates enhancement of performer status, while avoiding separation between performer and audience that is often apparent in rock music. The location of an English folk-rock performance thus acts as a forum for aspects of rock performance, and as a communal gathering enabling a bonding process between audience and performer. Similarities are evident between ways in which folk music has been re-presented to audiences in popular music settings and the way in which the early collectors presented folk music to the Victorian and Edwardian public in edited, published formats. Changes to the performance practice of folk songs made by modern performers have arguably increased the popularity of British folk music. Perhaps, without this change in the period following the second folk revival, British folk songs might once again have faced relative obscurity. English folk-rock performers acted in a similar capacity to the early folk song collectors through their populist approach to performance practice and by their performance of folk music in a wide variety of venues to large audiences. The combination of folk music with various forms of popular music has increased folk music's accessibility. A similarity, therefore, exists between the modern performance of folk music and the views of collectors such as Sharp, who regarded the dissemination of folk music in easily accessible forms as vital to its preservation. Conversely, despite positive comments made by English folk-rock performers concerning folk and rock music amalgamations, there is also the possibility that the amalgamation of British folk music with other music styles might result in a homogeneous mix in which none of the elements is identifiable. The national heritage that the Victorian and Edwardian folk song collectors sought to preserve would thus be lost – a situation in which continuity of folk music performance might be regarded as ultimately destructive. English folk-rock music performance in the late twentieth and early twenty-first centuries presents folk music in new contexts, despite the potentially negative effect of homogenisation.

A canon of recorded English folk-rock has emerged since the late 1960s, which has been facilitated by contemporary audience expectation that live performance must match criteria set by production values in recorded media. As in rock music performance, live English folk-rock performance is expected to be an accurate representation of recorded work. Consequently, audience reception of English folk-rock performance relates less to perceived authenticity in adaptations of folk songs for rock performance than to the accurate live re-creation of recorded works that have become more recent 'source versions'. Audience reception is, however, not uniform. It differs within factions of the folk audience. Some descriptions from performers, as well as my own, indicate that a faction of this audience prefers to retain a nostalgic view of authenticity, tradition and preservation, keeping music 'like it once was'.[2] The traditional environment for folk performance is changing as folk-orientated festivals presented as world music festivals demonstrate audience growth. A new folk circuit has recently emerged concurrently alongside festival performance and whose performers appear at world music festivals. This demonstrates that the new audience does not share a critical view of commercial issues but embraces the notion of globalised folk music.

In conclusion, continuity, variation and selection are compatible and transferable. For example, continuity exists in English folk-rock performance enabled by a process of contemporisation of performance practice and by the use of modern instrumentation – two issues that have attracted audiences outside the British folk scene. The dimensions of variation and selection can be applied to commercial processes in folk-rock promotion and distribution, as business practices used by the popular music industry are adopted by the emerging English folk-rock music industry and by its performers. World-music-orientated folk festivals may be regarded as encouraging growth in eclecticism in the musical tastes of the audiences attending them, as well as in the performance styles of the artists performing at them. As UK folk festival audience sizes have increased, English folk music performed in rock music contexts has undergone variation and selection, while retaining continuity.

English folk-rock of the late 1960s and 1970s, including the musical amalgamations that followed it, was separate from the second folk revival. Folk-rock music performance in the late twentieth and early twenty-first centuries presents folk music in new contexts. Audiences experience folk music played in circumstances that are often musically varied and, perhaps, outside their musical tastes. As with the audience reception of early music, there are factions within the modern folk audience to whom perceptions of 'authenticity' in folk music performance are no longer pivotal issues. Moreover, growth in audience attendance at folk and world music festivals, combined with the influence folk music has had on popular music styles, has enabled the UK to experience what can be regarded as a 'third' folk revival. This started in the mid-1990s as a separate phenomenon, to which there has been no formal reference before now.

This revival is festival-based and has occurred during a period in which British folk music has adopted a world music perspective, nonetheless avoiding becoming part of any homogeneous mix. The modern folk festival of the late twentieth and early twenty-first centuries has provided its own musical context as audiences may experience varied and foreign concepts. Preservationist perceptions of 'authenticity' and 'tradition' in folk music performance are therefore no longer central issues in modern folk music, adding a new, non-Darwinian context to concepts of continuity, variation and selection. The revival is also performer-based, as many modern folk performers use combinations of traditional and modern music instrumentation, as well as music technology, as new means of cultural expression. The audience perception within a unified folk community of rapport between performer and audience supports notions of elevated performer status. This becomes a significant change in twentieth-century folk audience perceptions of the standing of performers, which formerly related to notions of equality between established performers and floor singers. Finally, the revival is audience-based. Festival audiences are presented with a broad cultural mix that includes folk music from the British Isles in modern contexts – while the music's cultural relevance and identity remain intact despite the variety of settings in which it is performed.

At the time of writing, Fairport Convention's annual Cropredy Festival has provided a performance forum for the band, and for bands formed by past members, for over twenty-five years. It is significant therefore that Steeleye Span performed at the first 'Spanfest' in July 2007, and was engaged in an anniversary tour between 2009 and 2010, indications of the commodity status of English folk-rock in which preservation, commercialism and authenticity co-exist in a process of continuity, variation and selection.

Notes

1 Heylin, *Dylan*, 100–7.
2 I paraphrase a statement made by Maddy Prior in an interview by Ralph McTell (*Who Knows Where the Time Goes*, BBC Radio 2, 9 November 1994). See chapter 5 for the statement in context.

Appendix 1

Stylistic diversity at United Kingdom rock music festivals

Headline artists appearing at events generally regarded as rock festivals that were promoted between 1969 and 2002 are listed below along with a description of their musical styles.

Table A1.1 Stylistic diversity in artist rosters at archetypal United Kingdom 'rock' festivals between 1969 and 2009[a]

Date	Festival	Artists appearing	Musical styles
1969	Isle of Wight Festival	The Who, The Band, The Nice, Joe Cocker, Pentangle, Bob Dylan, Julie Felix, Tom Paxton, Richie Havens	Rock, country-rock, progressive rock, folk music performed in a jazz context, folk music performed in a rock context and solo folk performers

Table A1.1 (*Continued*)

Date	Festival	Artists appearing	Musical styles
1970	Isle of Wight Festival	The Doors, The Jimi Hendrix Experience, The Who, Emerson, Lake and Palmer, The Moody Blues, Miles Davis, Joan Baez, Richie Havens, Ralph McTell, Leonard Cohen	Rock, blues-based rock, progressive rock, jazz fusion and folk music
1970	The 10th National Plumpton Blues Festival	Deep Purple, Yes, Elton John, The Incredible String Band, Magna Carta	Blues-based rock, progressive rock, pop and folk music
1970	The Yorkshire Folk Blues and Jazz Festival	The Who, Yes, The Pretty Things, Pentangle, Fotheringay, The Amazing Blondel	Rock, progressive rock, folk music performed in a jazz context, folk-rock and folk music
1972	Great Western Express, Lincoln	The Beach Boys, The Faces with Rod Stewart, The Strawbs, The Boys of the Lough	Pop, rock, progressive rock and folk music
1973	National Jazz, Blues and Rock Festival, Reading	The Faces with Rod Stewart, Aerosmith, Genesis, Richard and Linda Thompson, Tim Hardin, John Martyn	Rock, progressive rock and folk music
1975	National Jazz, Blues and Rock Festival, Reading	Hawkwind, Thin Lizzy, Yes, Mahavishnu Orchestra, Alan Stivell, String Driven Thing	Rock, progressive rock, jazz fusion and folk music
1975	Crystal Palace Garden Party	Jack Bruce, Carla Bley, Billy Cobham, Steeleye Span	Progressive rock, jazz and folk-rock

(*Continued*)

Table A1.1 (*Continued*)

Date	Festival	Artists appearing	Musical styles
1978	Reading Rock	Status Quo, Foreigner, Patti Smith, The Albion Band	Rock, punk and folk-rock
1979	Knebworth	Led Zeppelin, Fairport Convention	Rock, folk-rock
1982	The Glastonbury Festival	Van Morrison, Aswad Richie Havens, Roy Harper	Blues- and jazz-based rock, reggae and folk music
1984	The Glastonbury Festival	The Smiths, Elvis Costello, Ian Dury, Joan Baez	Rock and folk music
1987	The Glastonbury Festival	Elvis Costello, Robert Cray, Paul Brady	Rock, blues and folk music
1992	The Glastonbury Festival	Primal Scream, Shakespears Sister, The Levellers	Rock, pop and folk-rock
1997	The Cropredy Festival[b]	Osibisa, The Julian Dawson Band, Fairport Convention	African-influenced rock, blues-based rock and folk-rock
1997	The Glastonbury Festival	The Smashing Pumpkins, Radiohead, Sting, The Oysterband, The Levellers, Billy Bragg, Beth Orton	Rock, folk-rock and folk music
2000	The Cropredy Festival	All About Eve, The Hamsters, Robert Plant, Fairport Convention, The Albion Band, The Incredible String Band	Pop, blues-based rock, folk-rock and folk music
2001	The Glastonbury Festival	Bill Wyman's Rhythm Kings, Suzanne Vega, Richard Thompson, The Levellers, The John Tams Band, Show of Hands	Blues and jazz, pop, folk-rock and folk music

Table A1.1 (*Continued*)

Date	Festival	Artists appearing	Musical styles
2001	Guildford Live 2001	Pulp, Cast, James, The Saw Doctors, Bert Jansch, Lonnie Donegan	Pop, rock, folk-rock, folk music and skiffle
2001	Reading Festival	Manic Street Preachers, Teenage Fan Club, Folk Implosion	Rock, pop and folk music
2002	Guildford Live	Hawkwind, The Pretenders, Echo and the Bunnymen, Lonnie Donegan	Rock, pop and skiffle
2002	Isle of Wight Festival	Ash, The Charlatans, Robert Plant, Tin Lids, Kevin West, Arlen	Pop, rock and folk music
2004	The Glastonbury Festival	Paul McCartney, Muse, Oasis, Franz Ferdinand	Pop and rock
2006	V Festival	Radiohead, The Charlatans, Seth Lakeman, Paul Weller	Progressive rock, folk and rock
2007	The Cropredy Festival	Wishbone Ash, Seth Lakeman, Fairport Convention, Jools Holland's Rhythm and Blues Orchestra	Progressive rock, folk, folk-rock, rhythm and blues
2008	The Glastonbury Festival	Kings of Leon, Jay-Z, The Verve, Neil Diamond, Shakin' Stevens, The Levellers	Rock, rap, pop, rock and roll and folk-rock
2009	V Festival	Oasis, Snow Patrol, Seth Lakeman	Rock and folk

Notes: [a] This table does not include WOMAD world music festivals, which have been promoted since 1982.

[b] This festival is promoted annually by Fairport Convention. It presents a mixture of folk and rock artists as well many past and present members of Fairport.

Source: www.ukrockfestivals.com and www.efestivals.co.uk in addition to personal communications in a number of internet chat rooms.

Table A1.2 Artists appearing at the Cambridge Folk Festival between 1986 and 2009

Year	Artists appearing and their musical styles[a]
1986	Flaco Jiminez (Texan/Mexican conjunto music), Bo Diddley (rock and roll), Lindisfarne (rock music), Martin Carthy (folk music), Neil Innes (singer-songwriter with an emphasis on satire), Charlie Musselwhite (blues) and Danny Thompson (jazz)
1987	Beausoliel (Cajun/Zydeco dance music), Michelle Shocked (singer-songwriter in a rock music style), Dick Gaughan (folk music), The Albion Band and Magna Carta (English folk-rock)
1988	Christy Moore (folk music), Tanita Tikaram (pop music), Martin Carthy (folk music), The OysterBand (English folk-rock), 10,000 Maniacs, Tom Robinson, Nick Lowe (rock music)
1989	Nanci Griffith (country music), Lyle Lovett (country music), Fairground Attraction (pop music), The Kursaal Flyers (rock music), Ali Farka Tourè (guitarist from Mali, West Africa), The Watersons (folk music)
1990	Rory Gallagher Band (blues/rock), Michelle Shocked (rock), June Tabor (folk), The Albion Band (English folk-rock), Jo Ann and Dave Kelly (acoustic blues)
1991	Clannad (Irish folk-rock), Suzanne Vega (pop music), Roddy Frame (pop music), Rumillajta (Andean music played with pan pipes, guitar and drums), The Charlie Musselwhite Band (blues)
1992	Nanci Griffith (country), Buddy Guy and Band (blues), The Blues Band (blues), Gallagher and Lyle (pop), Robyn Hitchcock and The Egyptians (rock)
1993	Christy Moore, The Dubliners (folk music), John Mayall and The Bluesbreakers (blues), Tom Robinson (rock music), C. J. Chenier and The Red Hot Louisiana Band (Cajun/Zydeco dance music)
1994	Joan Baez (folk music), The Saw Doctors (Irish folk and pop music), Billy Bragg (folk music), Jools Holland (rhythm and blues), Steeleye Span (English folk-rock), Ralph McTell (folk music)
1995	Elvis Costello, Nick Lowe and The Impossible Birds, Lindisfarne (folk-influenced rock music), Clarence Gatemouth Brown (blues), Ashley Hutchings Dance Band (English folk-rock), Sharon Shannon (folk music)

Table A1.2 (*Continued*)

Year	Artists appearing and their musical styles[a]
1996	Ray Davies (seminal singer-songwriter), Penguin Café Orchestra (jazz), Oysterband (English folk-rock), Altan (Irish folk-rock)
1997	Jackson Browne, Hothouse Flowers (rock music), Eddie Lejeune and The Morse Playboys (Cajun/Zydeco dance music), Afro Celt Sound System (combination of Celtic folk music with Afro-American dance music), Steve Earle (country-rock music), Jools Holland and his Rhythm and Blues Orchestra (jazz influenced rhythm and blues), the London Community Gospel Choir (Afro-American gospel music), Richard Thompson (English folk-rock), the Boys of the Lough (folk music)
1998	Taj Mahal (blues), The Dillards (country), Nick Lowe (rock), Klezmer Festival Band (klezmer)
1999	Nick Cave (rock music), Suzy Bogguss (country music), The Blind Boys of Alabama (blues), James Taylor (acoustically orientated singer-songwriter whose music varies between folk and jazz), Norma Waterson and Martin Carthy (folk music), Oysterband (English folk-rock)
2000	Juan De Marcos' Afro-Cuban All stars (Latin), Dr John (funk), Glenn Tilbrook (rock), Ani Difranco (singer-songwriter in a rock style), Eddi Reader and Boo Hewerdine (pop)
2001	The Levellers, Richard Thompson Band (English folk-rock), Suzanne Vega (pop music), Bill Wyman's Rhythm Kings (rhythm and blues), Black Umfolosi (Zimbabwean a cappella group)
2002	Joe Strummer and The Mescaleros, Indigo Girls, Chumbawumba (rock), Billy Bragg, The Dubliners, Eliza Carthy and Martin Greene (folk), Taraf De Haidouks (Romanian folk music), John Prine (folk)
2003	Steve Earle (country-influenced rock), The Saw Doctors (Irish rock), Afro Celt Sound System (electronic dance with Celtic influences), Rosanne Cash (country), Orchestra Baobab (Senegalese pachanga band), Julian Cope (rock), Linda Thompson (folk), Eliza Carthy Band (folk with rock influences), Roddy Frame (pop)

(*Continued*)

Table A1.2 (*Continued*)

Year	Artists appearing and their musical styles[a]
2004	Jimmy Cliff (reggae and ska), Beth Orton (folk influenced pop), The Levellers (folk-rock), The Divine Comedy (pop), Mariza (Portuguese fado performer), Asleep At The Wheel (country and western swing), Keb' Mo' (blues), Ralph McTell, Loudon Wainwright III, Sharon Shannon, Bert Jansch (folk)
2005	Christy Moore (folk), Lucinda Williams (country), The Blind Boys Of Alabama (gospel *a cappella* group), The Proclaimers (pop), Mavis Staples (soul), Jimmy Webb (composer of seminal pop songs), Kate Rusby (folk), KT Tunstall (pop), Rodney Crowell (country), Kathryn Tickell Band, Karine Polwart, Bellowhead (folk)
2006	Emmylou Harris (country), The Chieftains (folk), Richard Thompson (English folk-rock), Cerys Matthews (singer-songwriter), Eddi Reader (singer-songwriter), Capercaillie (folk)
2007	Joan Baez (folk), Nanci Griffith (country), The Waterboys (rock), Steve Earle (country-influenced rock), Kate Rusby (folk), Toots & The Maytals (rock steady and reggae), Ricky Skaggs & Kentucky Thunder (country), Toumani Diabaté & Symmetric Orchestra (West African Mande performers), Sharon Shannon, Bellowhead (folk)
2008	k.d. lang, Joan Armatrading (rock), The Imagined Village (folk collective drawing on world music styles), Billy Bragg, Judy Collins (folk), Allen Toussaint (New Orleans rhythm and blues), Seth Lakeman, Eliza Carthy (folk)
2009	Lucinda Williams (country), Los Lobos (Mexican rock), The Saw Doctors (Irish rock), Booker T. (soul), Paul Brady, The Waterson Family, Buffy Sainte-Marie (folk), Oumou Sangare (Malian Wassoulou performer), Beth Nielsen Chapman (country), Bellowhead, Cara Dillon (music)

Note: [a] Descriptions of artists not performing in mainstream rock or pop music styles taken from Broughton *et al.*, *World Music: A Rough Guide*.
Source: Laing and Newman, *Thirty Years of the Cambridge Folk Festival*, 88–105 and information supplied by the festival coordinator, Eddie Barcan.

Appendix 2

Examples of performance differences in folk songs recorded by traditional folk singers and by English folk-rock performers

The following oscillographic illustrations are further comparative analyses of two folk songs that have been recorded by traditional folk singers and by English folk-rock performers. The first song is 'Lord Bateman' recorded by Joseph Taylor in 1906 and it is one of several that were collected from Taylor by Percy Grainger in Brigg in Lincolnshire between 1906 and 1908. Jim Moray also recorded the song in 2003. The second song is 'Copshawholme Fair', recorded by Bob Forrester in 1953, as well as by Steeleye Span in 1970. Each pair of performances presents its own issues of pulse and timing, with some unaccompanied singers performing with a pulse constancy that is normally associated with rock music. There are, nevertheless, differences arising that are similar to those discussed in chapter 4 of this book. Oscillographic representations of unaccompanied vocal performances can be easily identified. Representations of vocal performances with rock band accompaniment have, however, been identified with the use of the digital clock in the transport window of the Pro Tools software used in these examples. This means of timing identifies each syllable sung in the rock band performances.

I have again measured the spaces between the oscillographic spikes that occur on the emphasised syllables of each line of the first verse of each song. The unaccompanied versions mostly demonstrate a level of interpretive freedom for the performer that is not available to performers singing in a rock music context, which is restricted by the use of constant pulse.

'Lord Bateman'

The first verse of Joseph Taylor's version of 'Lord Bateman' is as follows, with emphasised syllables in capitals:

Lord BATEman WAS a NOBLE lord,
A NOBLE lord of HIGH deGREE.
He SHIPP'D himself on BOARD a ship,
Some FOReign country he WOULD GO SEE.

'Lord' is on the final quaver of bar 1 and 'Bate' falls on beat 1 of bar 2. The spacing of each emphasised syllable in millimetres is as follows (see Figure A2.1 for the oscillographic representation). The spaces between each emphasised syllable are as follows:

BATE – 11 mm – WAS – 17 mm – NOBLE – 33 mm – NOBLE – 31 mm – HIGH – 9 mm – GREE – 25 mm – SHIPP'D – 31 mm – BOARD – 30 mm – FOR – 30 mm – WOULD – 4 mm – GO – 6 mm – SEE.

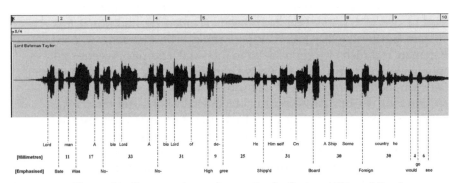

A2.1   Oscillographic diagram of sound waves in the first vocal line of 'Lord Bateman' by Joseph Taylor

Taylor starts the verse with three differently spaced syllables, although from the second line the distance between each emphasis is often between 30 and 33 millimetres indicating a sense of constant pulse in the performance. The non-emphasised syllables are mostly between 4 and 6 millimetres apart, a further indication that Taylor intended to sing within the framework of a rhythmical structure, albeit without the restriction that would be imposed by accompaniment. Jim Moray's first verse of 'Lord Bateman' is as follows, with emphasised syllables in capitals:

Lord BATEman WAS a NOBLE LORD,
NOBLE LORD of HIGH deGREE.
He PUT himSELF on BOARD a SHIP,
Some FOReign COUNtry he WOULD go SEE.

As with Taylor's version, Moray starts this verse with 'Lord' on the final quaver of bar 1, and the first syllable of bar 2 is 'Bate'. Moray omits 'A' at the beginning of the second line. The emphasised syllables are shown in an oscillographic representation in Figure A2.2. The spaces between each emphasised syllable are as follows:

BATE – 14 mm – WAS – 18 mm – NOBLE – 14 mm – LORD – 17 mm – NOBLE – 14 mm LORD – 18 mm – HIGH – 13 mm – GREE – 18 mm – PUT – 14 mm – SELF – 18 mm – BOARD – 13 mm – SHIP – 19 mm – FOR – 13 mm – COUN – 19 mm – WOULD – 14 mm – SEE.

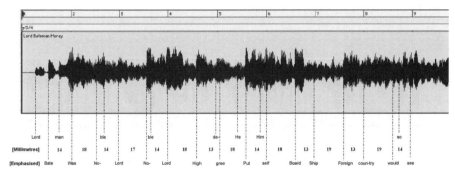

Oscillographic diagram of sound waves in the first vocal line of 'Lord Bateman' by Jim Moray

A2.2

Whereas Taylor's performance is in an approximate $\frac{4}{4}$ metre, Moray's contemporary accompaniment is in $\frac{5}{4}$ metre and his performance is regulated by the resulting pulse. Moray's $\frac{5}{4}$ metre uses an additive 3 + 2 structure and it is illustrated by the alternate spacings of between 17 and 19 millimetres and 13 and 14 millimetres that start at bar 2.

'Copshawholme Fair'

Bob Forrester's version of 'Copshawholme Fair' starts with two semi-quavers at the end of bar 1 with the words 'On a'. The first downbeat of bar 2 is 'Fri' of 'Friday'. Forrester sings in an approximate $\frac{6}{8}$ metre. The spaces between emphasised syllables are irregular, although, towards the end of the verse, there are four spaces that vary between 21 and 26 millimetres and suggest an almost regular pulse.

The emphasised syllables are as follows:

On a FRIday it FELL in the month of ApRIL,
O'er the HILLS came the MORN with her BLYTHE sunny SMILE,
And the FOLK were a'THRONGing the ROADS everyWHERE,
Making HASTE to be in at COPshawholme Fair.

An oscillographic representation of these emphases is shown in Figure A2.3. The spaces between each emphasised syllable are as follows:

FRI – 10 mm – FELL – 30 mm – RIL – 23 mm – HILLS – 11 mm – MORN – 10 mm – BLYTHE – 15 mm – SMILE – 26 mm – FOLK – 12 mm – THRONG – 21 mm – ROADS – 5 mm – WHERE – 22 mm – HASTE – 24 mm – COP.

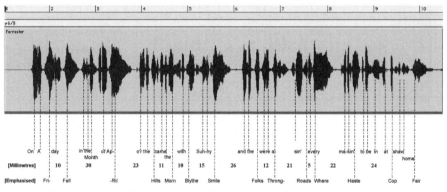

A2.3   Oscillographic diagram of sound waves in the first vocal line of 'Copshawholme Fair' by Bob Forrester

Steeleye Span's version of the song is also in $\frac{6}{8}$ metre, with the words 'On a' falling on the final two quavers of bar 1. The text is slightly different to Forrester's performance of the song, although the words scan with the melody in exactly the same way as the earlier version.

On a FINE ev'en FAIR in the MONTH of APRIL
O'er the HILL came the MORN with a BLYTHE sunny SMILE,
And the FOLKS they were THRONGING the ROADS everyWHERE,
Making HASTE to be IN at COPshawholme FAIR.

An oscillographic representation of these emphases is shown in Figure A2.4. The spaces between each emphasised syllable are as follows:

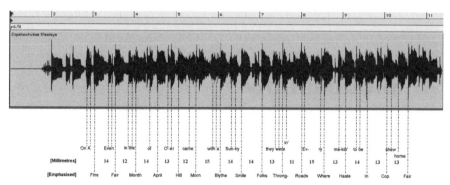

Oscillographic diagram of sound waves in the first vocal line of   A2.4
'Copshawholme Fair' by Steeleye Span

FINE – 14 mm – FAIR – 12 mm – MONTH – 14 mm APRIL – 13 mm – HILL
– 12 mm – MORN – 15 mm – BLYTHE – 14 mm SMILE – 14 mm – FOLKS –
13 mm – THRONGING – 11 mm – ROADS – 15 mm – WHERE – 13 mm –
HASTE – 14 mm – IN – 13 mm – COP – 13 mm – FAIR.

The Steeleye Span accompaniment demonstrates a constant pulse that
dictates the timing of the vocal performance, as illustrated by each
emphasised syllable being consistently between 11 and 15 millimetres
apart, with an average of 13 millimetres between them.

Bibliography

Abbott, Kingsley. *Fairportfolio*. Norfolk: Abbott, 1997.

Adorno, Theodor W. *Introduction to the Sociology of Music*. Translated by E.B. Ashton. New York: Continuum International Publishing Group, 1988.

——. *Aesthetic Theory*. Translated by Christian Lenhardt. London: Routledge and Kegan Paul, 1984.

——. *Jargon of Authenticity*. Translated by Knut Tarnowski and Frederic Will. London: Routledge and Kegan Paul, 1977.

—— and Max Horkheimer. *The Dialectic of Enlightenment*. London: Verso, 1979.

Anderson, Benedict. *Imagined Communities: Reflections on the Origin and Spread of Nationalism*. London: Verso, 1991.

Anderson, Ian. 'A Weekend of Britfolk', *fROOTS* 27:10 (2006): 34-7.

Appadurai, Arjun. *Modernity at Large: Cultural Dimensions of Globalization*. Minneapolis: University of Minnesota Press, 1996.

Armstrong, Frankie and Brian Pearson. 'Some Reflections of the English Folk Revival', *History Workshop Journal* 7 (1979): 95-100.

Arthur, David. 'Editorial'. *English Dance and Song* 63:3 (2001): 1.

Atkinson, David. 'Folk Songs in Print: Text and Tradition'. *Folk Music Journal* 8:4 (2004): 456-483.

——. 'Revival: Genuine or Spurious?' In *Folk Song: Tradition, Revival, and Re-Creation*, edited by Ian Russell and David Atkinson. Aberdeen: Elphinstone Institute, University of Aberdeen, 2004.

Atton, Chris. ' "Living in the Past?": Value Discourses in Progressive Rock Fanzines', *Popular Music* 20:1 (2001): 29-46.

Bacon, Tony. *London Live.* London: Balafon Books, 1999.

Badahir, Sefik Alp. 'Wohin treiben die Regionkulturen?' In *Kultur und Region im Zeichen der Globalisierung*, edited by Sefik Alp Badahir. Neustadt a. d. Aisch: Verlag Degener und Co. (Schriften des Zentralinstituts für Regiolforschung der Universität Erlangen: Nürnberg), 2000.

Baker Jr., Houston. 'Critical Memory and the Black Public Sphere'. In *Cultural Memory and the Construction of Identity*, edited by Dan Ben Amos and Liliane Weissberg. MI: Wayne State University Press, 1999.

Barnard, F. M. *Herder On Social And Political Structure.* London: Cambridge University Press, 1969.

Bartmann, Manfred. 'Spotlights on Festival History and Communication: Folk Legends Work on the Great Hits of Rock and Popular Music'. *The World of Music* 43:2 and 3 (2001): 193–206.

Baumann, Max Peter. 'Festivals, Musical Actors and Mental Constructs in the Process of Globalization'. *The World of Music* 43:2 and 3 (2001): 9–30.

Bearman, Alan. *Sidmouth 43rd International Folk Arts Festival Working Programme.* Buckinghamshire: Sidmouth International Festival Limited, 1997.

——. *The Sidmouth News.* Buckinghamshire: Sidmouth International Festival Limited, 1997.

Bearman, C. J. 'Who Were The Folk? The Demography of Cecil Sharp's Somerset Singers'. *The Historical Journal* 43:3 (2000): 751–5.

Bell, Helen. 'Session Culture'. *fROOTS* 27:10 (2006): 52–5.

Ben Amos, Dan. 'Afterword'. In *Cultural Memory and the Construction of Identity*, edited by Dan Ben Amos and Liliane Weissberg. Detroit, MI: Wayne State University Press, 1999.

Bennett, Andrew. 'Going Down the Pub!: The Pub Rock Scene as a Resource for the Consumption of Popular Music'. *Popular Music* 16:1 (January 1997): 97–108.

Bernstein, J. M., 'Introduction'. In *Culture Industry: Selected Essays on Mass Culture*, edited by J. M. Bernstein. London: Routledge, 1991.

Bessman, Jim. 'The Billboard Report: Rising Singer/Songwriters Redefine Folk In The '90s'. *Billboard*, 14 July 1994.

Bhabha, Homi K. *The Location of Culture.* London: Routledge, 1994.

Biddle, A. and L. Dolby. *Music: A Practical Guide For Teachers.* London: Murray, 1996.

Bird, John. *Percy Grainger.* London: Elek Books Limited, 1976.

Blacking, John. *A Common Sense View of All Music.* Cambridge: Cambridge University Press, 1987.

——. 'Making Artistic Popular Music: The Goal of True Folk'. *Popular Music* 1, Folk or Popular? Disfunctions, Influences, Continuities (1981): 9–14.

Blake, Andrew. *The Land Without Music*. Manchester: Manchester University Press, 1997.

Blaustein, Richard. 'Rethinking Folk Revivalism: Grass Roots Preservationism and Folk Romanticism'. In *Transforming Tradition*, edited by Neil V. Rosenberg. Chicago: University of Illinois Press, 1993.

Bohlman, Philip V. 'World Music at the "End of History"'. *Ethnomusicology* 46:1 (Winter 2002): 1–32.

——. 'Ethnomusicology's Challenge'. In *Disciplining Music: Musicology and its Canons*, edited by Katherine Bergeron and Philip V. Bohlman. Chicago and London: University of Chicago Press, 1992.

——. *The Study of Folk Music in the Modern World*. Bloomington and Indianapolis: Indiana University Press, 1988.

Boiko, Martin. 'The Latvian Folk Music Movement in the 1980s and 1990s: From "Authenticity" to "Postfolklore" and Onwards'. *The World of Music* 43:2 and 3 (2001): 113–18.

Bommes, Michael and Patrick Wright. '"Charms of Residence": The Public and the Past'. In *Making Histories: Studies in History Writing and Politics*, edited by Richard Johnson, Gregor McLennan, Bill Schwartz and David Sutton. London: Hutchinson, 1982.

Boyes, Georgina. *The Imagined Village-Culture, Ideology and the English Folk Rvival*. Manchester: Manchester University Press, 1993.

Bragg, Billy. *The Progressive Patriot*. London: Bantam Press, 2006.

——. 'That England'. *fROOTS* 22:11 (2001): 28–35.

Brocken, Michael. *The British Folk Revival 1944–2002*. Aldershot: Ashgate, 2003.

Bronson, Bertrand H. *The Ballad as Song*. Berkeley: University of California Press, 1969.

Brooks, Simon. *Diwylliant Poblogaidd a' Gymraeg*. Tal-y-Bont: Y Lolfa, 1996.

Burdon, Eric, and Jeff Marshall Craig. *Don't Let Me Be Misunderstood*. New York: Thunder's Mouth Press, 2001.

Burns, Robert G. H. 'Continuity, Variation and Authenticity in the English Folk-Rock Movement'. *Folk Music Journal* 9:2 (2007): 192–218.

——. Review of *Electric Folk: The Changing Face of English Traditional Music*, by Britta Sweers. *Folk Music Journal* 9:1 (2006): 111–13.

——. 'British Folk Music in Popular Music Settings'. In *Folk Song: Tradition, Revival, and Re-Creation*, edited by Ian Russell and David Atkinson. Aberdeen: Elphinstone Institute, University of Aberdeen, 2004.

——. 'Advanced Rock Techniques: Fairport Convention'. *Bassist*, July 1998, 72–6.

Cannadine, David. 'The Context, Performance and Meaning of Ritual: The British Monarchy and the "Invention of Tradition"'. In *The*

Invention of Tradition, edited by Eric Hobsbawm and Terence Ranger. Cambridge: Cambridge University Press, 1983.

Cantwell, Robert. 'When We Were Good: Class and Culture in the Folk Revival'. In *Transforming Tradition*, edited by Neil V. Rosenberg. Chicago: University of Illinois Press, 1993.

Carthy, Martin. Interview by Ralph McTell. *Who Knows Where The Time Goes: The Story of English Folk-Rock*, BBC Radio 2, 9 November 1994.

—— and Norma Waterson. Review of *The British Folk Revival: 1944–2002*, by Michael Brocken. *Folk Music Journal* 8:5 (2005): 646–9.

Castle, Pete. 'Is English Music Too Awkward?' *Traditional Music Maker* 43 (June 2000): 11.

Clarke, Donald. *The Rise and Fall of Popular Music*. New York: St Martin's Press, 1995.

Clarke, Robert T. Jr. *Herder: His Life And Thought*. Berkley: University of California Press, 1955.

Clayton-Lea, Tony and Richie Taylor. *Irish Rock: Where It's Coming From, Where It's Going*. Sidgwick and Johnson: Dublin, 1992.

Cohen, Sara. 'Identity, Place and the Liverpool Sound'. In *Ethnicity, Identity and Music*, edited by Martin Stokes. Oxford: Berg, 1994.

Commons Hansard, 'Culture, Media and Sport', Parliament Publication and Records, www.publications.parliament.uk/pa/cm200506/cmhansrd/cmo50712/debtext/50712-27.htm.

Cook, Deborah. *The Culture Industry Revisited*. Lanham, MD: Rowman and Littlefield, 1996.

Cook, Nicholas. *Music, Imagination and Culture*. Oxford: Clarendon Press, 1990.

Coombes, Annie E. 'The Recalcitrant Object: Culture Contact and the Question of Hybridity'. In *Colonial Discourse, Post-Colonial Theory*, edited by Patrick Williams, Nahem Yousaf and Jane Jacobs. New York: Manchester University Press, 1994.

Cope, Peter. 'Community-Based Traditional Fiddling as a Basis for Increasing Participation in Instrument Play'. *Music Education Research* 1:1 (1999): 61–73.

Cousins, Dave. Interview by Ralph McTell. *Who Knows Where The Time Goes: The Story of English Folk-Rock*, BBC Radio 2, 16 November 1994.

Crehan, Kate. *Gramsci, Culture and Anthropology*. Los Angeles: University of California Press, 2002.

Crick, Bernard. 'The English and the British'. In *National Identities*, edited by Bernard Crick. Oxford: The Political Quarterly Publishing Co, 1991.

Dallas, Karl, Robin Denselow, David Laing and Robert Shelton. *The Electric Muse: The Story of Folk Into Rock*, edited by Karl Dallas. London: Methuen Publishing, 1975.

Davenport, Paul. 'Five Men and an Idea'. *English Dance and Song* 66:3 (Autumn 2004): 17.

De Chiara, Marina. 'A Tribe Called Europe'. In *The Post Colonial Question: Common Skies, Divided Horizons*. London: Routledge, 1996.

De Ledesma, Charles and Simon Broughton. 'Out of the Orchid House: Calypso and Soca from Trinidad and Beyond'. In *World Music: The Rough Guide*, edited by Simon Broughton. London: Penguin, 1994.

Denisoff, R. Serge. *Great Day Coming: Folk Music and the American Left*. Urbana: University of Illinois Press, 1971.

Denselow, Robin. 'So, Who's it Going to Be? Pulp, Oasis or the Granny on your Right?' *Guardian*, 9 September 1996.

Department for Education and Employment. *About Music in the National Curriculum*. London: Qualifications and Curriculum Authority, 1999.

DeTurk, David A. and A. Poulin Jr. *The American Folk Scene: Dimensions of the Folksong Revival*. New York: Dell, 1967.

Dewe, Mike. *The Skiffle Craze*. Aberystwyth: Planet, 1998.

Donington, Robert. *The Interpretation of Early Music*. London: Faber, 1974.

Downing, Dave. *Future Rock*. St Albans: Panther, 1976.

Eden, Muriel. 'Letters'. *English Dance and Song* 62:4 (Winter 2000): 24.

Elschek, Oskár. 'Folklore Festivals and their Current Typology'. *The World of Music* 43:2 and 3 (2001): 153–69.

——. 'Traditional Music and Cultural Politics'. In *Music in the Dialogue of Culture: Traditional Music and Cultural Policy*, edited by Max Peter Baumann. Berlin: International Institute for Comparative Music Studies and Documentation, 1991.

Epstein, David. *Beyond Orpheus: Studies in Musical Structure*. Cambridge, MA: MIT Press, 1979.

Erlmann, Veit. 'The Aesthetics of the Global Imagination: Reflections on World Music in the 1990s'. *Public Culture* 8 (1996): 467–87.

——. 'Tradition, Popular Culture and Social Transformation'. In *Music in the Dialogue of Culture: Traditional Music and Cultural Policy*, edited by Max Peter Baumann. Berlin: International Institute for Comparative Music Studies and Documentation, 1991.

Everitt, Phil. 'Exploring Folk Culture in the Classroom'. *Lore and Learning: The Newsletter of the Folklore Society Education Group* 1 (1993): 16–24.

Featherstone, Mike. *Undoing Culture: Globalization, Postmodernism and Identity*. London: Sage, 1995.

——. *Consumer Culture and Postmodernism*. London: Sage, 1991.

Feintuch, Bert. 'Musical Revival as Musical Transformation'. In *Transforming Tradition*, edited by Neil V. Rosenberg. Chicago: University of Illinois Press. 1993.

Feist, Andy. *British Invisibles: Overseas Earnings Of The Music Industry*. London: British Invisibles, 1995.

Fletcher, Tony. *Dear Boy: The Life of Keith Moon*. London: Omnibus Press, 1998.

Floyd, M. *World Musics in Education*. Aldershot: Scholar Press, 1996.

Ford, Charles. '"Gently Tender": The Incredible String Band's Early Albums'. *Popular Music* 14:2 (1995): 175–83.

Ford, Robert. *Vagabond Songs and Ballads of Scotland*. Paisley: Alexander Gardner, 1899.

Forgacs, David and Geoffrey Nowell-Smith. *Antonio Gramsci: Selections from Cultural Writings*. London: Lawrence and Wishart, 1985.

Fox-Strangways, A. H. *Cecil Sharp*. London: Oxford University Press, 1933.

Francmanis, John. 'National Music to National Redeemer: The Consolidation of a "Folk-Song" Construct in Edwardian England'. *Popular Music* 21:1 (2002): 1–25.

Friedman, Jonathan. *Cultural Identity and Global Process*. London: Sage, 1994.

Frith, Simon. *Performing Rites*. Oxford: Oxford University Press, 1998.

——. 'Music and Identity'. In *Questions of Cultural Identity*, edited by Stuart Hall and Paul du Gay. London: Sage, 1996.

——. 'Popular Music and the Local State'. In *Rock and Popular Music: Politics, Policies and Institutions*, edited by Tony Bennett, Simon Frith *et al*. London and New York: Routledge, 1993.

——. *Sound Effects*. London: Pantheon, 1983.

——. '"The Magic that Can Set You Free": The Ideology of Folk and the Myth of the Rock Community'. *Popular Music* 1, Folk or Popular? Disfunctions, Influences, Continuities (1981): 159–68.

—— and Howard Horne. *Art Into Pop*. London: Routledge, 1987.

Fyfe, Pete. *Musicians' Union Folk, Roots and Traditional Music Directory*. London: Musicians' Union. 1999.

Gammon, V. 'One Hundred Years of the Folk Song Society'. In *Folk Song: Tradition, Revival, and Re-Creation*, edited by Ian Russell and David Atkinson. Aberdeen: Elphinstone Institute, University of Aberdeen, 2004.

——. 'Introduction: Cecil Sharp and English Folk Music'. In *Still Growing: English Traditional Songs and Singers from the Cecil Sharp Collection*, edited by Steve Roud, Eddie Upton and Malcolm Taylor. London: English Folk Dance and Song Society in association with Folk South West, 2003.

——. Review of *Two For The Show*, by David Harker. *History Workshop: A Journal of Socialist and Feminist Historians* 21 (1986): 147–56.

——. 'Folksong Collecting in Sussex and Surrey, 1834–1914'. *History Workshop Journal* 10 (1980): 61–89.

Gardiner, Michael. *The Cultural Roots of British Devolution*. Edinburgh: Edinburgh University Press, 2004.

Garnham, Nicholas. 'Contribution to a Political Economy of Mass Communication'. *Media, Culture and Society* 1 (1979): 123–46.

Gellner, Ernest. *Nations and Nationalism*. Oxford: Blackwell, 1983.

——. *Thought and Change*. London: Weidenfeld and Nicolson, 1964.

Gerstin, Julian. 'Reputation in a Musical Scene: The Everyday Context of Connections between Music, Identity and Politics'. *Ethnomusicology* 42:3 (Autumn 1998): 385–414.

Giddens, Anthony. *The Consequences of Modernity*. Cambridge: Polity, 1990.

Gillett, Charlie. *The Sound Of The City*. London: Souvenir Press, 1983.

Goertzen, Chris. 'The Norwegian Folk Revival and the Gammeldans Controversy'. *Ethnomusicology* 42:1 (Winter 1998): 99–127.

Goldstein, Kenneth. 'A Future Folklorist in the Record Business'. In *Transforming Tradition: Folk Music Revivals Examined*, edited by Neil V. Rosenberg. Chicago: University of Illinois Press, 1993.

——. 'Bowdlerization and Expurgation: Academic and Folk'. *Journal of American Folklore* 80 (1967): 374–86.

Green, Christopher. *BPI Statistical Handbook*, edited by Peter Scaping. Penryn: Troutbeck Press, 2001.

——. *BPI Statistical Handbook*, edited by Peter Scaping. Penryn: Troutbeck Press, 1998.

——. *BPI Statistical Handbook*, edited by Peter Scaping. Penryn: Troutbeck Press, 1995.

Green, Lucy. *How Popular Musicians Learn: A Way Ahead for Music Education*. Aldershot: Ashgate, 2001.

Grun, Bernard. *Timetables of History*. New York: Simon and Schuster/ Touchstone, 1991.

Hall, Stuart. 'Introduction: Who Needs Identity?' In *Questions of Cultural Identity*, edited by Stuart Hall and Paul du Gay. London: Sage, 1996.

——. 'The Local and the Global: Globalization and Ethnicity'. In *Culture, Globalization and the World-System*, edited by Anthony D. King. New York: State University of New York at Binghamton, 1991.

——. 'Cultural Identity and Diaspora'. In *Identity: Community, Culture, Difference*, edited by Jonathan Rutherford. London: Lawrence and Wishart, 1990.

——. 'Culture, the Media and the Ideological Effect'. In *Mass Communication and Society*, edited by J. Curran *et al*. London: Arnold, 1977.

Hammond, J.L. and Barbara Hammond. *The Skilled Labourer: 1760–1832*. London: Longmans, Green and Co., 1919.

Hanneken, Bernhard. 'Concepts and Contexts of the Tanz and FolkFest Rudolstadt'. *The World of Music* 43:2 and 3 (2001): 31–47.

Hardy, P. and D. Laing. *The Faber Companion To Popular Music*. London: Faber and Faber, 1990.

Harker, Dave. *Fakesong: The Manufacture of British 'Folksong' 1700 to the Present Day*. Milton Keynes: Open University Press, 1985.

——. 'May Cecil Sharp Be Praised'. *History Workshop Journal* 14 (1982): 44–62.

——. *One For the Money*. London: Hutchinson and Co., 1980.

——. 'Cecil Sharp in Somerset: Some Conclusions'. *Folk Music Journal* 2 (1972): 220–40.

Hebdige, Dick. *Subculture: The Meaning of Style*. London: Richard Clay Ltd, 1988.

Hewson, Robert. *The Heritage Industry: Britain in a Climate of Decline*. London: Methuen, 1987.

Heylin, Clinton. *Dylan: Behind the Shades*. London: Penguin, 1992.

Hinton, Brian and Geoff Wall. *Ashley Hutchings: The Guv'nor and the Rise of Folkrock*. Bath: The Bath Press, 2002.

Hobsbawm, Eric. *Nations and Nationalism since 1780: Programme, Myth, Reality*. Cambridge: Cambridge University Press, 1990.

—— and Ranger, T. *The Invention of Tradition*. Cambridge: Cambridge University Press, 1983.

Holmes, Edmond. *What Is and What Might Be: A Study in General and Elementary Education in Particular*. London: Constable, 1912.

Hood, Mantle. *Perspectives in Musicology*. New York: W. W. Norton, 1972.

Horne, Donald. *The Great Museum: The Re-Presentation of History*. London: Pluto Press, 1984.

Howes, Frank. *Folk Music of Britain and Beyond*. London and Southampton: Methuen, 1969.

Humphries, Patrick. *Fairport Convention: The Classic Years*. London: Virgin Books, 1997.

——. *Richard Thompson: Strange Affair*. London: Virgin Books, 1996.

Irvin, Jim. 'The Angel Of Avalon'. *Mojo* 49 (1998): 76.

Irwin, Colin. 'The New Folk Uprising'. *fROOTS* 27:11 (2006): 25–31.

——. 'The Face of Folk'. *fROOTS* 27:6 (2005): 20–7.

——. 'The New English Roots'. In *World Music: The Rough Guide*, edited by Simon Broughton. London: Penguin, 1994.

Jabbour, Alan. 'American Folklore Studies: The Traditions and the Future'. *Folklore Forum* 16 (1983): 235–47.

Jackson, Bruce. 'The Myth of Newport '65: It Wasn't Bob Dylan They Were Booing'. *Buffalo Report* (August 2002), http://buffaloreport.com/020826dylan.html.

——. 'The Folksong Revival'. In *Transforming Tradition*, edited by Neil V. Rosenberg. Chicago: University of Illinois Press, 1993.

Johnson, Julian. *Who Needs Classical Music?* New York: Oxford University Press, 2002.

Johnson, Robb. 'Does Folk Still Exist?', *Musician: The Journal of the Musicians' Union* (June 1998): 23.

Kärjä, Antti-Ville. 'A Prescribed Alternative Mainstream: Popular Music and Canon Formation'. *Popular Music* 25:1 (2006): 3–19.

Karpeles, Maud. *Cecil Sharp's Collection of English Folk Songs*. London: Oxford University Press, 1974.

——. *Cecil Sharp: His Life and Work*. London: Routledge and Kegan Paul, 1967.

Kartomi, Margaret. 'The Processes and Results of Musical Culture Contact: A Discussion of Terminology and Concepts'. *Ethnomusicology* 25 (May 1981): 227–49.

Katriel, Tamar. 'Sites of Memory: Discourses of the Past in Israeli Pioneering Settlement Museums'. In *Cultural Memory and the Construction of Identity*, edited by Dan Ben Amos and Liliane Weissberg. Detroit, MI: Wayne State University Press, 1999.

Kaufman Shelemay, K. 'The Ethnomusicologist and the Transmission of Tradition'. *The Journal of Musicology* 14:1 (1996): 35–51.

Keil, Charles. 'Motion and Feeling Through Music'. *Journal of Aesthetics and Art Criticism* 24:3 (1966): 337–49.

Kellner, Douglas. *Media Culture*, London and New York: Routledge, 1995.

Kennedy, Peter. 'Drop the Dead English'. *English Dance and Song* 62:4 (Winter 2000): 9.

——. *Folksongs of Britain and Ireland*. London: Oak Publications, 1984.

——. *Folksongs of Britain and Ireland: A Guidebook to the Living Tradition of Folksinging in the British Isles and Ireland*. London: Cassell, 1975.

Kent, Jeff. *The Last Poet: The Story of Eric Burdon*. Stoke-on-Trent: Witan Books: 1989.

Kenyon, Nicholas. 'Introduction: Some Issues and Questions'. In *Authenticity in Early Music*, edited by Nicholas Kenyon. Oxford: Oxford University Press, 1988.

Kerman, Joseph. 'A Few Canonic Variations'. *Critical Enquiry* 10:1 – Canons (September 1983): 107–25.

Kinsley, James. *The Poems and Songs of Robert Burns*. Oxford: Clarendon Press, 1968.

Laing, Dave and Richard Newman. *Thirty Years of the Cambridge Folk Festival*. Cambridge: Music Maker Books, 1994.

Leach, R. and R. Palmer. *Folk Music in School*. Cambridge: Cambridge University Press, 1978.

Leppard, Raymond. *Authenticity in Music*. London: Faber and Faber, 1988.

Lessem, Alan. 'Bridging the Gap: Contexts for Reception of Haydn and Bach'. *International Review of the Aesthetics and Sociology of Music* 19:2 (December 1988): 137–48.

Livingston, T. E. 'Music Revivals: Towards A General Theory'. *Ethnomusicology* 43:1 (Winter 1999): 66–85.

Llewellyn, Meic. 'Popular Music in the Welsh Language and the Affirmation of Youth Identities.' *Popular Music* 19:3 (2000): 319–39.

Lloyd, Albert Lancaster. *Folk Song in England*. London: Lawrence and Wishart, 1967.

Mabey, Richard. *The Pop Process*. London: Hutchinson, 1969.

Macan, Edward. *Rocking The Classics: English Progressive Rock and the Counterculture*. New York: Oxford University Press, 1997.

MacColl, Ewan. *Journeyman*. London: Sidgwick and Jackson, 1990.

MacColl, Ewan. *Traveller's Songs From England and Scotland*. London: Routledge and Kegan Paul, 1977.

MacDonald, Ian. *Revolution in the Head*. London: Fourth Estate, 1994.

Mach, Zdzislaw. 'National Anthems: The Case of Chopin as a National Composer'. In *Ethnicity, Identity and Music*, edited by Martin Stokes. Oxford: Berg, 1994.

MacInnes, Colin. '1958: Pop Songs and Teenagers'. In *The Faber Book of Pop*, edited by Hanif Kureishi and Jon Savage. London: Faber and Faber, 1995. (This essay was originally published as *England, Half English*. London: MacGibbon and Key, 1958).

MacKinnon, Niall. *The British Folk Scene: Musical Performance and Social Identity*. Buckingham: Open University Press, 1993.

Maniates, Maria Rika. 'The Reception of New Music Today: A Response'. *New Literary History* 17:2 – Interpretation and Culture (Winter 1986): 381–390.

Mayer Brown, Howard. 'Pedantry or Liberation? A Sketch of the Historical Performance Movement'. In *Authenticity in Early Music*, edited by Nicholas Kenyon. Oxford: Oxford University Press, 1988.

McCrone, David. *Understanding Scotland: The Sociology of a Stateless Nation*, London and New York: Routledge, 1992.

McGarr, Paul. 'Show Red Card to Nationalism', *SocialistWorkeronline*. www.socialistworker.co.uk/article.php?article_id=5400.

McLaughlin, Noel and Martin McLoone. 'Hybridity and National Musics: The Case of Irish Rock Music'. *Popular Music* 19:2 (2000): 181–99.

McNaughton, Adam. 'The Folksong Revival in Scotland'. In *The People's Past*, edited by E. J. Cowan. Edinburgh: Polygon, 1991.

Meyer, Leonard. *Style and Music: Theory, History and Ideology*. Philadelphia: University of Pennsylvania Press, 1989.

Middleton, Richard. *Studying Popular Music*. London: Taylor and Francis, 1991.

Mitchell, Gillian. *North American Folk Music Revival: National Identity in the United States and Canada 1945–1980*. Aldershot: Ashgate, 2007.

Moore, Allan F. 'Authenticity as Authentication'. *Popular Music* 21:2 (2002): 209–23.

——. *Rock: The Primary Text: Developing a Musicology of Rock*. Aldershot: Ashgate, 1993.

Morgan, Robert P. 'Rethinking Musical Culture: Canonic Reformulations in a Post-Tonal Age'. In *Disciplining Music: Musicology and its Canons*, edited by Katherine Bergeron and Philip V. Bohlman. Chicago: University of Chicago Press, 1992.

——. 'Tradition, Anxiety, and the Current Musical Scene'. In *Authenticity in Early Music*, edited by Nicholas Kenyon. Oxford: Oxford University Press, 1988.

Munro, Ailie. *The Folk Music Revival in Scotland*. London: Kahn and Averill, 1984.

Nairn, Tom. *The Break-Up of Britain: Crisis and Neo-Nationalism*. London: New Left Review Editions, 1977.

Nederveen Pieterse, Jan. *Globalization and Culture: Global Mélange*. Lanham, MD: Rowman and Littlefield, 2004.

Nettl, Bruno. *The Study of Ethnomusicology: Thirty-One Issues and Concepts* (2nd edition). Urbana and Chicago: University of Illinois Press, 2005.

——. 'Relating the Present to the Past: Thoughts on the Study of Musical Change and Culture Change in Ethnomusicology', *Music and Anthropology* (1996), www.muspe.unibo.it/period/MA/index/number1/nettl/number1/nettl/ne1.htm.

——. *The Western Impact on World Music: Change, Adaptation and Survival*. London: Collier Macmillan, 1985.

——. *Eight Urban Musical Cultures*, Urbana and Chicago: University of Illinois Press, 1978.

——. 'Some Aspects of the History of World Music in the Twentieth Century: Questions, Problems and Concepts', *Ethnomusicology* 22:1 (January 1978): 123–36.

Noyes, Dorothy and Roger D. Abrahams. 'From Calendar Custom to National Memory: European Commonplaces'. In *Cultural Memory and the Construction of Identity*, edited by Dan Ben Amos and Liliane Weissberg. Detroit, MI: Wayne State University Press, 1999.

Nunn, Dave. 'Folk Britannia'. *English Dance and Song* 68:2 (Summer 2006): 25.

Osborne, Elle. *The Art Class*. *fROOTS* 27:6 (2005): 35–8.

Paddison, Max. *Adorno's Aesthetics of Music*, Cambridge: Cambridge University Press, 1993.

Paine, Thomas. 'The Rights of Man'. In *The Complete Works of Thomas Paine*. Vol. 2, Part 2, Political and Miscellaneous. New York: The Freethought Press Association, 1954.

Palmer, John R. 'Yes "Awaken", and the Progressive Rock Style'. *Popular Music* 20:2 (2001): 243–61.

Palmer, Roy. *The Sound of History: Songs and Social Comment*. London: Pimlico, 1996.

——. *A Touch On The Times: Songs of Social Change 1770–1914*. Harmondsworth: Penguin Education, 1974.

Pearson, Roberta. 'Custer Loses Again: The Contestation over Commodified Public Memory'. In *Cultural Memory and the Construction of Identity*, edited by Dan Ben Amos and Liliane Weissberg. Detroit, MI: Wayne State University Press, 1999.

Pegg, Bob. Review of *One For The Money: Politics and Popular Song*, by Dave Harker. *Folk Music Journal* 4 (1981): 176–8.

——. *Folk: A Portrait of English Traditional Music, Musicians and Customs*. London: Wildwood House, 1976.

Peluse, Michael S. 'Not Your Grandfather's Music: Tsugaru Shamisen Blurs the Lines Between "Folk", "Traditional" and "Pop" '. *Asian Music* (Summer/Fall 2005): 57–80.

Perry, Charles. *The Haight Ashbury*. New York: Random House, 1984.

Phillips, Caryl. *The European Tribe*. London: Faber and Faber, 1987.

Pickering, Michael. 'The Study of Vernacular Song in England'. *Jahrbuch für Volkliedforschung* 33 (1988): 95–104.

——. 'Song and Social Context'. In *Singer, Song and Scholar*, edited by Ian Russell. Sheffield: Sheffield Academic Press, 1986.

—— and Tony Green. 'Towards a Cartography of the Vernacular Milieu'. In *Everyday Culture: Popular Song and the Vernacular Milieu*, edited by Michael Pickering and Tony Green. Milton Keynes: Open University Press, 1987.

Pollard, Michael. *Discovering English Folksong*. Princes Risborough: Shire, 1982.

——. *Folk Music in School*. London: Cambridge University Press, 1978.

Porter, James. 'Convergence, Divergence, and Dialectic in Folksong Paradigms: Critical Directions for Transatlantic Scholarship'. *Journal of American Folklore* 106:419 (1993): 61–97.

Prior, Maddy. Interview by Ralph McTell. *Who Knows Where The Time Goes: The Story of English Folk-Rock*, BBC Radio 2, 9 November 1994.

Prögler, J. A. 'Searching for Swing: Participatory Discrepancies in the Jazz Rhythm Section'. *Ethnomusicology* 39:2 (1995): 21–54.

Radulescu, S. 'Traditional Musics and Ethnomusicology'. *Anthropology Today* 13:6 (1997): 8–12.

Ramnarine, Tina K. *Ilmatar's Inspirations: Nationalism, Globalization, and the Changing Soundscapes of Finnish Folk Music*. Chicago: University of Chicago Press, 2003.

Reeves, James. *Idiom of the People*. London: Heinemann, 1958.

Rosenberg, Neil V. 'Introduction'. In *Transforming Tradition*. Chicago: University of Illinois Press, 1993.

——. 'Starvation, Serendipity, and the Ambivalence of Bluegrass Revivalism'. In *Transforming Tradition: Folk Music Revivals Examined*, edited by Neil V. Rosenberg. Chicago: University of Illinois Press, 1993.

Rösing, Helmut. 'Listening Behaviour and Musical Preference in the Age of "Transmitted Music"'. *Popular Music* 4, Performers and Audiences (1984): 119–49.

Russell, Ian. 'Stability and Change in a Sheffield Singing Tradition'. *Folk Music Journal* 5 (1987): 317–58.

Rutherford, Jonathan. 'A Place Called Home: Identity and the Culture Politics of Difference'. In *Identity: Community, Culture, Difference*, edited by Jonathan Rutherford. London: Lawrence and Wishart, 1990.

Schofield, Derek. *The First Week in August: Fifty Years of the Sidmouth Festival*. Matlock: Sidmouth International Festival, 2004.

——. 'Seaside Shuffles'. *fROOTS* no. 133 (1994): 28–32.

Scott, Derek B. *Music, Culture, and Society: A Reader*. Oxford: Oxford University Press, 2000.

Seeger, Pete. *The Incompleat Folksinger*, edited by Jo Metcalf Schwartz. Lincoln: University of Nebraska Press, 1972.

Shapiro, Anne Dhu. 'The Tune: Family Concept in British-American Folksong Scholarship'. PhD dissertation, Music Department, Harvard University, 1975.

Sharp, Cecil. *English Folk Song: Some Conclusions*. London: Simpkin, Novello, 1907. (Republished London: Methuen, 1954.)

——. *A Book of British Song for Home and School*. London: John Murray, 1904.

Sheldon Posen, I. 'On Folk Festivals and Kitchens: Questions of Authenticity in the Folksong Revival'. In *Transforming Tradition*, edited by Neil V. Rosenberg. Chicago: University of Illinois Press, 1993.

Shepard, L. 'A. L. Lloyd: A Personal View'. In *Singer, Song and Scholar*, edited by Ian Russell. Sheffield: Sheffield Academic Press, 1986.

——. 'Correspondence'. *Folk Music Journal* 2 (1973): 318–19.

Shepherd, John. 'The "Meaning" of Music'. In *Whose Music?*, edited by John Shepherd. London: Latimer New Dimensions, 1977.

——. 'Media, Social Process and Music'. In *Whose Music?*, edited by John Shepherd. London: Latimer New Dimensions, 1977.

Silverman, Carol. 'Learning to Perform, Performing to Learn'. *Journal of American Folklore* 108 (Summer 1995): 307–16.

Slobin, Mark. *Subcultural Sounds*. Hanover, NH: Wesleyan University Press, 1993.

——. 'Micromusics of the West: A Comparative Approach'. *Ethnomusicology* 36:1 (Winter 1992): 1–87.

——. 'How the Fiddler Got on the Roof'. In *Folk Music and Modern Sound*, edited by William Ferris and Mary L. Hart. Jackson: University Press of Mississippi, 1982.

Small, Christopher. *Musicking*. Middleton, CT: Wesleyan University Press, 1998.

——. *Music of the Common Tongue*. London: John Calder, 1987.

Smith, Anthony D. 'Towards a Global Culture?' In *Global Culture*, edited by Mike Featherstone. London: Sage, 1990.

Smith, Graeme. 'Irish Meets Folk: The Genesis of the Bush Band'. In *Music – Cultures in Contact: Convergences and Collisions*, edited by Margaret J. Kartomi and Stephen Blum. Sydney: Currency Press, 1994.

Stanford, Charles Villiers and Geoffrey Shaw. *The New National Song Book*. London: Boosey and Co., 1906.

Stevens, Halsey. *The Life and Music of Béla Bartók* (2nd edition). New York: University of New York, 1981.

Stokes, Geoffrey. 'American Made'. In *Rock of Ages: The Rolling Stone History of Rock and Roll*, edited by Ed Ward, Geoffrey Stokes and Ken Tucker. New York and Upper Saddle River, NJ: Rolling Stone Press/ Prentice Hall, 1986.

Stokes, Martin. 'Introduction'. In *Ethnicity, Identity and Music: The Musical Construction of Place*, edited by Martin Stokes. Oxford: Berg, 1994.

Stratton, Jon. 'Capitalism and Romantic Ideology in the Record Business'. *Popular Music* 3 (1983): 143–56.

Stump, Paul. *The Music's All That Matters: A History Of Progressive Rock*. London: Quartet, 1997.

Stutzmann, Alexandre. 'Europe's Fake ID'. *International Politics* 38:2 (June 2001): 94.

Sweers, Britta. *Electric Folk: The Changing Face of English Traditional Music*. Oxford: Oxford University Press, 2005.

——. 'Ghosts of Voices'. In *Folk Song: Tradition, Revival, and Re-Creation*, edited by Ian Russell and David Atkinson. Aberdeen: Elphinstone Institute, University of Aberdeen, 2004.

Sykes, Richard. 'The Evolution of Englishness in the English Folksong Revival 1890–1914'. *Folk Music Journal* 6:4 (1993): 446–490.

Symon, Peter. 'Music and National Identity in Scotland: A Study of Jock Tamson's Bairns'. *Popular Music* 16:2 (1997): 203–16.

Taruskin, Richard. *Text and Act*. New York: Oxford University Press, 1995.

——. 'The Pastness of the Present and the Presence of the Past'. In *Authenticity and Early Music*, edited by Nicholas Kenyon. Oxford: Oxford University Press, 1988.

Taylor, Timothy. *Global Pop: World Music, World Markets*. New York: Routledge, 1997.

Thompson, Richard. 'The Day the World Turned Day Glo'. *Mojo* 49 (January 1998): 76.

Todd Titon, Jeff. 'Reconstructing the Blues: Reflections on the 1960s Blues Revival'. In *Transforming Tradition*, edited by Neil V. Rosenberg. Chicago: University of Illinois Press, 1993.

Tomlinson Gary. 'Authentic Meaning in Music'. In *Authenticity and Early Music*, edited by Nicholas Kenyon. Oxford: Oxford University Press, 1988.

Tucker, Ken. 'Hard Rock on the Rise'. In *Rock of Ages: The Rolling Stone History of Rock and Roll*, edited by Ed Ward, Geoffrey Stokes and Ken Tucker. New Jersey: Rolling Stone Press/Prentice-Hall, 1986.

Unterberger, Richie. *Eight Miles High: Folk-Rock's Flight from Haight-Ashbury to Woodstock*. San Francisco: Backbeat Books, 2003.

Van Der Merwe, Peter. *Origins of The Popular Style*. Oxford: Oxford University Press, 1992.

Vaughan Williams, R. *National Music and Other Essays*. Oxford: Oxford University Press, 1947.

—— and A. L. Lloyd. *The Penguin Book of English Folk Songs*. Harmondsworth: Penguin, 1961.

Von Appen, Ralf and André Doehring. 'Nevermind The Beatles, Here's Exile 61 and Nico: "The Top 100 Records of All Time" – A Canon of Pop and Rock Albums from a Sociological and an Aesthetic Perspective'. *Popular Music* 25:1 (2006): 21–39.

Von Schoenebeck, Mechthild. 'The New German Folk-Like Song and its Hidden Messages'. *Popular Music* 17:3 (1998): 279–92.

Vulliamy, Ed. 'Cropredy'. *Guardian Guide: Festivals '97*, June 1997.

———. 'The Alter-Ego of Englishness'. *Guardian*, 11 August 1995.

———, and Graham Lee. *Pop, Rock and Ethnic Music in School*. Cambridge: Cambridge University Press, 1982.

Walker, Annie. 'It's Monday, So this Must Be Sidmouth'. *English Dance and Song* 63:3 (2001): 4.

Walser, Robert. *Running with the Devil: Power, Gender, and Madness in Heavy Metal Music*. Middletown, CT: Wesleyan University Press, 1993.

Watson, Ian. *Song and Democratic Culture in Britain*. New York: St Martin's Press, 1983.

Weber, William. 'The History of Musical Canon'. In *Rethinking Music*, edited by Nicholas Cook and Mark Everist. Oxford: Oxford University Press, 1999.

———. 'The Intellectual Origins of Musical Canon in Eighteenth Century England'. *Journal of the American Musicological Society* 47:3 (Autumn 1994): 488–520.

Weissberg, Liliane. 'Introduction'. In *Cultural Memory and the Construction of Identity*, edited by Dan Ben Amos and Liliane Weissberg. Detroit, MI: Wayne State University Press, 1999.

Welch, Chris. 'Gryphon: The 13th Century Slade'. *Melody Maker*, August 4, 1973.

Westwell, Paul. *Folk Music Report*. London: Executive Committee of the Musicians' Union, 1997.

Whiteley, Sheila. *The Space Between the Notes*. London: Routledge, 1992.

Wiggershaus, Rolf. *The Frankfurt School: Its History, Theories, and Political Significance*. Translated by Michael Robertson. Cambridge, MA: MIT Press, 1994.

Wildblood, Kate. 'The New Folk'. *M: The MCPS/PRS Members Music Magazine* 24 (June 2007): 24–9.

Witkin, Robert W. *Adorno on Popular Culture*. London: Routledge, 2003.

Witts, Richard. 'I'm Waiting for the Band: Protraction and Provocation at Rock Concerts'. *Popular Music* 24:1 (2005): 147–52.

Woods, Fred. *Folk Revival: The Rediscovery of a National Music*. Poole: Blandford Press, 1979.

Young, R. *Electric Eden: Unearthing Britain's Visionary Music*. London: Faber, 2010.

Zelizer, Barbie. 'The Liberation of Buchenwald: Images and the Shape of Memory'. In *Cultural Memory and the Construction of Identity*, edited by Dan Ben Amos and Liliane Weissberg. Detroit, MI: Wayne State University Press, 1999.

Ziff, Bruce and Pratima V. Rao. *Borrowed Power: Essays on Cultural Appropriation*. New Brunswick, NJ: Rutgers University Press, 1997.

Discography

Alan Price Set. 'I Put a Spell on You' (Nina Simone). Decca F12367. 1966. Seven-inch single.

The Albion Band. *The Prospect Before Us.* Harvest SHSP 4059. 1977. LP.

The Animals. 'Please Don't Let Me Be Misunderstood' (Nina Simone). MGM 13311. 1965. Seven-inch single.

The Battlefield Band. *At The Front.* Topic 12TS381. Originally recorded in 1978. CD.

The Beach Boys. *Pet Sounds.* Capitol CDP 7484212. 1967. CD.

The Beatles. *Sergeant Pepper's Lonely Hearts Club Band.* Parlophone PCS 7027. 1967. LP.

The Byrds. 'All I Really Want To Do' (Bob Dylan), *Mr Tambourine Man.* Columbia CL 2372. 1965. LP.

——. 'The Bells Of Rhymney' (Pete Seeger), *Mr Tambourine Man.* Columbia CL 2372. 1965. LP.

——. 'Chimes Of Freedom' (Bob Dylan), *Mr Tambourine Man.* Columbia CL 2372. 1965. LP.

——. 'Mr Tambourine Man' (Bob Dylan), *Mr Tambourine Man.* Columbia CL 2372. 1965. LP.

——. 'Spanish Harlem Incident' (Bob Dylan), *Mr Tambourine Man.* Columbia CL 2372. 1965. LP.

——. 'The Times They Are A'Changin'' (Bob Dylan), *Turn! Turn! Turn!* Columbia CS 9254. 1965. LP.

——. 'Turn! Turn! Turn! (To Everything there Is a Season)' (Pete Seeger), *Turn! Turn! Turn!* Columbia CL 9254. 1965. LP.

——. 'Eight Miles High' (Roger McGuinn, David Crosby and Gene Clarke). Columbia COL 483707 2. 1966. Seven-inch single.

——. *Sweetheart Of The Rodeo*. CBS 63353. 1968. LP.

Carthy, Eliza. *Red Rice*. Topic TSD2001. 1998. CD.

Carthy, Martin. *Sweet Wivelsfield*. Deram SML 1111. 1975. LP.

—— and Dave Swarbrick. *Life and Limb*. Special Delivery SD 1030. 1990. CD.

Castle, Pete. *Mearcstapa*. Steel Carpet Music MAT 5022. 2000. CD.

Coope, Boyes and Simpson. *Jerusalem Revisited*. World Music Network RGNET 1014. 1997. CD.

The Dave Brubeck Quartet. *Take Five* (Paul Desmond). Bluenite BN006. 1960. Seven-inch single.

Denny, Sandy. *The Northstar Grassman and The Ravens*. Island ILPS 9165. 1971. LP.

——. *Sandy*. Island ILPS 9027. 1972. LP.

Dransfield, Barry. *Unruly*. Proper Records CD 126943. 2005. CD.

Dylan, Bob. *The Freewheelin' Bob Dylan*. Columbia CS 8786. 1963. LP.

——. *Another Side Of Bob Dylan*. Columbia CS-8993. 1964. LP.

——. *Highway 61 Revisited*. CBS Records SBP 233279. 1965. LP.

Fairport Convention. *Fairport Convention*. Polydor 2384047. 1968. LP.

——. *Liege and Lief*. Island Records ILPS 9115. 1969. LP.

——. *Unhalfbricking*. Island ILPS 9102. 1969. LP.

——. *What We Did On Our Holidays*. Island ILPS 9092. 1969. LP.

——. *Angel Delight*. Island ILPS 9162. 1971. LP.

——. *Full House*. Island ILPS 9130. 1971. LP.

——. *Nine*. Island ILPS 9246. 1973. LP.

——. *Rosie*. Island ILPS 9313. 1973. LP.

——. *Gladys' Leap*. Varrick Records 023. 1985. LP.

——. 'Wat Tyler' (Ralph McTell and Simon Nicol), *Gladys' Leap*. Varrick Records 023. 1985. LP.

——. 'Here's To Tom Paine' (Steve Tilston). *Who Knows Where The Time Goes*. Woodworm Records WRCD 025. 1997. CD.

——. *35th Anniversary Concert*. Secret Films SMADVD236. 2002. DVD.

——. *Over The Next Hill*. Matty Grooves Records MGCD041. 2004. CD.

Gryphon. *Gryphon*. 1973. Transatlantic TRA 262. LP.

——. *Midnight Mushrumps*. Transatlantic TRA 282. 1974. LP.

——. *Red Queen To Gryphon Three*. Transatlantic TRA 287. 1974. LP.

——. *Raindance*. Transatlantic TRA 302. 1975. LP.

Hutchings, Ashley and Friends. *Morris On*. Island HELP 5. 1972. LP.

——. *Son of Morris On*. Harvest SHSM 2012. 1976. LP.

Jethro Tull. *Living In The Past* (Ian Anderson). Chrysalis CHS 2081-A. 1969. Seven-inch single.

Killen, Louis. *Ballads and Broadsides*. Topic 12T126. Originally recorded in 1964. CD.

Lindisfarne. *C'mon Everybody*. Stylus Records SMR738. 1987. CD.

McShee, Jaqui, Gerry Conway and Spencer Cozens. *About Thyme*. Pinnacle Records GJSCD 012. 1996. CD.

Moray, Jim. *Sweet England*. Niblick is a Giraffe Records NIBL003. 2003. CD.

Mr Fox. *Mr Fox*. Transatlantic TRA 226. 1970. LP.

——. *The Gypsy*. Transatlantic TRA 236. 1971. LP.

Pink Floyd. *Dark Side Of The Moon*. Harvest SHVL 804. 1973. LP.

Procul Harum. *A Whiter Shade Of Pale* (Gary Brooker and Keith Reid). Deram DM 126. 1967. Seven-inch single.

The Rolling Stones. *Little Red Rooster* (Willie Dixon). London Records LL 3420. 1963. Seven-inch single.

The Spencer Davis Group. 'Keep On Running' (Jackie Wilsono. Fontana TL 5359. 1966. Seven-inch single.

Steeleye Span. *Hark! The Village Wait*. Mooncrest Records 22. 1970. LP.

——. *Please To See the King*. B and C Records 1029. 1971. LP.

——. 'Rave On' (Sonny West, Bill Tilghman and Norman Petty). B and C Records CB164. 1971. Seven-inch single.

——. *Ten Man Mop Or Mr Reservoir Butler Rides Again*. Pegasus PEG9. 1971. LP.

——. *Below The Salt*. Chrysalis CHR1008. 1972. LP.

——. *Parcel of Rogues*. Chrysalis CHR1046. 1973. LP.

——. *All Around My Hat*. Chrysalis CHR1091. 1974. LP.

——. *Now We Are Six*. Chrysalis CHR1053. 1974. LP.

——. *Commoners Crown*. Chrysalis CHR1071. 1975. LP.

——. 'To Know Him Is to Love Him' (Phil Spector). *Commoner's Crown*. 1975. Chrysalis CHR1071. LP.

——. 'Twinkle, Twinkle Little Star' (Jane Taylor). *Commoner's Crown*. 1975. Chrysalis CHR1071. LP.

——. *Storm Force 10*. Chrysalis 1151. 1977. LP.

——. *The Black Freighter* (Bertolt Brecht and Kurt Weill). Chrysalis CHR1151. 1977. *Storm Force 10* LP.

——. *They Called Her Babylon*. Park Records B0001KJ038. 2004. CD.

The Strawbs. *All Our Own Work*. Pickwick SP1–70719. 1968. LP.

——. *Strawbs*. A and M Records AMS 936. 1969. LP.

——. *Just a Collection of Antiques and Curios*. A and M Records AMLS 994. 1970. LP.

——. *From the Witchwood*. A and M Records AMLH 64304. 1971. LP.

——. *Grave New World*. A and M Records MS 10111202. 1972. CD.

——. 'Lay Down' (Dave Cousins and Tony Hooper). A and M Records AMLH 68144. 1972. Seven-inch single.

——. 'You Won't Get Me, I'm Part of the Union' (Dave Cousins and Tony Hooper). A and M Records AMLH 68144. 1973. Seven-inch single.

Swarbrick, Dave with Martin Carthy. *Folk On 2*. Cooking Vinyl MASH CD 001. 1996. CD.

Various Artists. *The Iron Muse*. Topic 12T86. 1963. LP.

——. *The Electric Muse: The Story of Folk into Rock*. Island/Transatlantic Folk 1001. 1975. Four LPs.

——. *When the May Is all in Bloom*. Veteran Tapes VT131CD. 1995. CD.

——. *Hidden English*. Topic Records TSCD 600. 1996. CD.

——. *The New Electric Muse: The Story of Folk into Rock*. Essential Records ESB CD 416. 1996. Three CDs.

——. *Come All My Lads that Follow the Plough: The Life of Rural Working Men and Women*. Topic TSCD 655. 1998. CD.

——. *The Imagined Village*. Real World B000T4F0J8. 2007. CD.

Waterson, Lal and Mike. *Bright Phoebus*. Trailer LES 2076 (Leader Sound Ltd, London). 1972. LP. Re-released on Trailer/Leader LESCD 2076. 2000. CD.

Yes. *The Yes Album*. Atlantic Super 2400101. 1970. LP.

——. *Fragile*. Atlantic 7567–82667–2. 1971. LP.

Index

Note: Page numbers in italic indicate an illustration or a caption